Beyond Ruins
Reimagining Modernism

Beyond Ruins
Reimagining Modernism

Edited by Raafat Majzoub and Nicolas Fayad

Table of Contents

12
Foreword
Farrokh Derakhshani

16
Introduction
Raafat Majzoub

CONTEXT

22
Exhibiting the State in the City
Fadi El Abdallah

32
It Shouldn't End Like This
Nora Akawi and George Arbid in Conversation with Raafat Majzoub

40
The Forgotten History
Bernard Khoury

BRACING

72
Modern Memoir
EAST Architecture Studio

88
The Scaffolds of Modernism
Aaron Betsky

94
A Regenerative Invitation for the Tripoli Fair
Sarah Mineko Ichioka

PRESERVATION

106
Architecture in Scale
A Discussion with Ana Tostões and Farès el-Dahdah

118
Collaborative Conservation: Revitalising African Modernism
Aziza Chaouni

MANUAL / ANTI-MANUAL

138
Traduttore, Traditore: Reflections on Collective Restoration
Jozef Wouters

150
Organic Regeneration: Muharraq as a Resource
Noura Al-Sayeh Holtrop

160
Practice as Context
Civil Architecture

ADDITIONS / MATERIALITY

174
Stone Matters
Elias and Yousef Anastas

184
Small Touches, Big Hopes: Renovating an Icon of Global Modern Architecture in Tripoli, Lebanon
Sibel Bozdoğan

204
Activating Heritage
Nader Tehrani in Conversation with Nicolas Fayad

CULTURE

222
Life amid Ruins
Costica Bradatan in Conversation with Raafat Majzoub

230
Convened by Buildings and by Building Alike
Sumayya Vally

244
Architecture as Archive
Marco Costantini

SPECULATIVE FUTURES

256
MetaNiemeyer
Charles Kettaneh

270
Play is Progressive
Amale Andraos in Conversation with Raafat Majzoub

284
Restitution against the Ruins of a Modern Temptation
Akram Zaatari

296 Contributor Biographies
303 Image Credits
304 Imprint

Foreword
Farrokh Derakhshani

The Rachid Karami International Fair in its huge scale and its vicinity to the city and the sea

In search of modernisation, numerous countries in the early twentieth century called upon "international" architects to design iconic projects as representations of the "new nation", in order to reinforce their vision for generations to come. In the majority of cases, the political leaders could not see the completion of their dreams due to political changes, lack of resources, or natural and man-made disasters, or due to simply not understanding the realities of their time.

Large spaces were allocated in the vicinity of historic cities for these new schemes. In numerous cases, during the standstill state of these projects, the rapid formal and informal expansion of the cities encircled these sites, building up on gardens and the agricultural lands. The unfinished buildings turned into ruins, but they saved important locations in the middle of the urban agglomerates, creating opportunities for public and green spaces in service of all citizens. The Rachid Karami International Fair, designed by Oscar Niemeyer, never saw its planned grand opening in the 1970s. What was designed and built from 1962 to 1979 was mummified for four decades, until the renovation of a small portion, the Guest House, by EAST Architecture Studio brought life back to this abandoned place – giving hope to Tripolitans that soon the entire complex might be open, accommodating the new functions needed today. A lively place for public events and festivities for all.

The Rachid Karami complex is a good example of our "recent heritage". The notion of "heritage" as described by westerners has tended to address only whatever was created up to the nineteenth century. On the other hand, in the countries which were once colonised, anything created that differed from traditional examples was considered alien and not a part of their culture and heritage. Even in the West, movements such as Docomomo paying attention to modern heritage did not start until the late 1980s; and the term "recent heritage" covers new interventions in the built environment since the late nineteenth and early twentieth centuries, using non-traditional architectural vocabulary of a place, new construction technologies, and universal values. Gladly in recent decades this reading of heritage has changed, and the good examples of the built environment – regardless of time, place, and author – are part of societies' collective memory.

Restoration, conservation, renovation, rehabilitation, reconstruction, and adaptive reuse are different terms used for interventions in the existing built environment, regardless of the age of the building. The triennial Aga Khan Award for Architecture, since its inception in 1977 by His Highness the Aga Khan, has been in search of exceptional achievements in the field as examples to be showcased. During the first Award Cycle, culminating in 1980, the Master Jury recognised projects focused on restoration and on an informal settlement upgrading along contemporary buildings. At the time, such projects were not acknowledged as inclusive forms of architecture by the mainstream architectural community. Hence, the Aga Khan Award's recognition played a crucial role in broadening the scope of international architectural discourse, emphasising the importance of inclusive and socially responsive approaches in the field. In consecutive Award Cycles, focusing on area conservation and reconstruction among premiated projects continued to expand the discourse. In the most recent Award Cycle (2020–22), a number of projects dealing with the "recent heritage" were included in the jury's selection, and the renovation of the Niemeyer Guest House, conceptualised and carried out by EAST Architecture Studio, was among the six recipients of the 2022 Aga Khan Award for Architecture.

In the spirit of seeking contemporary and innovative solutions for the challenges of the built environment today, particularly those confronting new generations, the Aga Khan Award for Architecture aims to recognise projects that give hope and inspire. The design solutions implemented in the Niemeyer Guest House, along with the activities it accommodates, is one of them! It not only addresses current architectural and social needs, but also serves as a beacon of inspiration, demonstrating the transformative power of thoughtful and visionary design.

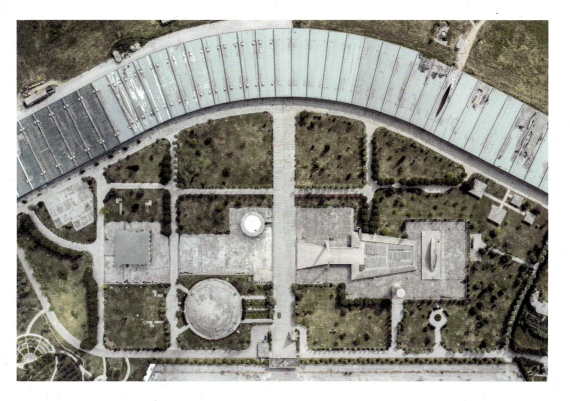

The Rachid Karami International Fair from above

 Please scan the QR code to view the Aga Khan Award for Architecture visual portraits of the Restoration of the Great Omari Mosque, Saida, Saleh Lamei-Mostafa (1989); Samir Kassir Square, Beirut, Vladimir Djurovic Landscape Architecture (2007); Issam Fares Institute, Beirut, Lebanon, Zaha Hadid Architects (2016); Renovation of the Niemeyer Guest House, Tripoli, EAST Architecture Studio (2022), all recipients of the Aga Khan Award for Architecture in Lebanon.

Introduction
Raafat Majzoub

There is something flattening about the word "ruin" when speaking of buildings. It reduces their present stories to ontologies of their past—levelling a contemporary experience into heritage. In buildings and works of cultural stature, the connotation of decay embedded in "ruins" invites an impetus to heal and fix them. To stunt their decomposition. To enable them to be experienced as protected facilities or within facilities that protect them, or protect us from them.

What is particularly exciting about ruins, however, is that moment before they are expropriated into "facilities", when they are still liberated from the legitimising power of function. Before being recruited as heritage, ruins are traces of both the past and the future simultaneously. Their legitimacy comes from the imagination afforded by their existence, such as where the visceral experience dominates the logical, seducing us to dream about possible futures beyond the existing contracts with reality.

Even more exciting are ruins within ruins, ruined buildings in ruined systems, as is the case of most postcolonial nations struggling to move forward from the exploitative legacies of their oppressors. While political unrest could obliterate or render these buildings dispensable, it also freezes real-estate markets that, along with the challenging sluggishness of urban planning and policy, provide a latency whereby these buildings transform into landscapes seeded with traces of the historical transformations of their worlds. The lack of preservation guidelines provides the space to reinvent the brief of how to move forward. There is no manual, and acknowledging the risks that come with it, the anti-manual is a site of critical creative reimagination.

In 2022, an almost invisible, reversible adaptive reuse of the Niemeyer Guest House at the Rachid Karami International Fair in Tripoli, Lebanon, won the Aga Khan Award for Architecture. Designed by the Beirut-based EAST Architecture Studio, the project is a case study of an architectural intervention that becomes a scaffold bracing the life of a building rather than claiming to restore it to its original architectural intent.

In the present volume, we inspect this metaphor of the scaffold through conversations with experts that challenge classical, top-down strategies for architectural preservation, not only by adopting grassroots alternatives, but mostly by re-examining the logical frameworks that define our cultural relationships with transformation. Architecture as a scaffold acknowledges both power and transience as mutually inclusive. It does not aim to mummify a building in/to a facility, but rather respectfully facilitates its growth with additions that enable the natural respiration of its essence and materiality.

One of the recurring lessons from our contributors is that a scaffold necessitates a form of partnership, and that it can never exist alone. It reminds us to acknowledge the architectural intervention as a temporary participation in an ongoing transfer of human knowledge and planetary intelligence. With this framework, there is no ruination, only milestones and opportunities to reflect and speculate on futures that are more intersectional and just than the ones before.

How can we conceive of such progress in a context that places so much value on the image? What is the value of nation-building at a time of ecological crises on a planetary scale? Where does the investment in heritage preservation fit into the strained budgets of postcolonial economies? How can we envision new modes of authorship that acknowledge collective participation? And how can new methodologies reshape future approaches to preservation?

We begin to address these considerations in the first chapter, *CONTEXT,* where **Fadi El Abdallah** draws a parallel between the relationship between Tripoli and the Fair and that of Tripoli and the State. **George Arbid** and **Nora Akawi** continue to excavate this relationship, and discuss the reverberations of a failed nation-building megaproject, notwithstanding the evocative nature of such failures for the imaginations of generations of architects internationally. **Bernard Khoury's** "Episode 5: The Forgotten History", taken from his unpublished book *Toxic Grounds,* introduces fiction as a scaffold for engaging with Lebanon's modern heritage.

Opening the second chapter, *BRACING,* **EAST Architecture Studio** situates preservation as a scaffold towards the construction of relevant and contemporary lived experiences through architecture. **Aaron Betsky** defines imaginative reuse as an adaptation "not by merely placing the new in, over, or through the existing, but through an intuitive form of excavation that collages what is found with the new". **Sarah Mineko Ichioka** builds an ecosystem of peers and case studies around the renovation of the Niemeyer Guest House as an invitation to consider preservation as an ecologically regenerative practice.

A conversation between **Farès el-Dahdah** and **Ana Tostões** opens the *PRESERVATION* chapter, delving into the history of building protection, the links between Niemeyer's Tripoli and Brasília projects, and the critical relevance of heritage preservation in the Global South amid socio-political and economic challenges. **Aziza Chaouni,** in turn, through examples of her own work on modernist heritage in North Africa, shares strategies for building cooperative legacies that outlive the project management lifespans of preservation projects and ensure lasting growth through self-determination.

A main pillar of our argument in this book is our mindfulness of the pitfalls of turning any strategies into shortcuts or standardised guides. In the chapter *MANUAL/ANTI-MANUAL,* we consult the work of **Jozef Wouters** who uses scenography as a scaffold for collective labor, particularly in his project Soft Layer, which was initiated as a performance to preserve the historical Dar Baïram Turki in the Medina of Tunis. **Noura Al-Sayeh Holtrop,** through her work on the Pearling Path project in Muharraq, reflects on the importance of "considering heritage, as an opportunity to rethink the present" outside an immediate economic need to profit from history, in order to afford preservation work the "possibility to imagine different futures". **Civil Architecture** unpack their position that an architectural practice "must generate its own context" through a collection of their publications that is part of a "recursive operation of research, arguments and theoretical frameworks which in turn produce architecture".

In the *ADDITIONS/MATERIALITY* chapter, we consider the stratification of matter and skill that occurs with historical practices. **Elias and Yousef Anastas** speak to the interconnectedness of material, economy, and culture through stone in Palestine through their project Stone Matters. **Sibel Bozdoğan** asks, "What exactly is the 'original' to be preserved when most modern buildings and complexes are added on and transformed several times along the way?" **Nicolas Fayad** and **Nader Tehrani** discuss cultural continuity and authorship in the translation between heritage craft and contemporary architecture, and speak to the architectural project as a site of humility, learning, and knowledge exchange.

Opening the *CULTURE* chapter is an interview with **Costica Bradatan** on translation and failure in lieu of architecture's role as a narrator of civilisation, unpacking preservation as a grounding human instinct. **Sumayya Vally** uses her Serpentine Pavilion to illustrate how she considers architecture to have "a profound role to play in expanding the cultural domain by simply listening to the contexts within which we work." **Marco Costantini** compares the Corm Foundation in Beirut and the Niemeyer Fair in Tripoli, proposing buildings themselves as public cultural archives that "testify to the crucial role that architecture plays in the collective memory of a nation and the importance of preserving its most striking witnesses."

In the last chapter, *SPECULATIVE FUTURES,* **Charles Kettaneh** expands this conversation to include the domain of the virtual, and explores the potential of digital platforms to democratise and reclaim neglected architectural spaces. **Amale Andraos** discusses with us the evolution of public spaces in the modern Arab city and the architect's responsibility to redefine the brief. Lastly, through an examination of film, art, and architectural works, **Akram Zaatari** establishes that "the wider avenue of restitution is a creative practice and not an expression of nostalgia for origins or authenticity", a crucial key to operating beyond ruins, into imagination.

Through this framework, *Beyond Ruins: Reimagining Modernism* presents preservation as an architecture of relationships, mediating the importance of knowledge transmission through buildings and the significance of understanding their contemporary relevance in relation to the transformations of their provenance. Our contributors challenge us to encounter opportunities to reimagine the notion of heritage – not as a fixed point in history that needs to be protected, but as a dynamic, evolving grammar that needs to be made accessible. As a mediator, preservation has a responsibility – surpassing the built form – to translate this grammar into a language that enables multiple actors on social and ecological levels to co-author their shared futures.

CONTEXT

Exhibiting the State in the City
Fadi El Abdallah

Many residents of Tripoli can sum up their demands from the Lebanese state under three headlines: the fair, the refinery, and the seaport. Some might add an airport in Qoleiat, north of the city, to the list of stalled projects. But residents' criticism focuses mainly on three key failures: the failure to restore the operations of the oil refinery, which used to transport Iraqi oil to Europe until it was halted due to disagreements between the two ruling Ba'ath Party regimes in Iraq and Syria; the failure to ensure that international exhibitions are held exclusively on the grounds of the Rachid Karami International Fair in Tripoli; and the failure to develop the city's port, despite its location and capabilities, which are superior, according to the Tripolitans, to those of the Beirut Port.

These are three indicators of the existing relationship between the Lebanese state and the people of Lebanon's "second city" – or its "true city", if we follow the opinion of Issam El Abdallah (1941-2017), a southern poet who sees Beirut as a "sprig of villages", a gathering of smaller towns rather than a real city with cohesive historical and social continuity. More precisely, these are the signs held up by Tripoli itself as evidence of the deprivation imposed on it by the state, preventing it from utilising its resources. However, the truth may be less a calculated decision on the part of the state and more indicative of its confusion on how to deal with Tripoli, compounded by the city's own confusion about its "Lebaneseness", as becomes evident from tracing the story of the fairgrounds itself.

The land that would eventually house the fairgrounds, purchased by the state in the early 1960s, was mostly owned, it is said, by the Karami family, adding financial wealth to their prominence and prestige. The establishment of the Fair is a legacy of the Fouad Chehab[1] era and his attempts to modernise Lebanon's institutions, as well as attempts to expand the parameters of state attention to the regions beyond the Beirut–Jounieh and Beirut–Damascus road axes, the two areas to which it had long been confined.[2]

The Fair space was officially established by decree in 1960. Brazilian architect Oscar Niemeyer completed his designs shortly thereafter, which strikingly contrasted with the city's traditional architecture. Construction of the fairgrounds began in 1967, around the time of the June War,[3] and halted in 1975 with the onset of the Lebanese Civil War, which lasted until 1990.

The two dates are significant in their own right: the 1967 defeat, of course, resulted in a shift of influence from the region's official armies to the Palestinian guerrillas, and it was followed by the Cairo Agreement in 1969[4] and the end of the reign of Fouad Chehab's successor, Charles Helou. The Cairo Agreement moved the arena of guerrilla action to the Lebanese border, the first sign that the right to bear arms would no longer be the sole purview of the state, as well as a beginning of the collapse of the doctrine of Chehabism, which had tried to keep Lebanon isolated from and neutral in regional conflicts, as part of an agreement with Egypt's Gamal Abdel Nasser.

Figure 1. Tripoli Bab al-Raml Cemetery

No doubt that the choice of Niemeyer himself, famous for his designs in the new Brazilian capital, reflected a desire to modernise a city that was famous in Lebanon for its conservatism and traditionalism like most second cities in comparison with the capital. In neighbouring Syria, efforts to modernise were more frequently focused on the capital, Damascus, compared to Aleppo. Damascus had a higher concentration of wealth, foreign communities, and diplomatic ties.

At the time, the fairgrounds demarcated the city from the southwest, and for a long time it was surrounded only by orchards that later became Tripoli's richest, most affluent neighbourhood known as the *maarad,* Arabic for "fair", given that it had been built overlooking it. Now, however, if you look at a map of "the balad", as Tripolitans call their city, you'll notice that the urban expanse has extended south of the Fair, and a newer rich and affluent area has emerged known as "Damm wa Farz", literally, "annexation and sorting", denoting the legal process of reallocation of land, whereby smaller plots were annexed and larger ones sorted, part of the massive movement to monetise agricultural land during the post-war real-estate speculation boom of the Rafik Hariri era.

The city seems to swallow its fairgrounds, just as it swallowed the Bab al-Raml Cemetery (fig. 1). This cemetery, with its marble tombstones carved with verses from the Koran, had long bordered the city. Nearby were hills of red sand that, according to local legend, would one day be roused by a fierce, howling wind and blown over the city, settling over it and heralding its end.

Like the cemetery, the fairgrounds have become a witness to what is no longer there, or perhaps never was, a forgotten realm within the belly of the city, a blind unseen spot, a gap in time from which we look towards another, infinitely distant era.

The state tried to extend a bridge of modernity to its second city, which, since the establishment of Greater Lebanon, had refused to belong to it, for reasons that are worth understanding. Tripoli was the capital of an Ottoman province that extended well into what we today call Syria, and its familial, commercial, and sectarian allegiances made it much closer to Homs, Hama, and even Aleppo than to Metn, Keserwan, and the mountainous heart of the Mount Lebanon Mutasarrifate,[5] which the French would seek to expand by creating Greater Lebanon, with borders specifically designed to protect the mountain's Maronites from concerns of further famine like the one seen during the First World War.

The creation of Greater Lebanon served not only to sever relations between Tripoli and its extended interests in Syria, but also to subjugate a Sunni city to a state created by the French for the Maronites. That would happen at the same time when other confessional states were created: the Alawite state, the Jabal Druze state, and the two Sunni states of Damascus and Aleppo. The modern Syrian state would be born from the Syrian rejection of these four states and their great revolt (1925–27).

Tripoli originally opposed the creation of Greater Lebanon and its annexation into it until the French army violently imposed that reality on the city. Although some of the city's elites, especially the clergy, later became involved in the Lebanese political community, beginning with Sheikh Muhammad al-Jisr and moving on to Mufti Abdul Hamid Karami and then his son Rachid, after whom the Fair was named upon the latter's assassination, the deep state met the city with a similar rejection. In fact, the project of the Fair may have been a reconciliatory offering of sorts.

After the end of the war, the situation became even more schizophrenic. In 1995, the state recognised the "exclusivity" of the Tripoli Fair, agreeing that it would be the sole space to host international exhibitions, but also maintained that it would lose that exclusivity if it failed to organise at least one international exhibition per year. While one or two major exhibitions have indeed been organised over the past thirty years, far more international exhibitions have been held in Beirut, compounding the sense of injustice among Tripoli residents.

The lack of interest in developing the city's port, following the destruction of the Beirut port in the 4 August 2020 explosion, suggests that this sense of discrimination is only set to continue and deepen. There seems to be no reason for not developing the port other than the fact that, unlike Beirut, Tripoli is beyond the reach of Lebanon's multiple sectarian parties. In a city that is largely mono-sectarian, it is difficult for rival sects to jostle for control over its docks and use it as a corridor for their weapons, explosives, and contraband.

I don't recall ever setting foot on the fairgrounds, nor do I know anyone who did, not my friends nor my parents' generation. It simply stood there, like ruins, until I left the city at the age of twenty-five for Paris. I never even visited the book fair when they moved its location from Al Rabita Al Thaqafiya[6] to the Rachid Karami fairgrounds, nor do I remember any truly important fair that took place there.

Instead, what I have in my memory are fleeting scenes: maybe Facebook photos of a choral concert near a theatre reflected in a body of water, images that could be memory or a dream of strange-looking buildings we see in passing as we drive around the Fair to get to the port or to the Beirut highway.

Back in the day, when citrus groves still dotted the area around the Fair, the air was perfumed with the scent of orange blossom. I fondly recall the sight of morning joggers weaving their paths around the fairgrounds, and I occasionally joined them. I also remember traces of unresolved grief and unhealed wounds from times when a car veered off the road and struck a jogger.

It was the vast parking lot surrounding the Fair, not the fairgrounds itself, that was a vibrant space in the city! That is where most of us learned the basics of driving, and in its empty rectangles the official driver's licence exams were held (fig. 2). Sometimes the state examiners would suggest, with innocence and ease, that the young person could, in exchange for a simple fee, return without even doing the exam at all and find the driver's licence waiting for them at home with their parents. And sometimes, if they were related to or close in any way to the state examiner, the fee wasn't even necessary!

From behind the walls of the fairgrounds, a trail of monuments looked down on us, joggers, student drivers, state examiners with their faces accustomed to the humiliation of bribery, boyfriends seeking a dark space in which to hide away with their girlfriends at night, Red Cross paramedics rushing to the site of a traffic accident. We paid no heed to any lingering trace of past dwellings, and no one halted us to lament their absence.

In October of 2019, before Covid and the economic collapse would hit, during a moment of unprecedented hope, tens of thousands of citizens, maybe even more, came together in the streets. They swept the roads clean, they decorated the unfinished and abandoned buildings from a bygone Ba'athist era, when the city had lived under a twenty-year occupation by the Syrian army and its intelligence services. They sang, danced, and cheered, created a code of conduct for the protesters, and produced monologues satirising politicians in a proudly local dialect. Meanwhile, all of Lebanon delighted in a new image of Tripoli, a city previously dubbed the "Kandahar" of Lebanon, mentioned only in relation to the frequent clashes between Bab al-Tabbaneh (Sunnis) and Baal Mohsen (Alawites) against the backdrop of the Syrian revolution against the Assad regime.

When the "revolution" began in Lebanon, rife with scenes from previous uprisings such as the March 14 and You Stink movements in 2015 and 2016, that is, rich in a folklore of songs,

Figure 2. Driving practice in the parking lot outside the fence of the Rachid Karami International Fair

flags, general cheerfulness, and elegance in dress and speech, Tripoli joined in, full-throated, at a time when other areas, especially Beirut, seemed to be under the threat of repeating the "glorious" days of May.[7]

Tripoli affirmed its belonging to the nation, and others hailed it as the "bride" and capital of the revolution – a striking paradox. A century after the country's creation, Tripoli embraced its Lebanese identity at the very moment the nation seemed to falter and fade. As what remained of Lebanon dissolved, the future stretched into an uncertain and shadowy expanse, devoid of any glimmer of hope.

But even in that moment, in the fervour of newfound belonging to the nation, the fairgrounds remained a stranger apart, with the old central square known under multiple names – Statue Square, Abdel Hamid Karami Square, Al-Nour Square, Square of God – becoming the central theatre of protest and gathering (fig. 3). The fairgrounds remained empty, abandoned and threatened, endangered, as UNESCO put it, "given its alarming state of conservation, the lack of financial resources for its maintenance and the risks inherent in development proposals for the complex that could jeopardize its integrity".[8]

The Tripoli Fair project was approved during the time of Fouad Chehab, who was the patron of a massive modernisation movement and process of institutionalisation in Lebanon. The Chehab era saw the establishment of the Banque du Liban, the Civil Service Council, the Central Inspection, Social Security, and other such institutions. He was seemingly highly aware of the importance of strengthening ties specifically between Tripoli and the nascent Lebanese government of the time. Mona Fayyad[9] notes that Chehab didn't make visits to events or inaugurate institutions during his presidency, so as not to be accused of favouritism or of reportedly neglecting certain regions in favour of others. According to Fayyad, he made only two exceptions to

Figure 3. People demonstrating at Al-Nour Square in Tripoli, on 9 November 2019, the twenty-third day of protests against government corruption

this rule: one visit to the south upon the death of a former Speaker of Parliament, and one visit to Tripoli to unveil the statue of Abdel Hamid Karami, which was later replaced by a sculpture of the word "Allah" during the time of the extremist "Tawhid Emirate" in the 1980s. Fayyad recalls that this was undertaken explicitly to say to the people of Tripoli, though not in these exact words, "Here you are, once again Lebanese", referring to the aftermath of the 1958 Mini-War[10] and the Tripolitans' unitary tendencies with Nasser's Egypt. He also requested that the statue be turned to face Beirut, the capital of the country.

These two facts are inseparable: the fairgrounds were one of the "institutions" of the Chehabist era in the new state; and, like the face of the statue of Abdel Hamid Karami – father of Rachid Karami, whose name the fairgrounds would later bear – it was another sign emphasising the link between Tripoli and the state capital.

That link was only finally secured by Tripoli's own full-fledged declaration of belonging to Lebanon in 2019. Before that, there is a noticeable difference between Tripoli's experience and that of Beirut, before, during, and after the civil war. In his article in *Al-Anbaa* newspaper,[11] Tawfiq Sultan mentions how Camille Chamoun, then president in the 1950s, grew angry at news of the development of the Tripoli port, favouring the exclusive development of the Beirut port. During the war, Tripoli had only a few rival militias fighting over power of the streets of the city, and unlike Beirut, it remained undivided. It did however fall under Islamist religious control, and the Syrian occupation took it over relatively early as compared to Beirut, especially the east Beirut. There is also considerable difference between what each city experienced after the war, with Beirut being the focus of all major reconstruction efforts.

These differences in experience between the capital and the ancient city, and the subsequent entrenchment of post-war sectarian quotas on national resources, may have contributed to the failure of completing the process of linking Tripoli to the state, a process that had to be undertaken in terms of "modernisation", especially in light of the founding myth of the Lebanese state as a bridge between European modernity and the Arab interior.

But the process of Tripoli's modernisation is actually older than the Lebanese state itself. As early as the days of Sultan Abdul Hamid II, the Ottomans began attempts to modernise "the most beautiful city on the eastern coast of the Mediterranean", as it was described by some travellers. The inauguration of the clock tower in the city's downtown "Tall" area symbolised a new relationship with time, while Azmi Bey built a road that would bear his name, linking Tripoli to its port and turning it into an important commercial market that for the first time divested from the usual logic of the interior markets in the Islamic and Levantine metropolises. The Mamluk initiative to rebuild Tripoli without defensive walls, after its recapture from the Crusaders, may have been the precursor of a new relationship and more modernised way of conceiving of military affairs and defence engineering; in contrast, Beirut, for example, remained behind its walls until the mid-nineteenth century.

During and after the French Mandate in the 1920s, attempts on behalf of the city's inhabitants, individuals and investors both, converged within the space of modernisation that overlooked them, and some semi-demolished buildings at the southern entrance to the city still bear evidence of the factories, industries, and warehouses that were established to manufacture biscuits, soft drinks, and other such things that the city had never enjoyed before. Cinemas and theatres opened up their doors (fig. 4), stages upon which Umm Kalthoum sang in the early

Figure 4. Empire Cinema, on Al-Tall Square in Tripoli, is one of the city's first cinemas, built in 1932 and renovated in 2022.

Figure 5. Concrete fence surrounding the fairgrounds

1930s, giving further evidence of the deep ties that have linked Tripoli to Egypt since the Ottoman era. Ibrahim al-Ahdab (d. 1891) wrote scripts for the plays of the Damascene Abu Khalil al-Qabbani that were staged in Cairo; Sheikh Ali Mahmoud sang the words of Sheikh Mahmoud bin Abdullah al-Shahal al-Tarabulsi (d. 1907); and Abdel Salam al-Nabulsi (b. Tripoli, 1899 – d. Beirut, 1968) launched his career in the Egyptian film industry, paving the way for Mohammed Jamal (b. Tripoli, 1934 – d. Los Angeles, 2023) and Walid Tawfiq (b. Tripoli, 1954) after him. Despite the complaints of deprivation against the Lebanese state, Tripoli was in a state of constant flux, witnessing significant changes in women's status and education, new areas of entertainment and consumption, and increased migration, especially to Arab countries.

Ottoman modernisation was quickly integrated into the city's fabric, allowing it to break out of the confines of the souq, to expand, connect to the port market, and to adopt new approaches to engineering, construction, and commerce. While the Lebanese state did not actually accomplish much in the city, Tripoli didn't seem to accept any of the crumbs on offer either. The fairgrounds remained empty, and the new "Olympic" football stadium, built during the Hariri era to host the 2000 Asian Cup matches, remained far from it as well, perched at the edge of the sea. The "Olympic" stadium had been intended to replace the "municipal" stadium as it was known, which abutted to the old city's neighbourhoods north of the Mitein road and adjacent to Zahiriya and the northern orchards on the banks of the Abu Ali River.

It would be simplistic to place the blame for all this exclusively on sectarianism. Part of it, of course, stems from Tripolitans' nearly century-long yearning to belong to a place beyond Lebanon and their reluctance to take advantage of the few opportunities they have been offered, preferring instead to complain constantly about injustice. But none of that exempts sectarianism, of course.

In my opinion, Tripoli is likely to remain the deprived Sunni capital in a state defined by sectarian quotas. The most valuable resources – sectarian spoils – are located where sects intersect, particularly in Beirut, where assets like port docks, airport hangars, and even devastated streets are divided among sects. This pattern of deprivation is not unique to Tripoli but extends across the country. As long as the state operates on a system of quotas and plunder, as Professor Ahmed Beydoun describes,[12] it will only offer superficial promises that barely mask its deep-seated deprivation and disdain (fig. 5).

Behind the fairground walls, we stood alone, with no one to beckon our tears.

It is said that poets lament over ruins, because those who once inhabited them are now gone. But who cries over a ruin that was never inhabited in the first place?

In the fairgrounds, I see an arch looming over emptiness, or perhaps it was a bridge that was once extended to the city, while the hand that extended it has long since disappeared.

The bridge no longer leads to an elsewhere, but its restoration and preservation are perhaps a promise of an elsewhere that has not yet been created. This time, if by some miracle it comes to exist, it will not break its promises, and the arch, like a rainbow, will remain a fleeting witness to that promise.

1 Fouad Chehab was the President of Lebanon from 1958 to 1964 and is often remembered for his policies focused on nation-building and administrative reforms. He worked towards modernising Lebanon's infrastructure, reducing corruption, and fostering social and economic development.

2 I recall, for example, the great satirist Maroun Abboud's complaint, in the 1950s, about the chronic deprivation affecting the Christian villages around Jbeil, including his village Ain Kifa.

3 In June 1967, during the Six-Day War, Israel seized control of the Gaza Strip, the West Bank, including East Jerusalem, from Palestine, the Sinai Peninsula from Egypt, and the Golan Heights from Syria. This war, referred to as the "Naksa" or "the defeat" by Arabs, marked a pivotal moment as it shattered the Arab people's faith in their governments and catalysed the rise of Palestinian armed resistance movements committed to reclaiming Palestine over subsequent decades, using other neighbouring countries as a basis for their activities.

4 The Cairo Agreement (2 November 1969) between the Palestinian leader Yasser Arafat and the Lebanese General Emile Bustani, facilitated by the Egyptian President Gamal Abdel Nasser, formalised the conditions allowing Palestinian guerrilla operations from South Lebanon.

5 Around the mid-nineteenth century, during Ottoman rule, recurring conflicts between the Druze and Maronite communities led to the creation of a special administrative status for Mount Lebanon called the Mutasarrifate to ensure balanced governance structures. This new status was established with the active involvement of European powers.

6 Founded in 1943, Al Rabita Al Thaqafiya (The Cultural League) in Tripoli, Lebanon, is a cornerstone in promoting arts and education in the city. It launched its first annual book fair in 1974, establishing a key cultural event that was held at the Rabita's headquarters embedded in one of the city's residential and commercial districts informally named "Al Thaqafa" in reference to it. The book fair continues to enrich Tripoli's public life after it was relocated to the Rachid Karami International Fair in the 1990s.

7 In May 2008, Hezbollah militants took control of parts of Beirut, marking a significant moment in Lebanese politics where the armed party directed its weapons towards fellow citizens rather than fighting Israel. This action was a response to the Lebanese government's decisions aimed at dismantling Hezbollah's telecommunications network and removing the head of airport security, who was seen as having close ties with Hezbollah.

8 Rachid Karami International Fair in Tripoli, Lebanon, recognised as a cultural and architectural landmark, has been included in UNESCO's World Heritage list, UNESCO, https://www.unesco.org/ar/articles/adraj-mrd-rshyd-kramy-aldwly-fy-trabls-lbnan-fy-qaymt-alywnskw-lltrath-alalmy.

9 Mona Fayyad, "Fouad Chehab: The President Who Built Lebanon", *Al Hurra*, 4 August 2019.

10 In May 1958, armed unrest erupted in Lebanon when President Camille Chamoun sought a constitutional amendment for re-election. The conflict, originating in Tripoli and spreading to Beirut and the Syrian border, escalated into a civil war, persisting until October 1958.

11 Tawfiq Sultan, "Tripoli: Capital of Arab Culture and the Lebanese Misery", *Anbaa Online*, https://anbaaonline.com/news/234805.

12 Ahmed Baydoun, "The Spoliation or the Political Structure of the Lebanese State's Path to Bankruptcy", *Almodon*, 27 November 2019.

It Shouldn't End Like This
Nora Akawi and George Arbid in Conversation with Raafat Majzoub

Raafat Majzoub I'm very happy we were able to make time for this. I know both of your schedules are packed . . . And Nora, I hope the faculty and students for justice in Palestine groups in your school are active and doing well. George, you have studied and contextualised the Rachid Karami International Fair extensively as part of your work on modernism in Lebanon, and a lot of credit goes to you in familiarising architecture students with the Fair through your design studios. Nora, although you haven't worked on the Fair specifically, your extensive engagement with the Arab city – with emphasis on nation-building, cartography, bordering, and erasure in a postcolonial framework – would be an interesting provocation to unpack its context. Shall we start there?

George Arbid The project created a polemic from day one. During Fouad Chehab's era, the notion of promoting the nation in all sectors emerged. The government struggled to decide whether to establish a zoo or a fair in Tripoli, for example. At that time, the government was not subject to any colonial ideals. I say the contrary because the French Mandate encouraged an "Orientalised" Art Deco style in the 1930s in Beirut, while the Lebanese architects and their patrons wanted to avoid having that image projected onto them. They wanted modernism.

Nora Akawi The design of the Tripoli Fair, as part of a nation-building project, is adopting colonial structures for the construction of the narrative, image, and social imaginary of the nation-state as defined by the modern-colonial world order.[1] Oscar Niemeyer's architecture has participated in such constructions around the world, but I'm specifically thinking of a text by Paulo Tavares that traces Niemeyer's design of the altar for the "First Mass of Brasília", which took place on 3 May 1953, to mark the foundation of the construction site of the state's new capital. This historical landmark, Tavares writes, "was carefully designed to evoke the mass celebrated in 1500 by the Cabral fleet on the beach of Coroa Vermelha, . . . which symbolically marked the possession of the Amerindian territories by the Portuguese Empire"[2]. How might this lineage impact our reading of the Fair in Tripoli in the context of Niemeyer's larger body of work?

GA Nation-building, of course, drove such costly projects. It had to do with marking the northern territory with a project that is on a national and regional scale. There is no other project like this one, not even in the Bekaa Valley or the South. What is truly significant in the context of the Fair is its lack of success from today's perspective; Tripoli remains impoverished to this day. The presence of the Syrian army during the war stalled it for a long time. Up until now, the people of Tripoli are still in conflict in Bab al-Tabbaneh and Jabal Mohsen, yet the politicians are not doing anything to change the situation. Much more could have been done to secure a decent living for the people in Tripoli. The Fair could have contributed to that, and it may have a role in the future. So far, it remains a site where imagination goes to waste. Fortunately, successive harmful projects

Figures 1 and 2. Student site visit to the Rachid Karami International Fair with George Arbid in 2004

for the use of the Fair were not implemented, starting with Cedarland, a sort of fake world including Fiji huts, followed by Chinamex, and ending with the Knowledge and Innovation Center that proposed to build 60,000 square metres on the site in two phases, instead of using the existing buildings.

NA In their Guest House project, Nicolas and Charles put forward their ideas as one possible interpretation of the site. They emphasised the possibility of dismantling their intervention if necessary to accommodate a different interpretation or use. So, George, from the archive and from teaching for so many years, did you come across different types of interpretations of the Fair?

GA There are many student projects. I did two studios; one of them when Nicolas and Charles were second-year students at the American University of Beirut, and I took them on site and showed them the Fair (figs. 1 and 2). We worked under the boomerang, creating a 7-metre-long model of 1:100 scale. At that time, Charles's project was completely crazy because he said, "I did not wish to build under the canopy; I wanted to build outside." I recommended that he construct a mobile structure, and that's exactly what he did. At that time, he constructed the mobile structure by folding an aluminium sheet and adding wheels. It was completely insane, yet powerful.

RM I'd like to pick up George's note on the Tripoli Fair as a site for imagination, without the "going to waste" part. George, I think the way you describe abandoned buildings connects a lot with Nora's point that they afford a loophole outside the metrics of what infrastructure, planning, or logic allow. With no responsible governing bodies, there cannot be any pragmatic steps forward,

only imagination, and one of these exercises ended up being the Guest House renovation. I just feel like the potentiality of these layers of imagination is worth speaking about.

NA The 1974 film *Kuneitra: Death of a City* by Jim Cranmer documents the destruction and looting of Quneitra by the Zionist occupation's military. In an interview with a woman who remained in Quneitra and refused to leave, describing the events as "destruction by design", she said that Quneitra needed to stay exactly as it is, in its destroyed form, as a reminder of the colonial violence perpetrated against her people, to ensure that future generations do not forget the injustices inflicted upon them and their lands, alongside the destruction and violence perpetrated against the rest of the occupied Syrian Golan Heights. I don't mean to propose a comparison between these two types of ruins: Quneitra, on the one hand, as a ruin purposefully created by a settler colonial regime in its attempts to erase and annihilate Indigenous populations, and the Fair in Tripoli, on the other hand, as a ruin that embodies the failures of the nation-state as a model, and the shortcomings of its attempt to construct images of hegemonic power and homogenous societies. Nor am I necessarily advocating for this approach. I bring this up only to ask you for your thoughts on such forms of memorialisation. In this case, what might be thought of as a monument to the failure of the nation-state?

GA I will counter this idea. My answer would be yes, but not always and not everywhere. Because I have this theory that I constantly speak about, which is that when the war in Lebanon ended, you had what I call vultures coming in, and they wanted us to keep the city as is, in order for them to come and do some war tourism and to take selfies with the bullets and the holes in the buildings. Suddenly, we found ourselves betraying ourselves, unable to envision a future devoid of these sometimes-excessive traces. I can use the work on the Beit Beirut project as an example, where the intervention overplayed war traces as a statement, while other aspects of the life of the building were disregarded. The alibi of memory works here against the mnemonic performance. In the case of Quneitra, it makes sense; in other cases, it is counterproductive.

NA Raafat had mentioned earlier Fadi El Abdallah's piece where he establishes the Fair's relationship with the state as a kind of mirror of Tripoli, and of city residents' relationship with the state. Currently, we observe a significant disconnect between the state and the street or the people. Projects like the Rachid Karami International Fair are generally state-run. So, what are the possible political organisations that can actually enter into these places, potentially outside of the framework of the state, and is this something that you see already happening? Can we imagine inhabitations, interpretations, and occupations of the Fair that can exit the framework of the state, and make these spaces more in line with what's happening in the streets, and with the aspirations of the people who live around it?

GA Think of abandoned buildings in Beirut such as the Holiday Inn, Saint Georges, Burj El Murr, the Egg (City Palace cinema), et cetera. Something interesting happened during the recent demonstrations, whereby people started entering these buildings, and they would appropriate them and do all sorts of activities. Before the 2019 revolution, they staged events like concerts and exhibitions. However, during the demonstrations, people started entering the Egg, and they somehow reappropriated it. The appropriation also took place at the Grand Theatre and other buildings in downtown Beirut. There was a general sentiment calling for change. Professors started giving lectures in these buildings and young crowds started gathering there. As a result, the buildings began to take on a certain life – the ordinary life of the street – that had not existed before. For me, the future of the Rachid Karami International Fair itself is just that – let's open it and see what happens.

RM There is a not-so-subtle connection between the reclamation process and a narrative of "unsafety" by governing forces. The relationship between the coercive state and its people on the street is to contain them by making it unsafe, inaccessible. I remember as an architecture student, every time I used to try to enter the Egg or the Holiday Inn, this lack of safety was the device by which these spaces are walled off. It is a systemic strategy to erase these spaces from the memory of people in public. The action to reclaim safety and shelter in these spaces, either

36

collectively through non-governmental organisations as Nora suggested, or even formally, is critical in rebuilding the trust between people and their city. Tripoli remains a city heavily reliant on street life. When the October 2019 demonstrations started, Tripoli's people inspired the country in how they were expressing dissent on the street, but no one used the Fair for any activity. They just passed next to it on their way to demonstrate in Sahet al-Nour.

GA Similarly, in Horsh Beirut, the government argues that the Lebanese do not deserve a park, citing their potential to destroy it through burning or littering, making it also unsafe. So, there's this idea that the government deserves barricaded open spaces, but not the Lebanese people. In addition to being a space for coming together, rehabilitating the Tripoli Fair is necessary for both short-term and long-term reasons, and it can generate significant economic income. For example, to renovate the tower, which is the restaurant, one has to be accurate and not generic. If we consider the restaurant tower as a singular structure, the establishment of a high-quality restaurant there could potentially generate significant revenue, half of which could go towards the restoration of the building next to it, and so on and so forth.

RM Also relevant to this conversation is another point from Fadi's text, that Tripoli had entered Lebanon in 2019, through the revolution. I find this very interesting but also argue that this moment of assimilation with Lebanon was a moment of rupture for Tripoli. The city has maintained a unique and nuanced relationship with the Arab context, politically, economically, and socially, following a logic that differs from how Lebanon identifies and separates itself. I had always prided myself on how Tripoli was never plagued by the Lebanese separationist brand identity.

NA Do you mean that it entered Lebanon in its dissent towards the government?

RM There was always dissent, but it entered a performance of dissent I feel is more didactic and branded, slightly disconnected from reality, as is the case in Beirut. And the more youth groups with kiosks and logos, the more Beirut applauded.

GA But also, there's a recognition that their interests align with those of people from other regions, and they believe that by working together, they can forge a new nation. That wasn't present before, and even from the day of modern Lebanon's creation in the 1920s, there was this idea of disconnecting from Tripoli, especially voiced by the Christians. Even though there are Sunnis and Christians in Tripoli, there was this idea to create a smaller Lebanon without them. This is very telling.

NA It would be interesting to consider whether this is also related to the fact that it has been primarily disfranchised. In Palestine, for example, Munir Fasheh highlights that the fact the NGO-isation that happened in the West Bank did not catch on in Gaza, which enabled a resistance movement and a struggle for freedom that was outside of the framework of humanitarianism. In the case of Tripoli, is there a relationship evident between disfranchisement and the potentialities of dissent and resistance that exist outside of the chains of state structures and NGO development? What is the current state of neoliberal development in Tripoli today, and what is its relationship with the future of the Fair?

RM Following up on this from an urban perspective, can you speak to why this project is on the outskirts of the city and at that scale (fig. 3)? Tripoli is a historical hub for trade and traditional industry. Was this isolation intentional (figs. 4 and 5)? Are there any examples of such projects implemented in historic cities being more directly attuned to the energy of these cities?

GA At that time, everyone was building malls and large-scale projects on the outskirts because it made movement and ownership easier. The monumentality that they wanted could not have been achieved closer to the centre.

RM Well, yes, it's good they didn't raze the old city for it.

Figure 3. Aerial view of Tripoli showing the Fair in its urban context

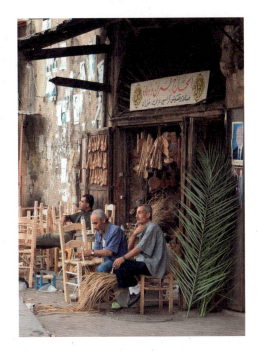

Figure 4. Traditional chair weaving at a workshop in downtown Tripoli

Figure 5. Khan al-Khayyatin (Tailors' caravanserai) in the old city

GA Solidere did. In the commercial centre of Beirut. It is especially inexcusable since it came after the lessons learned from the mistakes of the world; we redid the same mistakes thirty years later. When the Rachid Karami International Fair was done, it was the time of a trend, and Lebanon wanted to follow it. They weren't envisioning that the future of Lebanon is in agriculture and didn't see that it was in fact a very specific environment, ecology, and economy they were intervening on. This is why I say it is never too late to look at the Fair site from today's perspective and make it a place that lives more organically. One of the strategies is to find different, more connected, programmes. Listing it as a UNESCO World Heritage Site doesn't mean that we leave it as it is. It shouldn't end like this.

RM Definitely not. Thank you both for this talk. I think it's great to open up all these avenues to provoke and contextualise the different forces at play when speaking about the Fair. Let's continue this conversation when the book is out.

---

1 See Adrian Lahoud, "Fallen Cities: Architecture and Reconstruction", in *The Arab City: Architecture and Representation*, ed. Amale Andraos and Nora Akawi (New York: Columbia Books on Architecture and the City, 2016).

2 See Paulo Tavares, "Brasilia: Colonial Capital", in *The Settler Colonial Present*, ed. Nick Axel, Andrew Herscher, Nikolaus Hirsch, and Ana María León, *e-flux Architecture* (October 2020), https://www.e-flux.com/architecture/the-settler-colonial-present/.

The Forgotten History

Bernard Khoury

Editors' note:

In this chapter excavated from *Toxic Grounds,* Bernard Khoury's unpublished book of architecture fiction, a character by the name of Dr Ramzi Mirza, a historian, takes us through the hidden history of Beirut's modernist heritage. As the city faces globalisation and reconstruction, Dr Mirza is committed to preserving the work of its pioneering architects like Joseph Philippe Karam and Khalil Khouri. His endeavour reveals the challenges of protecting historical buildings amidst rapid urban development and highlights the cultural significance of Beirut's modernist architecture and the socio-political forces that threaten its survival.

V

Episode 5
The Forgotten History

My name is Doctor Ramzi Mirza. I am a historian.

The etymological origins of my name are rooted in Persian history. The word, which means royalty in almost every old version of Persian, Arab and Caucasian languages is derived from the term Amirzade which means the child of the Amir, or the child of the ruler. Under Catherine the Great, empress of Russia, the Mirzas gained equal rights with the Russian nobility due to their extreme wealth. In return, the family financed the Russo-Turkush war against the Ottoman Empire and Abdul Mirza was given the title Prince Yusopov. His descendant, Prince Felix Yusopov married Princess Irina Alexandrovna of Russia, the only niece of Tsar Nicholas II.

I was born in Beirut in 1957 where I went to school at le College des Frères de La Salle, a Christian school that provided me with an exceptional education. I graduated from there with the highest honors and obtained a Baccalaureate in mathematics. As a young boy, I joined the catechism classes and never missed church that the whole family attended every Sunday. I was also a proud member of the religious choir. In 1975, our family moved to France where I first studied at the Faculte des Lettres de Strasbourg for 4 years. After that, I went to L'universite de Loraine in Nancy where I got a masters degree in Art History and Archeology. My passion took me to great locations such as the Ain Dara temple in Syria where I was a site assistant. I also worked with the British School of Archeology on the digs of San Vincenzo al Volturno back in 1986. By the late 1980's, my parents had settled in Paris so I took Philosophy courses at the Sorbonne University where I ended up getting a doctorate 4 years later. As if that wasn't enough, at the age of 35, I started studying Architecture at l'École Nationale Supérieure des Beaux-Arts. There, I wrote a 792-page doctorate thesis, which was entitled: Existentialism or Essentialism, an investigation of the Architecture of Safavid Persia. From that point on, Architecture research became my primary occupation. I published a number of important papers including: Spatial dimensions of the Freudian uncanny (1998), Architectural Heteropias and Socio-Spatial Practices of Alterity (1999), Changing the Architectonic of Philosophy / Rajchman's Interest in Folded Architecture (2001) In 2003, I published a book with Princeton Architectural press that was titled The Wittgenstein House and the poetic possibility of Architecture. My extensive research and writings earned me very prestigious academic positions in various universities including the Graduate School of Design at Harvard, Princeton University and many others.

You may ask yourself what my role in this book is. In fact, I don't know and I bear no resemblance to any of the other characters who testified here, before or after me and I have absolutely no interest in knowing them. Beirut is contaminated with individuals of that sort: immoral, irresponsible money driven opportunists. Unlike most vile figures that could only see financial opportunities in the post-war reconstruction projects, I came back to my dear city in 2004 for a noble cause. Our rich historical architectural heritage was in danger. Most of the buildings erected during the early years of the nation's independence were being whipped out, demolished or disfigured. There were no serious preservation mechanisms or institutions to protect our patrimony. In fact, none of the vibrant and distinctive early modern structures were protected or considered historical. The tangible traces of our political and social history were disappearing in a process that was making way for an ostentatious baseless modernity. Beirut was desperately trying to reinvent itself but it was subjected to globalization and hyper capitalist destructive forces. The city and its major actors were trying to get back in the spotlight that was more focused on Dubai and other Arabian Gulf cities. Since the early days of the so-called reconstruction period I had already written many articles on the matter. Unfortunately, that was not enough to trigger any serious reaction locally that would help resist or stop the damage that was being inflicted. I had to concentrate my efforts on the ground and focus on endangered buildings that were being disfigured or subject to demolition. One of the most visible architectural sacrileges at the time was the work done on the late 1960's former City Center project by Architect Joseph Philippe Karam, which was being converted to an entertainment venue. I was strongly opposed to the proposed scheme and was behind the Association for the Preservation of the Dome building, which was backed by a number of local intellectuals, architects and historians. We organized protests and sit-ins, wrote many articles in the local papers but we couldn't stop the project. A man by the name of Serge Salem had the power and the money to bribe the municipal authorities, get all the necessary permits and implement his hideous project. That was a big blow for me and for my allies. At that point, I had to reevaluate my strategy. If the conjuncture did not help us win the battle on the powerful developers' grounds, there was still a lot of work that needed to be done in the background. The disfiguration of Joseph Philippe Karam's City Center project was very symptomatic of a much larger phenomenon. The work of the first and second generation of local modernist architects was being forgotten. As the actual buildings were being demolished, the architects who conceived them were hard to find. Many had passed away, some had emigrated, and others were getting old. So I concentrated my efforts on archiving all the relevant historical documents I could get my hands on, building a database of what was there to be saved and what was worth documenting.

105

Joseph Philippe Karam was one of the first architects I researched. He had passed away back in 1976 at the age of 53, but his wife and his son were still around. They were the first who helped me put together the initial pieces of a huge puzzle that would later expand to include a large number of other influential figures from the post independence period. Karam was considered to be one of the leading figures of modern architecture in Lebanon. He had a prosperous 30-year career during which he designed and built an important number of iconic modern buildings in Beirut. Those included the City Center completed in 1966, which was at the time the largest shopping center in the region. He was also behind the second phase of the Phoenicia Hotel, originally designed by Edward Durell Stone, the Forest apartment building, La Gondole Center and many other great modern specimens. The story of Joseph Philippe Karam is rooted in the history of the young republic, which was born after the breakup of the Ottoman Empire. At the end of World War I, the country as we know it presently in its current borders was placed under French mandate by the League of Nations. The boy was given a French name and was sent to a Jesuit religious school. In 1946, Karam graduated from the Ecole Francaise d'Ingenieurs at the Saint Joseph University with a major in mathematics and Engineering. His French education led him to embrace modernist trends. After World War II, the young state, which had recently gained its independence from the French, profited from the new peace. Like many young local professionals of his generation, Joseph Philippe Karam benefited from a period of economic growth in the region that lasted 3 decades. It was impossible not to notice the literal connection between Karam's professional career, which started as the guns of World War II fell silent, and the end of it, with his premature death in 1976, at the onset of the Lebanese civil war. This also happened to be the end of the modern era in Lebanon and the region.

107

One of Karam's other great designs was the Tosbahji project located on Emir Omar Street in the Clemenceau district in Beirut. Due to its location at the edge of the demarcation line, a few meters away from the Holiday Inn tower, it had suffered from minor war damage. The harm that was done to the building through ad-hoc alterations and additions after the war was in fact far more severe. When I visited it recently, I could no longer identify Karam's original project that I only knew from historical photos we had collected and the initial architectural drawings from his archives. The Tosbahji complex was not only a pretty piece of architecture. In the 1960's and until the beginning of the hostilities in 1975, it housed a number of influential designers and urbanists who left a strong mark on the territory. At some point in time, Khalil Khouri and Gregoire Serof, both prominent architects of the second generation of local modernists, had offices there. Khouri and Serof were born and raised in Beirut. They had met on the benches of the College de La Salle in their early school years. The two young boys shared a passion for airplanes. They spent their childhood holidays designing and building model glider planes with left over pieces of wood they collected from the back of Khouri's father's woodshop. They would fly them around the sandy hills of Bir Hassan near the old airport. When there wasn't enough wind to keep their planes up in the air, they would ramp their way up to the fortified fences of the military hangars and get a closer look at the "Spitfire" fighter planes that the allies forces kept there, making sure the guards wouldn't notice them.

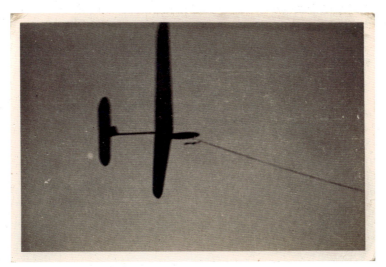

The two young kids thought they would eventually grow up to design more innovative jet propelled planes that the whole world would benefit from. They wanted to be aeronautic engineers. This was the 1940's in Beirut; a time when young kids of the small modern nation dreamed of embarking on the great modern project that seemed to be at reach. By the time the 2 boys grew up they were advised by their respective parents to make wiser, more realistic career choices. So they attended the Academie Libanaise des Beaux Arts where they both obtained an architecture degree. Way before their graduation, the 2 young men were already practicing and designing, amongst others, multiple housing schemes for Palestinian refugee camps that were commissioned by the United Nations. On the weekends, they would go flying over the Bekaa' valley piloting glider planes of the Lebanese Air Force. That's how they met Michel Ecochard, the prominent French urbanist who also flew as a hobby.

When I started this research project, Khouri who was already in his early seventies had left the country a couple of years earlier to settle in the U.S. I managed to get a hold of his younger brother who was still around, managing what was left of their industrial design operation, which was going down the drain. During my numerous sessions with him I got to visit many of Khouri's projects including their Interdesign showroom on Rome Street conceived in the early 1970's and completed in 1996. Khalil had designed and built this very innovative piece of brutalist architecture to showcase the furniture he produced. Years later, by the time I visited it, the exhibition spaces were packed with imported designer furniture of mediocre taste. There was very little left of the far more interesting creations that the Khouri brothers had produced in their golden age back in the 60's and early seventies. The operation was in decline, like most of the industrial sector in general and with it most other productive sectors in the country. As many other local industrialists, the Khouri brothers were under very heavy financial pressure. The banks, which were keeping them in artificial survival mode, were charging them absurdly high interest rates on their loans. As their debt was soaring, the bankers were slowly but surely eating away their patrimony, seizing their real estate properties and anything else they could get their hands on.

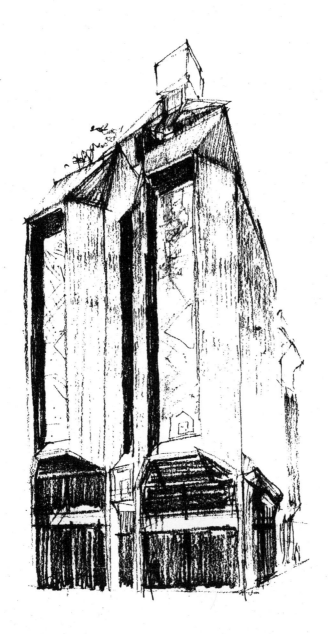

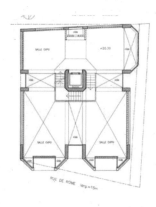

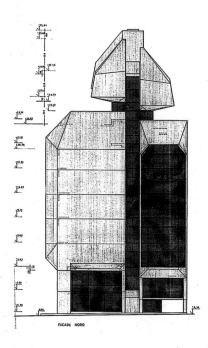
FACADE NORD

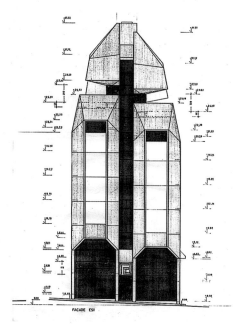
FACADE EST

The story of Khalil Khouri was quite a colorful one and full of contradictions. His mother was a nun who left the convent with Elias, the carpenter who was supposedly doing some woodwork there. They married and had 6 kids. Khalil, the eldest, grew up in the family's modest house adjacent to his father's carpentry shop. Elias El Khouri was one of the first 200 members to enroll the Phalangist Party. Initially a paramilitary youth organization, it was formed in 1936 by Pierre Gemayel, a Maronite Catholic who modeled it on the fascist organizations he had observed while in Berlin as an Olympic athlete. Consistent with their authoritarian beginnings, the Phalangists embraced the need to modernize but their ideology was on the far right of the political spectrum; the members used the Roman salute. The party's motto was "God, the Fatherland and the Family" and its policies were anticommunist, anti-Palestinian with no place for pan-Arab Ideals.

As a kid, Khalil was already an atheist and his beliefs were already not in line with his supposed Christian upbringing, both at home and at the religious school he attended. Later, as a young man, he embraced leftist ideals and became a member of the Lebanese Communist Party. He never missed the speeches of Gamal Abdelnasser that were broadcasted on the radio. At some point after the revolution in Cuba, he attended the 7th International Union of Architects Congress in Havana in 1963. The story says that he made it there via Vladivostok in a military soviet plane, bringing with him a cargo full of medical aid to the freedom fighters. His act of bravery led him to sit at the dinner table with Fidel Castro and the Che.

On his way back to Beirut, the pro-western authorities that had information on the incident took away his passport and forbid him from traveling for over a year. Back in the 1960's, Khouri had an oversized map of the globe in his office on which he had colored in all the Soviet and Communist nations in red. The other countries that were still under western control were crosshatched in red lines of different densities. More density of lines represented less time for the territory to fall under Communist influence. Less density of lines meant a longer time for that territory to become Communist. According to Khouri's projections, which he illustrated on his map, the whole globe should have turned red before the end of the1980's. Obviously, History proved him wrong but it didn't take the fall of the Berlin Wall for Khalil to reevaluate his political certainties. By the mid 1960's, after his father had passed away, he had already converted his dad's small carpentry woodshop into a prosperous furniture manufacture. The business expanded rapidly and by the early 1970's the Khouri brothers had built one of the largest furniture production plants in the region that employed over 400 artisans on 20000 square meters of surface. Besides his main occupation as an architect and designer Khalil also initiated a number of real estate development projects in which he was a shareholder. He was the "entrepreneur" who robbed Tony Texas around a poker table in his suite on the 7th floor of the Commodore hotel (Episode 1) However, those who knew him well said that despite the obvious contradictions, he remained throughout his life very close to the proletariat and often favored a humble meal with his workers over lunch with his banker.

On the numerous tours I took to the Mount Lebanon region I discovered an important number of great modern architectural works. Those included projects designed by Raoul Verney, a close friend of Khouri and Serof who designed the Red Cross building in Jounieh, a beautiful chapel in Faqra and a number of private villas. At that point, Verney's career had slowed down. Early into the meeting, I could feel the man was not very interested by my research as he was more motivated by the wine he was drinking.

Another great specimen I had the privilege to visit firsthand with one of its original designers was the College des Frères Mont La Salle, a large educational facility composed of modular units of fair-faced concrete. It was completed in the early seventies by the Khouri brothers in collaboration with Serof and Verney. Other projects by Khouri included the Fouad Chehab Municipal Stadium in Jounieh, commissioned by the President at some point in the early 1960's. It featured a sculptural oversized canopy and was one of the first pre-stressed concrete structures in the region. Unfortunately, in the later years, the municipality closed off its lateral facades in an attempt to interiorize what were initially open-air sports courts. Like many other neglected projects of that era, the stadium had now lost its glitter due to heavy-handed alterations, which were performed by unknown architects at a later stage. I continued my excursions with Khouri with a visit to the Manar resort, a project they designed and developed in the late 1970's, which seemed to follow the lessons of Le Corbusier's Unite d'Habitation. This massive concrete building features a swimming pool on its roof placed under a sculptural structure that resembles a whale.

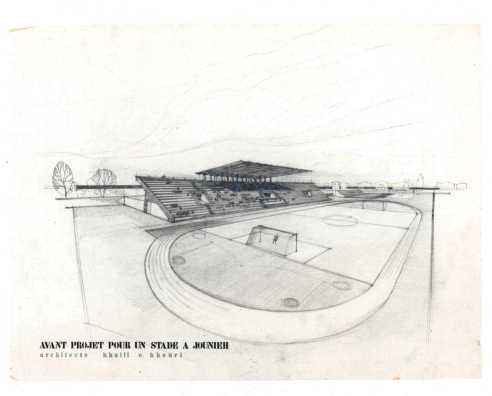

AVANT PROJET POUR UN STADE A JOUNIEH
architecte khalil e. khouri

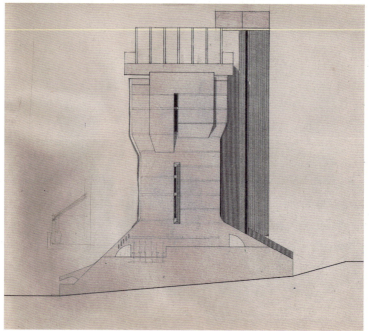

Another interesting architectural feature Khouri's brother pointed was the way gray and rainwater is collected from all terraces and channeled by very visible gargoyles that articulate the main façade of the edifice. The emphasis on architectural expression of water recuperation seemed unusual for that period. Khouri was very proud to note that the peripheral balcony landings that define the back façade of the building feed 3 levels while Le Corbusier's "coursive" of Marseille's Unite connects only to 2 levels.

During one of my last tours with Khouri's brother we stopped by Joseph Philippe Karam's Tosbahji building where I had the chance to hear his recollection of its history. Khalil had his office on the first floor, next to an extension of his ground floor showroom, which was located on a small island around which cars could drive in circles. The small exhibition pavilion, which was in Karam's initial plans, was redesigned by Khouri to be very transparent. The period's photographs showed very thin red I-beams holding an overhanging horizontal roof under which the designer's furniture was exhibited behind large glass panels on small-elevated plateaus. The showroom was damaged in the first days of the civil war and the Khouri brothers had to move out of there. Later, a beauty salon that moved in the space made alterations that butchered the initial design. The transparent glass panels were replaced by black tinted windows and the graceful horizontal overhang was closed off to extend the interior space. Khouri showed me where his older brother used to park his 1964 Alfa Romeo Sprint Veloce, the first one imported to Lebanon. A rare car that was bodied by Carrozzeria Bertone in Torino, which according to him was very unreliable. He also pointed at Gregoire Serof's parking spot. Serof had a Citroen DS, one of the prettiest and most forward-looking automobiles ever designed. Georgina Rizk, former Miss Universe made frequent visits to the building and had a parking spot under the pilotis of the elegant structure. She drove an orange Porsche 914 with a targa top. Residents of the building suspected her of having an affair with Cyril Chamoun, a playboy who owned the roof penthouse. He drove a Lancia Startos Zero. This one of a kind prototype was first presented at the 1970 Turin motor show. Back in the 1960's French eminent urbanist Michel Ecochard was commissioned by President Fouad Chehab the planning of many large infrastructural projects, including a new master plan for Beirut. During that time, Ecochard had a local liaison office and most of the work was done in an office space also located in the Tosbahji building.

124

Michel Ecochard, a graduate of the French Beaux Arts School started his career in 1930. Alongside Le Corbusier, he was given the task to plan and reorganize many cities of the region in the post-war period. When he was in his twenties, he had his first public works experience in Damascus under the colonial rule. In 1940, he became Director of the Syrian Urban Planning Department, which during French occupation included Lebanon. In 1945, during a trip to the Americas with Le Corbusier, Ecochard discovered the principles of Functionalist Urbanism that he applied on his later work. Better known as an urban planner, he was also an architect and an archaeologist. Ecochard's first solo project was the museum of Antioch, a marvelous architectural achievement that combined ancient Syrian architectural elements with modernist design. His plans for Damascus ensured the protection of its many historical monuments. In 1943, he designed the first master plan for Beirut. Back in Lebanon in 1963, he worked on integrating the capital into what he called a new national and regional urbanization strategy. In the course of his long career, Ecochard held a number of important institutional responsibilities. From 1946 till 1953, he was Chief Director of Urbanism in Morocco where he proposed his "new politics of inhabiting the territory for Muslim populations" also called the "Ecochard grid". After presenting his urbanism works for the Arabian cities at the 9th CIAM congress in 1953, he moved away from the region and worked on urban planning schemes for Guinea (1956-1958) the Ivory Coast (1961-1964) Senegal (1963-1979) Cameroun (1965-1974). In France, he worked on the master plan of Porto-Vecchio and Bastia (1962-1970) He was also in charge of the Urbanism section of the Beaux Arts school in Paris (1967).

2618   Vue prise du N-O   1935
        - mosquée des Ommeyades
        - Souq Midhat Pacha

Khouri's younger brother recalled many anecdotes that involved Khalil and Ecochard. Many of them reflected the contradictions between the pragmatism of the French urbanist and the very absurd reasoning of local politics. The most tragic one was about a supposed "fatwa" that was launched against the French urbanist in reaction to his proposed plan for the new North / South national highway in the early 1960's, during Fouad Chehab's presidential mandate. Like any conscientious urban planner would have done, Ecochard had outlined the course of the projected freeway at a reasonable distance from all the urban conglomerations it could cross along its path, giving them enough breathing space for future expansion. He rightfully considered that the speedy traffic was a nuisance to urban life and was to be kept as far as possible from the city fabric. The inhabitants of Jounieh, a little coastal town located about 20 kilometers north of Beirut did not agree with him. They were furiously opposed to his proposed trajectory and wanted the highway to pass smack in the middle of their beloved city. They considered that more traffic meant more exposure, more trade and commerce and therefor more immediate financial profit to all those who had land that would intersect the future 6-lane expressway. They wanted Michel Ecochard exterminated. In a desperate attempt to save his skin, the French urbanist found refuge at his friends' offices in the Tosbahji building before fleeing to Paris. Later, a compromise was found placing the highway half way in between its original location in Ecochard's plans and the old coastal road that ran in the center of the town. Soon enough, the old historical quarter and the little costal road that went through it were neglected. In an unprecedented phenomenon in the history of urban planning, the small Maronite Christian city of Jounieh had turned its back to the Mediterranean Sea.

The solution that was finally implemented did not provide the small town enough grounds to develop. Less than a decade later, the city's rapid expansion had already reached the edge of the highway, which provoked the unregulated proliferation of countless little shops that encroached on the high-speed lanes. Bakeries, small grocery stores, tire shops, tobacco and cigarettes stands were all looking to occupy every last inch of exposure to the vehicular circulation... You could find and buy anything on that highway. This provoked a catastrophic traffic bottleneck that the whole territory has since suffered from. The short-term mercantile mentality of the powerful feudal families who owned most of the land had overturned the long-term planning approach that characterized most of the development projects proposed during President Fouad Chehab's mandate. Ecochard's conflict with the people of Jounieh was perhaps very indicative of a cultural and socio-political phenomenon, which would later lead to the total bankruptcy of the state, its institutions and with it the notion of the modern nation.

129

BRACING

Modern Memoir
EAST Architecture Studio

Discovering Niemeyer

There's an unexplainable attraction to Lebanon that seems to defeat rationality. We – Charles Kettaneh and Nicolas Fayad – first met at architecture school at the American University of Beirut (AUB) before both of our careers as architects started in the United States and could have continued there. Nevertheless, there was this pull that brought us back, the same pull that brought many of our friends back, and generations before us, against the tide of logic, to participate in building – and often rebuilding – this small country full of contradictions, that same country where we were first introduced to architecture as a professional practice of cultural transmission and continuity.

The AUB campus itself is an enclave of coastal Levantine architecture mixed with a few modern and contemporary architectural gems by international architects. It was at AUB that we rediscovered our home through the lens of "architects in the making", with the introduction to the forgotten grounds of the Rachid Karami International Fair in Tripoli being one of our most notable experiences. This came about through a design studio exercise led by Dr George Arbid[1] – a mentor figure of sorts and, as we later discovered, a major caretaker of modern architecture in the country – who founded the Arab Center for Architecture, an invaluable repertoire of modernist gems that would later become a helpful resource for our work on the Guest House renovation some twenty years later.

Our first visit to the Niemeyer Fair felt like trespassing: barbwire fences were topping high concrete walls. Moving into the deserted site, we encountered in awe these monumental structures, their form, their scale and playfulness, which was unlike anything seen before. We could hardly believe that this was a part of "our" heritage.

Our experience discovering modernism through the work of Oscar Niemeyer was as unconventional as his architecture and as exhilarating as his imagination. From the boomerang, dome, and arches to structures seemingly defying gravity, we were learning the intent of each of his uncanny design decisions. His play with the notion of scale, manipulating monumental grandeur and human perspective, or his mastery of the curve are only a few of them. The bareness of the unfinished or looted structures did not detract from the understanding of his gestures – on the contrary, it seemed to sublime and abstract them at once.

In retrospect, from the exterior, this bare state does not differ immensely from what Niemeyer would have envisioned, other than the colour applied to the surfaces which would be white. The inexistent glass is probably what he would have desired from the material transparency – its absence. What could be understood as "modern ruins" was for us a full-scale architectural model, a real-life example of how to turn a line drawing concept into a three-dimensional construct. We were given the opportunity to wander into Niemeyer's creativity, and the

Figure 1. Nicolas Fayad and Charles Kettaneh at the Rachid Karami International Fair, 2018

abandoned site – emptied of function and human presence – made that experience personal and unique.

The studio exercise was to intervene "under the boomerang", as each student would occupy a chunk under the monumental canopy, in a similar fashion to what Niemeyer envisioned to "offer" to visiting counties during a World Exposition (fig. 1). Thirty-five iterations of a multi-purpose pavilion in an area of equal size, where we could express the learnings of our remarkable experience. While we are still uncovering meanings behind our design intentions, there is little doubt that this journey at the Tripoli Fair was a cornerstone that shaped our minds and our practice.

Preservation as Practice

Since the founding of EAST Architecture Studio, we have thoroughly engaged in preservation. Probably because of the richness and diversity inherent to the countries in which we practice, we have found ourselves more often than not in a position where we have to take into consideration existing structures, and therefore think of material conservation procedures, but also imagine a set of honest systems and possibilities to go beyond the existing. This involves, amongst other things, immersing ourselves in cultural practices, studying methodologies, and becoming acquainted with conservation charters through our own initiative.

Figure 2. Niemeyer Guest House construction progress photos, 2018

Our lack of formal training in architectural preservation offers us a unique perspective. We approach conservation by simultaneously considering the past and the future. From this standpoint, conservation emerges not just as a means of preserving a historical structure, but as a tool to manage and regulate societal change in the built environment. We have come to understand that, unlike contemporary architectural design, preservation as practice often necessitates more objective decision-making processes, fostering collaborations that are perhaps less obvious in the design practice alone (fig. 2).

Whether we are given a site in a natural setting or at a complex urban intersection, our approach builds on the idea that preserving the meaning of the extant needs to prevail. Preservation talks to memory; it reclaims context and builds upon it. We believe in preservation as a driver of design thinking because we're concerned with reactions and interpretation of places and environments. With projects that include existing structures, we are often invited to change the functions of these structures. Such projects share the particularity of being resolutely optimistic. Not only do they challenge us to acknowledge and preserve the past; they also force us to accept existing architectural expressions as hosts for new programmatic and tectonic use that often pays no respect to its original intent.

Preservation transcends space and time. The life cycle of a structure starts having meaning at different scales: it is not only about the materials but also about the usage and usability, and ultimately about the relevance to contemporary society. A vernacular Lebanese mountain house, for example, does not need its vaulted ground floor restored to recreate a home for animals. It is perfectly acceptable to suggest a programmatic function that corresponds to the present and future use of the house, thereby regenerating its programmatic life cycle. Ultimately, what is most crucial is to maintain the integrity of these vaults, to celebrate their presence as a reminder of their past use as well as their importance for the projected function.

Uncovering the Guest House

In the spring of 2017, we were invited to submit a proposal for the renovation of the Guest House, one of the fifteen pavilions designed by Oscar Niemeyer at the Rachid Karami International Fair in Tripoli. The new brief called for the transformation of the Guest House into a design platform and production facility that would promote the wood industry sector of Tripoli.

Tripoli is historically and culturally associated with its pioneering woodcraft industry. Since 2010, the sector has undergone a dramatic deterioration, fuelled by political unrest coupled with a growing emergence of low-cost imported furniture. Expertise France – a French public agency for international technical cooperation – was entrusted by the European Union to implement a development programme initiated by the Association of Lebanese Industrialists for the sustainable and inclusive promotion of Tripoli's woodcraft industry and carpentry cluster.

The Guest House renovation posed multiple challenges. How do we intervene in such a historical site while reconciling a client's needs and heritage conservation? This renovation, a first of its kind in the Fair, would surely mark a precedent. How could we embrace the significance of the past and the potential of its future use simultaneously?

Our endeavour to spark a dialogue between the old and the new, both symbolically and tangibly, through how we denote transitions or engineer tensions, would become paramount.

In such endeavours, the boundary between conservation and additions could be increasingly indistinct, or purposely obvious. A careful balancing of these protocols or operations would be key to the success of the project, as well as a deep dive into archival prints giving us clues on how Niemeyer intended to complete the structure. We thus embarked on an intensive research phase that pushed us to look for the original Niemeyer drawings. Thanks to Farès el-Dahdah,[2] who sits on the board of the Fundação Oscar Niemeyer, we were able to scrutinise original plans, sections, elevations, and intended material specifications. These valuable findings gave us clues on how Niemeyer would have sealed the Guest House, in terms of enclosure, material palette, and infrastructural systems. With this information at hand, we went back on site to absorb the spatial qualities and Niemeyer's original design intent.

Overwhelmingly opaque in appearance, the Guest House surprises with its light-flooded interior space, with an open floor plan punctured by a central courtyard (fig. 3). Its extensive floating roof sits on four columns and renders the "horizontal" space beneath as abstract. The compelling presence of the structural "ribs", which permeate through the roof slab, define the ceiling rhythmically, confirming the presence of an ornament that also has structural

Figure 3. Niemeyer Guest House north elevation after renovation

Figure 4. Niemeyer Guest House central courtyard

performance. Layers of burnt plaster had invaded the interior space, as the Guest House was used to inhabit militias during the Lebanese Civil War, but scratching through these layers revealed painted walls. The deliberate use of stone cladded on the internal face of the facades, along the internal side courtyards, as well as the presence of a stone cladded wall in the main space, introduces a sense of vernacular to the inside. From the outside, the fair-faced concrete roof dominates the Guest House's appearance, while the stained walls divulge a stucco application. There are no windows or punctures on the facade, other than the main entrances, as well as two service entrances at the back of the structure, which are not visible to passers-by. We were asked to intrude on a fundamentally introverted building.

Our intervention naturally considered the above-mentioned features, deliberately revealing and most importantly enhancing the "DNA" that composes the structure. We insisted on conceptually preserving the expansive open plan that revolves around the central courtyard, framed by several programmatic functions accommodating the needs of the desired platform. Defined by a series of lightweight steel and glass partitions registering the rhythmic ceiling structural grid, the spaces connect to each other and to the courtyard (fig. 4). Light, shadow, and transparency reverberate through a playful tempo of fixed and operable panels, allowing for openness or segregation when needed. The metalwork of these partitions, executed by local artisans, vertically projects the prevailing horizontal pattern of the ceiling ribs, highlighting their presence and their fragility at once. The imperfect yet precise craft that went into the making of these partitions intentionally allows for a detachment between the old and the new, a deliberate tension that aims to reconcile with the structural settling of the existing structure over time.

The proposed material palette and colour tones remained true to the state in which we first encountered the Guest House as architects, and the Fair as students – in its unfinished concrete grey colour. The resilience of concrete as a material and as a colour gives a sense of timelessness and austerity to the incomplete grounds in which the building resides. We've intentionally embraced this timelessness and introduced "monochromatism" as an integral part of the design intervention: ceilings, walls, floors, millwork and metal frames, all predominantly grey, help reveal the building's original weightless interiors, blurring thresholds between inside and outside (fig. 5).

Paradoxically, the programmatic use of the new space is ephemeral. Used as a design platform and prototyping facility for the next three years, the Guest House could one day reclaim its original use, or another one altogether. It is the notion of ephemerality, together with our desire to keep the structure intact, that made our intervention reversible: the lightweight partitions, lighting fixtures, and machinery could be removed, leaving space for another programme to take over, yet with the integrity of the original design still untouched.

Abstract like the Fair, the intervention would feel as if nothing had been done, or as if it had always been present. That sobriety worked well with the programme, yet it did not hinder creativity. It posed a remarkable challenge that was overcome by a lot of back and forth with all the stakeholders involved in the project, and a rigorous sense of balance and restraint throughout all design stages.

Figure 5. Niemeyer Guest House exhibition space

Figure 6. Niemeyer Guest House entrance walkway after renovation

Preservation as Scaffold

As humans on this planet, we are passers-by. What links us is the baton we pass as time triumphs over us. The baton that is architecture and the built environment is one of the strongest storytellers, as it speaks of civilisations, techniques, politics, and economies, to name a few. As architects, but also as humans, we have a responsibility to continue passing that baton. Through acts of preservation and restoration, we brace a story in decay, creating a scaffold that will sustain its presence to at least the next generation.

When lacking a vision for preservation, we confine ourselves to operating within the realm of the past, where landscapes and cities are steeped in nostalgia – while our theories are built on the assumption that our city remains static and stable. In this approach, architecture becomes the sole means through which memory is preserved. Can preservation be as much about envisioning futures as it is about conserving the past?

In reality, the current structure of preservation practice often reinforces the validity of continuous historical narratives, perpetuating a nostalgia-driven impulse to preserve. Discontinuities or inconsistencies are viewed as deviations from an otherwise ideal built environment. It is at this juncture that blurring the disciplinary boundaries between conservation and urban planning becomes essential for the relevance of our historical built environments. Developing multidisciplinary approaches to conservation might help anchor the importance of conservation in the public awareness once again, so that transitionary political agendas and bureaucratic constraints are not the only agencies left to determine the fate of buildings and the worthiness of their conservation. By collectively and holistically examining the built environment through various disciplines, we can forge new narratives that shape appropriate conservation practices (fig. 6).

The ability to acknowledge the simultaneous validity of conflicting forms, histories, or narratives is not a task solely for conservation narratives to address. Instead, they must work in tandem to resonate with the pluralism inherent in our region's built environment – both historical and contemporary. Furthermore, the pursuit of creating an imagined world of lost grandeur appears increasingly futile, irrelevant, and unproductive for designers.

Notions of cultural significance must expand to reflect highly pluralistic societies where cultural memory is often a dynamic and enacted process. In conservation debates within this dynamic context, it may be necessary to focus more intensely on the concept of constructing significance. Understanding how significance evolves can truly clarify the role of conservation professionals – not merely as opponents of change but as managers or facilitators of it.

Preservation practice should aspire to be anticipatory – projecting and anticipating what we want to conserve because we should be equally concerned with the future and its possibilities. One can envision a future where civic establishments decide on the worthiness of preserving a building before granting approval for new architectures to coexist. Thus, preservation will be intrinsically linked with the very conception of architecture and our cities on a larger scale. It will precede planning, leading to a clearer perspective on what we wish to conserve while speculating on the returns it may yield in the future.

At this critical juncture, some urgent questions emerge: How can we redefine the boundaries of heritage conservation, considering that the existing definition of heritage typically requires a minimum of 100 years? Why does the potential demolition or destruction of modern buildings not elicit stronger public engagement? How can we reimagine modern buildings not just as historical artefacts but as dynamic settings for present-day life? What criteria might designate them as works of art of national significance in today's context? We do not ask these questions in pursuit of definitive answers. Similar to our engagement with the Niemeyer Guest House, we aim to translate them into architectural gestures that acknowledge their importance, and materialise their potency as critical scaffolds for our cultural continuity.

1   See "It shouldn't end like this. Raafat Majzoub in conversation with Nora Akawi and George Arbid" by George Arbid in the present volume, p. 32.

2   See the conversation with Farès el-Dahdah and Ana Tostões in the present volume, p. 81.

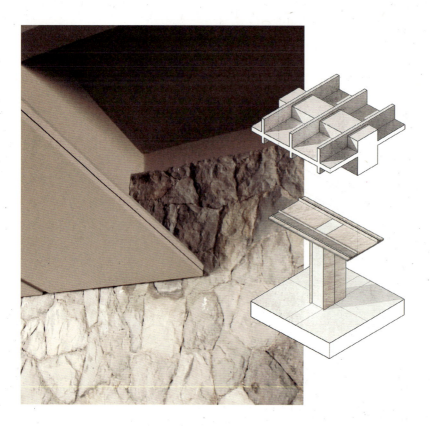

Axonometric drawing and photo of wooden sofit that conceals
the electromechanical devices and conduits

Collage depicting the north elevation before and after its renovation

1 Entrance Pavilion
2 Guest House
3 Administration Building
4 Lebanese Pavilion
5 Exhibition Hall
6 Domed Amphitheatre
7 Helipad
8 Nursery
9 Outdoor Theatre
10 Director's House
11 Collective Housing

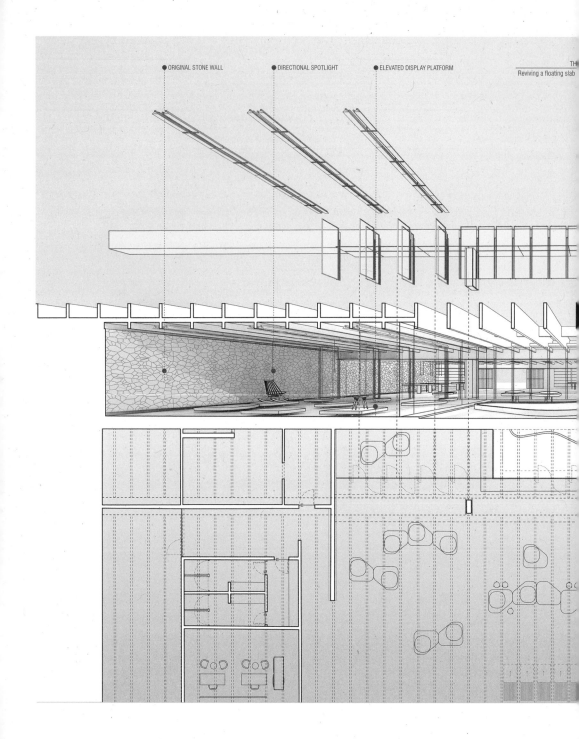

Composite drawing combining elements of the architectural intervention, such as the glazing partition and lighting system

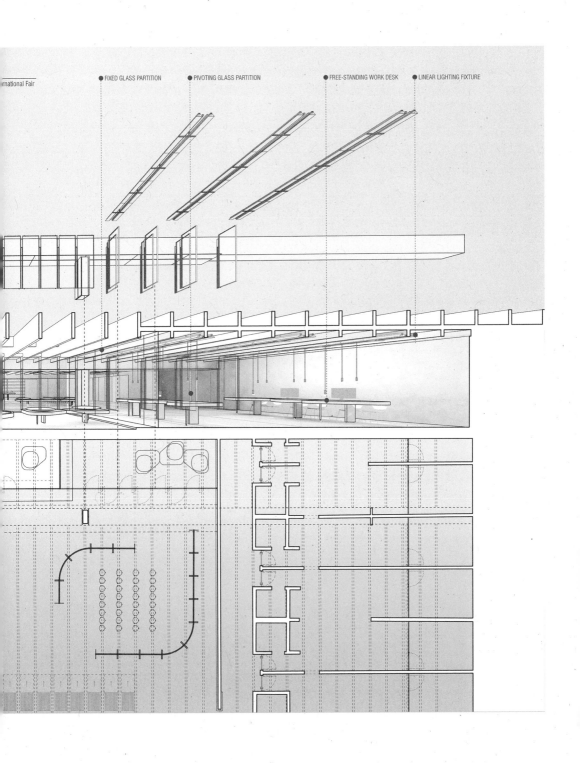

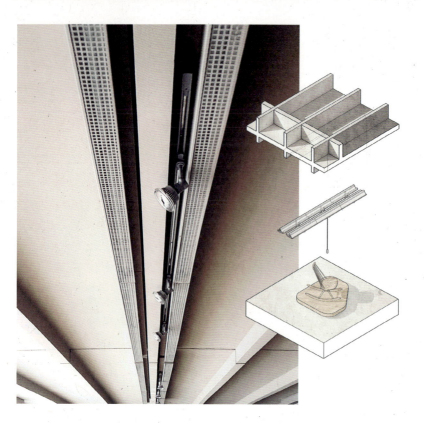

Axonometric drawing and photo of the integrated lighting system that borrows from the proportions of the ceiling ribs

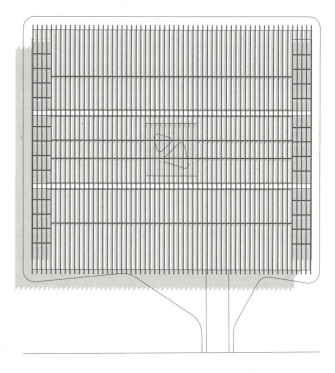

Roof plan

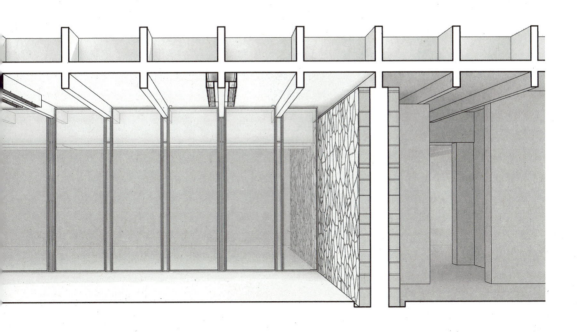

Axonometric drawing and photo of the glazing partition that references the rythmic structure of the ceiling ribs

The Scaffolds of Modernism
Aaron Betsky

When we build, we create a ghost of the building. That spectre consists, first, of the images, models, plans, and specifications we produce, usually in many iterations and layers. Then it arises as the clearing or emptying of the site, which awaits the imprint of the new, as well as settling into the materials we assemble in that place. Third, there are all the things we bury inside the building, from metal reinforcement bars to the seashells embedded in the concrete; the wires and pipes we also bury, never to be seen again; whole structures that disappear behind finished surfaces and complete chemical mixtures that freeze into the final building. Fourth, there is the second skin we construct – the scaffolding in and through which we make the building. Fifth, there are the accoutrements of use, whether planned by designers or installed and continually rearranged by users. Finally, there is one or many last versions of such others or ghosts of our buildings, which consist of the pictures and words we make to try to evoke not so much the result, as everything that we think and we, as designers or critics, want to explain is entombed within the building.

Often, that haunting other is much more beautiful than the actual structure we see and use. It is full of potential, it is infinitely evocative and flexible, and it can delight and scare us in ways reality can never hope to do. It is no wonder, then, that those who love architecture have engaged in seances to make these ephemeral spectres present. While many have engaged in drawing or building fanciful imagery that is meant to raise the possibilities of the ghost in unbuildable representations, others have argued that we should excavate our buildings to reveal what is buried inside them.

Yet others have spoken of the importance of the second skin or the scaffolding itself. Colin Rowe and Fred Koetter, in their seminal *Collage City*, posited that what was needed was an urban "protective membrane between the individual and the form of collective authority".[1] This in-between would imprint both the exigencies of daily life and the overall sense of control necessary to allow those lives to take place. The necessarily amorphous or slippery in-between would be expressed in that collage of buildings which were fragmentary, left over, and compromised exactly by those personal and collective histories, which would together present the "city as scaffold for exhibition demonstration".[2] Existing "between structure and event", as Rowe and Koetter quote Claude Lévi-Strauss in his analysis of "magical" thinking,[3] it is a realised and demonstratable (and actively demonstrating) reality that would allow buildings to remain as building blocks of a necessarily unrealisable utopia (or dystopia), which for them was the true ghost in these architectonic machines, while also impressing the necessary disorder and tragedy of human life upon our consciousness.[4]

To Bernard Tschumi, the result could be called an "event architecture": "The event is the place where the rethinking and reformulation of the different elements of architecture, many of which have resulted in or added to contemporary social inequities, may lead to their solution. By definition, it is the place of the combination of differences."[5] Tschumi proposed making forms that were open grids or three-dimensional frameworks in which a variety of events could take place, at best in a collage with each other.[6]

Such theories, which were further developed by Rowe's and Tschumi's students and collaborators, most notably Rem Koolhaas, remained theoretical.[7] Many other architects, however, have remarked quite simply that "a building under construction is much more beautiful than when it is finished".[8] They have also delighted in the beauty of scaffolding in particular, commenting on its openness, on the manner in which it indicates, rather than fixes, form, and on its gauzy presence as a result of the netting or accumulation of elements, at least in its bamboo version.

More recently, the architecture of scaffolding has also taken on an implicit form. In what I have called imaginative reuse, structures are rehabilitated, reoccupied, renovated, and adapted not by merely placing the new in, over, or through the existing, but through an intuitive form of excavation that collages what is found with the new.[9] The resulting architecture makes the evidence of the lives that have taken place within buildings present, engages in a kind of museum of scaffolding to make them come alive, and in that manner opens them up so as to make new ways of conscious occupation and inhabitation possible. The building itself becomes the scaffolding. It is stripped down, made more ephemeral and open, reveals what is buried inside of it, and

Figure 1. Renovation process view of the 1980s concrete floor of the second floor main room of Villa Tugendhat taken in 2010 as part of its two-year conservation and restoration

Figure 2. *The R4 Folie* is one of twenty-six bright red metal structures called *folies* scattered throughout Parc de la Villette in Paris

regains its unfinished potential. The architects of imaginative reuse work carefully, but without a preset plan or order, to tease out what is hidden within the building, so to then show and preserve what they have found. Whatever happens within the building can become yet another part of that revealed and embodied set of ghosts that haunt the structure.

Within this framework, the recuperation of modernist monuments takes a special place. By modernism, I refer here not to all the different reactions to modernisation that architects have formulated, but to the subset of those who have sought to embody the technological, democratic or open, and revelatory aspects these designers felt were intrinsic to the modern age. They sought to do so through abstraction, modularity, the openness of spaces to each other and to their surroundings, the revealing of structure, and the use of human-made materials such as glass, steel or other metals, concrete, and laminates based on chemical distillations and combinations.

Such architecture also sought to remove itself from both history and time in general. That was, of course, not possible. The very nature of many of the new materials very soon showed signs of wear. Steel rusted or coatings chipped off; concrete crumbled and cracked; artificial materials and glass discoloured. Joints were especially liable to show off the effects of time, whether because of the experimental nature of their fabrication or because exposing as much of the construction as possible increased the buildings to leakage of all sorts.

Modernist architects who created such structures did not care that this was the case. Their buildings were not meant for the ages, but for the specific time in which they were erected, and they imagined that the structures would be torn down as soon as their effectiveness had disappeared under the marching heels of progress. That very focus on the spirit of the age in architecture also meant that these buildings very soon appeared dated as well. Philosophically, what is new today is, as a result, already old. What had been the latest technology a few years ago now appeared as a relic. Moreover, it turned out that the very drive to represent modernisation as honestly as possible was an ephemeral one, replaced by a desire to make what was new recognisable in look and feel.

While the resistance to time as an issue created a long lag in the call to preserve modernist structures, by the 1960s the drive to fix up and reuse ahistorical historic monuments became an important force in architecture. The initial and still prevalent mode of such preservation is a highly regressive one. Buildings are restored to the way they appeared the moment they opened, and the actions taken by preservation architects are meant to keep them in that mode. This leads to such strange phenomena as the almost complete rebuilding of the Villa Tugendhat or the Villa Savoye as facsimiles of themselves that you can only enter wearing plastic booties, and that serve to merely remind you of what was once modernist (fig. 1). Even stranger are the attempts to resurrect buildings and make them permanent – ranging from a design by Ludwig Mies van der Rohe, the Barcelona Pavilion, to the dislocation and rebuilding of the annual Serpentine Pavilion – that were explicitly meant to be temporary in nature.

Only recently have we come to grips with another possibility. That is to understand what remains of modernism as ruins or after-effects that evoke, but will never be able to completely rebuild, the future we thought we were once going to have. Whatever is new is, in the mode of imaginative reuse, woven through the old in the manner of a scaffolding for new activities that can take place in and through what remains. Such architecture understands that modernism of the reductive and expositive sort has an elegiac quality, because, despite its claims to defy time and place, it remains rooted in those limited conditions (fig. 2).

This is even more so the case exactly in the case of those temporary structures, such as fairgrounds, that were part of a larger effort to show off modernity. There, what remains is even less, and what can be done with it is, paradoxically, more. Within the fragments of what was meant to be not much more than a scaffolding itself for exhibitions and events – for showing off the new products, materials, modes of life, and images of an always new age – we can erect a double to that open-ended, albeit temporary, but certainly adaptable construction. It can be dedicated not to the new as a fact, but to the activity of making, in an experimental and direct manner, the new. This is always also an act of rebuilding the past in a way that accepts, reuses, opens, reimagines, and thus unlocks the past, with all of its hopes, fears, and realities, in such a manner that we can engage in the daily activity of making the world we have inherited better.

1   Colin Rowe and Fred Koetter, *Collage City* (Cambridge, MA: The MIT Press, 1984), p. 111.

2   Ibid., p. 136

3   Claude Lévi-Strauss, *The Savage Mind* (1962; repr., Chicago: University of Chicago Press, 1966).

4   Rowe and Koetter, *Collage City*, p. 137.

5   Bernard Tschumi, *Architecture and Disjunction* (Cambridge, MA: The MIT Press, 1996), p. 258.

6   Ibid., p. 257.

7   See especially Rem Koolhaas's *Delirious New York* (New York: Rizzoli International Publications, 1978). Koolhaas has also developed a sophisticated and nuanced attitude towards preservation. See Rem Koolhaas and Jorge Otero-Pailos, *Preservation Is Overtaking Us* (New York: Columbia University Graduate School of Architecture, Planning, and Preservation, 2009).

8   Aaron Betsky, "Postscript from the 2016 Venice Biennale", *Architect*, 14 June 2016, https://www.architectmagazine.com/design/exhibits-books-etc/postscript-from-the-2016-venice-biennale_o.

9   My book *Just Don't Build: Imaginative Reuse* will be published by Beacon Press in 2025.

A Regenerative Invitation for the Tripoli Fair
Sarah Mineko Ichioka

As we, humans, hurtle headlong into conditions of ecological and technological destabilisation, we might benefit from asking ourselves: Which received truths, which cherished concepts, should we continue to carry with us? And which – if we chose to jettison them – might open paths towards other ways of being, better attuned with the fundamental conditions of life?

Within professional domains, this calls for our curiosity about the norms of thinking and practice that we have inherited, and how these serve us now, within dramatically changing circumstances. In the field of architecture, for example, we are accustomed to assessing a building's success and significance on the basis of various implicit and explicit assumptions.

At the time of the conception of the Rachid Karami International Fair (ca. 1962), overt assumptions would have included: nations should announce their modernisation, attract attention and investment by building large-scale attractions designed by international starchitects (*avant la lettre*). More recently, assumptions implied within the UNESCO World Heritage dossier on the Tripoli Fair (2023) and the critical praise for the Niemeyer Guest House's award-winning renovation include: the best approach to a heritage building is minimalist deference to its Master's original design intent.

EAST's interventions to the Guest House are indeed characterised by restraint, economy, and reversibility, and informed by their careful research into Niemeyer's work. The building has been resuscitated, yet not fully stabilised. For example, a pump is installed to remove water from its basement, but that basement has not been made impervious to regular flooding. It appears as a calm, beautifully lit oasis. At the same time, with the renovation, EAST and their programming and funding partners have created the conditions for the building's socio-economic reanimation, namely, the cultivation of right livelihoods for local craftspeople. This occupation connects with place-based heritage, extrapolating from regional woodworking traditions.

So, we might say that EAST have treated this declining uncle with loving care; they have helped to reduce his pain, to maintain his dignity, and they have celebrated his impeccable pedigree. But – whether intentionally, or otherwise – these actions don't suggest that he will live, or should live, forever. This is appropriate since the system of assumptions (economic, material, social) that brought him into being are dying. Or perhaps, more precisely, that system of assumptions is bringing our species itself to the brink of death, so it must be allowed to finally expire. On modernity's watch, we have overshot six out of the nine measurable boundaries of planetary health, including environmental pollution, freshwater availability, land system change, climate, and biodiversity loss.[1]

In this – perhaps too bluntly anthropomorphic – framing, I'm following the cues of Vanessa Andreotti, whose writing invites us "to witness and offer palliative care to modernity dying within and around" us.[2] Andreotti and her collaborators in the collective called Gesturing Towards

Decolonial Futures (GTDF) encourage us to hospice modernity "with care and integrity, as well as attention to the lessons these deaths offer, while also assisting with the birth of new, potentially wiser possibilities, without suffocating them with projections".[3]

Viewing the Niemeyer Guest House renovation through the lens of hospicing modernity (and, in the realm of the built environment, "carbon form",[4] for example, which arose from conditions of modernity) opens the possibility for new conversations about the future of the fairgrounds. Could a hospicing approach suggest a way to offer respect and thanks for the gifts of modernity, in this particular place and time, while declining to engage in delusions of its wholesale restoration to imagined glory days?

It is tempting to turn this into a public admonition to the politicians, financiers, construction conglomerates, and so on, who continue to commission and erect monumental architecture in the interest of perpetuating chauvinist nationalist narratives, extractive economic models, and so forth. But directing our focus onto external agents would miss, probably, the point of the exercise.

What might "hospicing modernity" feel like for those of us who write for and read books like this one, the circle who like to tell one another that we have meaningful things to say about architecture's place in the world? What might enable us to let go (really let go) of the underlying assumptions that brought the Fair about, about how a city should attract resources and command respect? To say goodbye to the received wisdoms that shape our expected behaviours in response to canonical architecture? And also – here's where it gets more challenging – to say goodbye to what we think it is important to say about a building? A key aspect of GTDF practice involves "interrupting modern-colonial addictions, in particular addictions to the consumption of knowledge [and] of critique".[5]

In place of the ecologically disastrous modernist palette of concrete, steel, and glass, biomaterials are gaining growing recognition from the architectural establishment[6] and construction industry. At their most exciting (and convincing), biomaterials are specifically tied into the ecologies of certain places (fig. 1).[7] Many biomaterials designers and makers work with the by-products of agriculture and food manufacturing. A report by Acted suggests that Lebanon's agricultural sector has a huge potential to reclaim an estimated US$100 million per year in lost nutrients and energy.[8] Beyond this immediate potential, given the economic crisis's impact on Lebanon's farmers (and business generally), diversified sources of income that turn additional organic "waste" into resources may be welcomed, while Lebanon's resident and diaspora design community may be well placed to create useful objects and building elements from these new materials, building on efforts such as the one currently housed in the Niemeyer Guest House.

Around the world, organisations are seeking to contend with the manufactured detritus of modern take-make-waste economies in ways that replace extractive models and create new

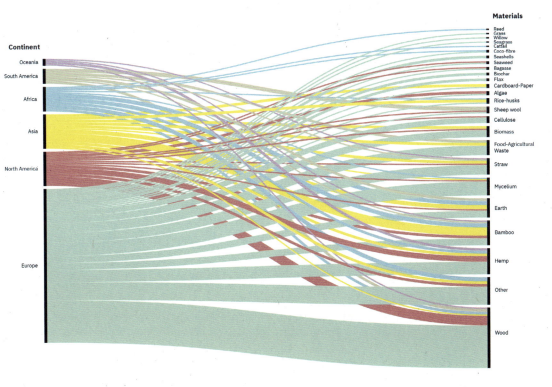

Figure 1. Built by Nature Prize 2024 submissions by geography and materials

social value. The port city of Rotterdam contains several inspiring examples of twentieth-century infrastructure repurposed to scaffold regenerative economies. Chief amongst these, BlueCity, designed by Superuse Studios,[9] repurposes the spectacular glass-domed 1980s leisure centre into an ecosystem that has grown from a small handful of initial experimental entrepreneurs to incubate over fifty circular economy businesses (figs. 2 and 3). The architecture of the renovation itself, which repurposed as many materials as possible from the old building, exemplifies creative "circular" approaches to architecture and construction.[10] Lebanon already has a circular economy hub in Beirut.[11] In complement to building organisational capacities for regenerative models, it would be a fascinating – if controversial – exercise to think about a "harvest mapping" approach to the Tripoli Fair and its environs, an approach that sought to document what elements are available, and how they might best be reused to meet contemporary needs, rather than seeking to preserve their originally intended form.

Working in the context of rapidly urbanising African societies, the enterprise Kubik aims to address some of the largest challenges facing cities like those they call home (Nairobi and Addis Ababa), namely waste (in the absence of formal waste management systems), housing access (via affordability), and the climate emergency (figs. 4 and 5). They do this by creating durable, affordable building components from upcycled, and otherwise wasted, plastics. Their business provides clean, easy-to-use, and affordable components which small contractors can use to build housing at speed, with dignity and safety for the poor as their driving purpose. The start-up also – by design – empowers female waste-pickers who previously were exploited by male brokers who charged massive mark-ups on the materials they collect. A recent report suggests that Lebanon's e-waste repair economy holds more promise than plastics or textile recycling, and that the majority of this economy currently constitutes micro businesses staffed by Syrian labourers.[12] What new business models might be incubated in a place like the Tripoli Fair, that build from these realities?

Figures 2 and 3. BlueCity in Rotterdam transforms a former tropical swimming facility into a circular economy hub for sustainable innovation.

Turning from buildings and their components to the landscapes they nest within, we can find many inspiring examples around the world of the restoration of land that had been previously depleted by human actions. Outside Jaipur, in India's dry northwestern state of Rajasthan, Manvendra Singh Shekhawat[13] and his colleagues have restored over 200 hectares of degraded land through a decade-long effort of tree planting, the restoration of historic water systems, food forest cultivation, and the selective introduction of grazing animals (figs. 6 and 7). At present, the site hosts over 140 species of migratory and resident birds, has the capacity to harvest 400 million litres of rainwater, and is moving towards self-sufficiency in food grown using traditional permacultural techniques.[14] This patient approach has sought to revive the ecosystem and understand its capacities for supporting life and right livelihoods for the traditional agricultural communities before reintroducing any significant built elements or newcomers. Any new buildings – planned to host a community centred on learning and wellness – are intended to be informed by a close study of indigenous construction methods, including the careful archiving of salvaged remnants of heritage buildings, earmarked for future adaptive reuse.

Deema Assaf, an architect and urban forester, established the TAYYŪN research studio to revive the forests that once grew across her native Jordan; the studio now works on projects across the Middle East. After years of more conventional architectural practice, Assaf says she "came to believe that the world needs many less structures and many more forests".[15] TAYYŪN has planted several native forests in Jordan, alongside creating a native forest database and conducting research into localising approaches to soil and planting (fig. 8).[16] Assaf notes that ecological landscaping practices "try to understand, mimic and accelerate the natural processes of any chosen locality".[17] And given the sometimes centuries-long absence of forests from the sites they've worked on, the studio has called upon paleobotanical research from neighbouring

Figure 4. Women waste collectors employed by Kubik in Harar

Figure 5. Kubik brick wall made of hard-to-recycle plastic waste

Figures 6 and 7. Ecological regeneration at Dhun Jaipur: 500 acres of degenerated land turned into a thriving ecosphere over a period of ten years

locations, to understand prehistoric vegetation patterns. Another international initiative, SUGi, planted micro forests in school courtyards in Beirut as part of recovery efforts after the port explosion of 2020 (fig. 9).[18] Rather than uprooting spontaneous vegetation as part of an architectural conservation exercise, it is exciting to imagine a future approach to the Fair site that works with regional experts to actively cultivate locally suited flora and fauna in the spaces between and within its structures.

    Might it be easier to hospice modernity in Tripoli, somewhat on the fringes of globalised capitalism? Meaning, might it be easier here to reconnect with the fundamental realities of place, distinct from modern-colonial abstract systems of value? Another possible route, if we

Figure 8. Amman Sanctuary, funded by SUGi and planted in collaboration with SUGi Forest Makers: TAYYŪN

seek to avoid suffocating the birth of new possibilities with "best practice" projections (as the GTDF collective also encourages), is instead to look to the past with curiosity. As David Graeber and David Wengrow relate in their book *The Dawn of Everything* (2021), our human ancestors lived—chose to live—in myriad different ways; which have fluctuated wildly across time, and sometimes varied radically between close neighbours. The archaeological record reveals a spectrum of governance, cultural practices, patterns of habitation, trade and social relations so broad, and so diverse, that a modernised mind can almost not comprehend its scope.

While the Niemeyer Guest House renovation breaks the isolation between the modernist ruin and the organic growth and heritage of its host city, it does not, on an architectural level, seek to engage with wider existential questions. Notably – and likely due to a combination of budgetary factors and aesthetic decisions – it does not strive towards planetary health in terms of its materials, energy sources, and approach to landscape.

In a place like Tripoli, reflection on three millennia of human habitation seems likely to offer more exciting food for our creativity than the bleak fare of the past fifty years. And perhaps in a way that reactivates other memories – of the fertile land beneath the Fair (where orange trees once grew), of an ancient port's relationship with the sea, and, most importantly, of the living metabolism connecting and sustaining all of these elements. How might we imagine the next iteration of the Guest House, and indeed the rest of the fairgrounds, with life at their centre?

Figure 9. Back to Play Forest at the Ecole Secondaire des Filles de la Charité in Beirut. Implemented by SUGi following the horrific blast on 4 August 2020, these micro Miyawaki forests have been planted as part of the rehabilitation of school playgrounds through de-paving and reintroduction of green spaces.

1 Stockholm Resilience Centre, "Planetary Boundaries", 2023, www.stockholmresilience.org/research/planetary-boundaries.html.

2 Vanessa Machado de Oliveira, *Hospicing Modernity: Facing Humanity's Wrongs and the Implications for Social Activism* (Berkeley, CA: North Atlantic Books, 2021).

3 Gesturing Towards Decolonial Futures (GTDF), decolonialfutures.net.

4 Elisa Iturbe, ed., "Overcoming Carbon Form", *Log* 47 (Fall 2019).

5 In full: "It is about interrupting modern-colonial addictions, in particular addictions to the consumption of knowledge, of self-actualisation, of experiences, of critique, of alternatives, of relationships and of communities." GTDF (see note 3).

6 At a recent Harvard symposium on the topic, the architect Paul Lewis, whose practice LTL has published case studies on "Biogenic" buildings made from earth- and plant-based materials, "advocated embracing ideas that are 'fundamentally at odds' with the 'given values we've inherited from modernism', aligning his explorations with the growing recognition that buildings as constructed throughout the past century have played a significant role in our current ecological predicament". On this, see A. Krista Sykes, "How Bio-Based Building Materials Are Transforming Architecture", Harvard GSD website, 30 April 2024, https://www.gsd.harvard.edu/2024/04/how-bio-based-building-materials-are-transforming-architecture/.

7 For example, the winners of the Built by Nature Prize, the first global awards programme dedicated to recognising the use of bio-based construction materials, with winners and finalists from places as varied as Nicaragua, Mexico, Senegal, Singapore, and the United Kingdom; see https://builtbn.org/prize.

8 Acted Lebanon, "Towards a Circular Economy in Lebanon", June 2020, www.acted.org/wp-content/uploads/2018/01 acted-lebanon-circular-economy-final.pdf.

9 Disclosure: a former collaborator of the author's.

10 Trying to design systems as neat "circles" is in itself probably a modernist trap, but this is certainly moving closer to a living systems approach.

11 https://www.thecircularhub.net/news/the-circular-hub-has-launched2

12 Deutsche Gesellschaft für Internationale Zusammenarbeit (GIZ), "Assessment Report: The Circular Economy Ecosystem in the MENA Region", 15 May 2023.

13 Disclaimer: a former client of the author's.

14 https://dhun.life/story-of-land.php

15 Transcript of "Deema Assaf on Greening the Desert", Alice Rawsthorn's interview for the Design Emergency Podcast, published in August 2023.

16 https://qr.biennale.org.sa/tayyun-pp-gd/

17 Transcript of "Deema Assaf on Greening the Desert" (see note 15).

18 https://www.sugiproject.com/forests/country/lebanon

PRESERVATION

Architecuture in Scale
A Discussion with Ana Tostões and Farès el-Dahdah

In this conversation, Raafat Majzoub and Nicolas Fayad consult Ana Tostões and Farès el-Dahdah on the evolution and significance of architectural preservation in Brazil and beyond. The discussion explores the history of building protection, the integration of host communities and intangible heritage in preservation efforts, the unique approach of preserving architectural grammar over style, the intricate connections between Niemeyer's projects in Tripoli and Brasília, and the broader relevance and urgency of heritage preservation in the Global South amidst socio-political and economic challenges.

Raafat Majzoub and Nicolas Fayad Could you speak to the history of protecting buildings? When and where did it start? What was the context and the reason behind such legislation?

Farès el-Dahdah In Brazil, it technically started in the 1930s with modern architects like Lucio Costa being in charge of preserving art and architecture, mostly Baroque churches at the time. To put this into perspective, the architect who masterminded the plan for Brasília was actually, for most of his life, a civil servant working for the agency in charge of historical and artistic preservation, what is now called IPHAN, or Instituto do Patrimônio Histórico e Artístico Nacional.

So you have to imagine that the architect who was in charge of preserving Baroque churches and Portuguese forts, which is what was considered architectural heritage back then in Brazil, was a fan of Le Corbusier. A good example that beautifully illustrates this paradox is found in Ouro Preto, a very-well-preserved eighteenth-century town and a World Heritage site in Brazil (fig. 1). The Baroque imaginary we see today does not represent what the town looked like 150 or so years ago, with all the accretions that an industrialising nineteenth-century Brazil brought about.

Modern architects in charge of preservation "cleaned" it all up and turned it into what they imagined the Baroque looked like. They removed and scraped everything back to the bare bones. Pilasters lost their gilding. Painted churches became white based on the pretext that the original colours could not be determined. They stripped everything down to the structure in order to abide by their own modernist convictions as applied onto an eighteenth-century urban fabric.

Figure 1. Ouro Preto

Figure 2. Church of Saint Francis of Assisi in Pampulha

Another interesting instance of early Brazilian building protection can be illustrated through Niemeyer's church in Pampulha (fig. 2). At the time, even before the project was completed, a local bishop had decided that it was too ugly for a church and rallied for its demolition. Lucio Costa, being in charge of the architectural division of the heritage institute, decided to protect it by law preemptively. He proposed that since the building would most likely become a monument in the future, it would be important to protect it even before it was finished, and this would eventually turn into law. I think this was how the Church of Saint Francis of Assisi in Pampulha was most probably the first modern building to be granted legal protection.

It also goes beyond that. The beginnings of architectural preservation in Brazil were very nuanced, in that they preserved grammar and not aesthetics. In 1936, when Oscar Niemeyer and Lucio Costa were in New York, designing the Brazilian Pavilion for the World Fair there, they were sent an image of a hotel project to be built in Ouro Preto in pseudo-Baroque style, with sweeping roof lines, et cetera. Costa intervened to stop the project, saying that if there is an empty lot, one should not mimic Baroque architecture, but rather just do "good" architecture that fits into the fabric.

The idea is that architecture should not be relegated to mere mimicry, and that there would not be a break between architectural heritage and modern architecture. For Costa, modern architecture is Brazilian by definition. Unlike modernisms elsewhere in the world, which have been argued on the basis of a break with tradition, in Brazil they argued that it was actually a continuation of tradition. This argument is how these architects also managed to turn modern architecture into the brand of the state, which remained solidly in place until the 1960s.

Ana Tostões Lucio Costa considered new and old architecture as two complementary components on the same path towards creating Brazilian architecture within the continuation of a tradition based on Portuguese Plain Architecture as defined by George Kubler. This was a pioneering and original approach to heritage because the protection of both "old and new" architecture was started simultaneously by the same institution, IPHAN. In one way, it recalls the past as a seed for the future; in another, it recognises the new – what is created now – as the continuity of heritage, essentially viewing the present as a heritage gift for the future. Furthermore, IPHAN collected various kinds of heritage, both material and immaterial, from the beginning of the 1930s, including architecture, painting, sculpture, music, poetry, and literature. This also included native Indigenous expressions that were identified, collected, and documented as part of Brazil's life and culture. In this sense, it is understandable how this process led to the recognition of modern Brazilian architecture as a symbol of the country.

In a way, this approach aligns with Jürgen Habermas's concept of the "unfinished modern project", reflecting the innovative heritage preservation in Brazil conducted through IPHAN. It adopts a transversal vision of time, recognising the past and present as part of an ongoing process, rejecting the idea of a tabula rasa. In other words, it opposes the notion of the modern movement as a complete break from the past. Modern architecture in Brazil is viewed not as a mere style but as a concept tied to the broader mission of architecture – its duty and power to shape society. By embracing this pioneering approach, modern architecture in Brazil continues the building process of spatial and formal thinking, deeply rooted in its time and context.

Lucio Costa's work eloquently expressed what he considered the values of heritage ensembles (anticipating the arguments of the Venice Charter – La Carta de Venezia – from 1964) in the cities of Minas Gerais, such as Ouro Preto and Mariana, as well as the Baroque Jesuit missions in southwest Brazil. Costa was among the first to recognise Baroque architecture's power as a current and even vernacular form of expression.

Architecture always reflects local differences. Even when the massing can be similar, the materials and applications are local. Lucio Costa had a global vision beyond prejudices about colonialism and travelled to Portugal to study the sources of this kind of eighteenth-century architecture in Brazil. Subsequently, it was Costa and his team's work that inspired architects in Portugal to conduct a comprehensive survey of their own architecture, focusing specifically on the vernacular architecture in the villages.

RM/NF Following up on this question, when did architecture preservation start accounting for the host communities and corresponding intangible heritage? What are interesting examples that would be useful to discuss?

FD In keeping with the Brazil experience, the municipality in Rio de Janeiro had always had master plans for the city. Corbusier designed one with an elevated highway that you could live in. They just made these mega plans. In 1965, there's a really psychedelic one, conceptualised by Sérgio Bernardes. This doesn't happen anymore, and these master plans were substituted with basic principles of how to live together, and how communities and community relations are to be formed. Basically, they totally gave up on the very idea of having a plan and proposed instead processes and methods to observe growth and intervene in it. This shift has been to the detriment of imaginary visions of spectacular architecture.

I might now sound like a bit of an extremist, but deep down, I can't help but feel a touch of loss when design is no longer at the forefront of plans and city-making imaginaries. In a way, it requires that the profession rethink what an architect does. It is definitely true that when we consider the plan for Rio de Janeiro from the 1920s, for example, it defined where people could live based on their buying power or lack thereof, and determined that they should no longer live together. The zoning was a deliberate urban design move around the time when the city itself was starting to become somewhat of a business administered by banks and developers. Design was ultimately used to segregate. Hence the paradox of City Beautiful Movements designed to conceal poverty and misery in order to protect land value, on the one hand, and a Brasília that prioritised design with the surprisingly successful goal of rendering social inequity visible, on the other.

AT I think that the moment when Docomomo International changed its constitution – which traditionally followed the acronym documentation and conservation of modern movement architecture – and embraced the concept of reuse, a new era was emerging. In fact, when one approaches the action of reuse, it means that the people, the users, matter beyond the pure architectural materiality. This shift occurred during my twelve-year mandate at the Seoul General Assembly. It is curious to note that this kind of complicity began to emerge beyond Eurocentric culture.

I would dare to state that one of the first actions considering people's involvement in heritage, identified and recognised as common ground, appeared in Brazil under the influence of Lina Bo Bardi. Initially, during the 1960s in São Salvador da Bahia, in the context of the "reuse" of the Solar do Unhão to turn it into a living museum (fig. 3). Lina's material intervention was reduced to the design of a magnificent staircase, leaving the entire environment in the original so as to receive vernacular and popular art, including craftsmanship participating in the project.

Figure 3. Solar do Unhão, São Salvador da Bahia

Speaking of the 1970s, it is necessary to mention the SESC Pompéia rehabilitation in São Paulo. This project transformed an abandoned factory with the active collaboration of the population, including many former workers. The factory's material structures were converted into a place for culture and sport, which proved to be a huge success at the community level and was later recognised by peers and the architectural culture.

RM / NF One of the important characteristics you mention of architectural preservation in Brazil is that the intention was to preserve the grammar rather than the building style. How did this materialise and who were the people behind this type of nuance?

FD In a way, cultural and historical preservation in Brazil has its own personality. It is unlike anywhere else. Instead of creating stylistic guidelines for design, heritage preservation in Brazil forbids architects from mimicking what's next door, or at least it used to. Another interesting thing to note is that when Brasília became a contender for a World Heritage Site, its application was first rejected by UNESCO on the basis that Brazil did not have strong enough laws to protect Brasília.

The applicable law, casually written by the president in 1960, was literally two sentences long. Much later, Lucio Costa interfered in the drafting of the law that eventually led to World Heritage status. He basically asserted that Brasília was designed according to four scales – the monumental, bucolic, residential, and aggregate scales – and that these scales ought to be

Figure 4. Hotel of Ouro Preto in Minas Gerais

preserved, not the buildings themselves. By 1989, the law was drafted with barely any mention of architecture. It only mentions landscape, distance, views, the sky, trees, et cetera.

The law that was finally passed at the federal level protected voids, since it was the only way to protect something like scale.

AT Following Farès, I agree that the best and most innovative example is the case of Brasília. The preservation, achieved through its classification as a heritage complex, was established while the construction was ongoing. That's why I prefer to call it a conceptual law rather than a series of rules to promote fragmentary actions. It is the spirit that is identified as the focus to be protected. This open and broad conception gives birth to an infinity of ways and projects of preservation and rehabilitation, because it is the safeguarding of the spirit that matters.

It is important to highlight Niemeyer's Hotel of Ouro Preto in Minas Gerais, from 1936. He was able to dialogue with the place in terms of topos, working brilliantly with the topographic levels, as well as with local materials and construction techniques, creating an innovative building while being respectful of the extraordinary built environment marked by the presence of the Baroque churches and the power of the current architecture as well (fig. 4).

Concerning the Baroque churches, it is necessary to consider a diversity of elements and materials. This expression arises from the lime finishing to the local stone mixed with sand

and earth colour, as well as from the power of the ceramic tiles (*azulejos*) within a magnificent light vibration to the indoor naive paintings.

RM / NF Could you speak to the formal conversation between Niemeyer's contribution to the Rachid Karami International Fair in Tripoli and to Brasília? Could we say there is a part of Tripoli in Brasília and not just the other way around?

FD Niemeyer was working on several projects in Brasília at the same time he was working on the Tripoli Fair, so while it may not be accurate that Tripoli was a prototypical device or inspiration for Brasília, it is definite that he was imagining both projects and designing parts of them simultaneously around 1962. There are many details that you can find in both places.

The University of Brasília, for example, is a long canopy covering volumes of classrooms, offices, auditoria, studios, et cetera (fig. 5), and is about the same scale and curvature of the so-called Grande Couverture (or the "boomerang") in Tripoli. There are also some structural details

Figure 5. Areal view of the Central Institute of Sciences (ICC), also known as Minhocão. It is the main academic building of the University of Brasília, designed by Oscar Niemeyer (1962).

Figure 6. View of the roof garden in Brasília's Itamaraty Palace (1962) by Oscar Niemeyer, showing blade-like beams that repeat in the Guest House

in Brasília's Itamaraty Palace (fig. 6) that repeat in the Guest House building. If you flip the elevation of Palácio da Alvorada – completed around 1958 as the official residence of the President of Brazil – upside down, you get the Lebanon Pavilion in Tripoli.

So one can notice that the same mind is working on many projects at the same time, cross-pollinating and exchanging details from one project to the other. These exchanges are details, not full buildings.

AT There's a particular power in how Niemeyer designed for seemingly different places and revealed their invisible similarities. In Tripoli, he plunged into the sensual atmosphere of the place, considering the climate constraints as well as geography (topos) and history (loci). Questions of ambience and comfort, such as permanent ventilation and praising the shadows while expressing himself through light nuances, are coordinated with form and materials. We all know that forms travel easily, but technologies and their materials do not do so as well. There's a cultural density inherent to the project.

In France, when intervening in Auguste Perret's plan for Le Havre, the approach is totally different from the Brazilian projects or even the Madeira hotel in Portugal. And we must not forget the iconic gesture at the Communist Party Headquarters in Paris. But the amazing thing is that all these works share a certain *air de famille,* immediately connecting and linking them with Niemeyer's expressive universes.

FD Oh, absolutely. I mean, there are the obvious ways to contextualise the project through building technologies and material selection, but Niemeyer went deeper than that in Tripoli to really reveal and employ the geological components of the area in which the Fair was being built. The entire stretch covered by the Fair today used to be highly irrigated agricultural land with an abundance of water, which can easily explain how Niemeyer used water as a design element that maintains the identity of the place, almost as a mirror on which the building would eventually sit.

RM/NF On the surface, preserving heritage buildings in the Global South appears to be an elite project, considering the humanitarian crises and emergencies resulting from postcolonial injustice, resource mismanagement, regional wars and violence, in addition to corruption at national and municipal scales. What is an argument that could present preservation as an urgent, relevant task that could be both generative and restorative?

FD Let's face it, historic preservation is often a project of colonial imaginary. Cairo, for example, had lost all its minarets over time, and, as far as I know, most were rebuilt or built under British colonial rule. The way the Taj Mahal looks today can also be credited to English Romanticism, with the vast lawns that replaced lush orchards.

This somehow applies to Tripoli, too. It's not enough to want to save a piece of Brazilian architecture, or to preserve a relic of Lebanon's nation-building project from decades ago. It is really tough to argue in favor of the monumental cost it will take to preserve the Niemeyer Fair here or elsewhere. It will most likely be impossibly expensive to fix, which makes it all the more difficult to justify in an impoverished city.

Hence, there is a need to think of possible virtues and added values that the Fair could bring to Tripoli. One way to find relevance is that – even without major renovation work – the Fair can be a remarkable park in Tripoli. Every city benefits from having a park, and Tripoli has one that seems dormant. Niemeyer argued intensely against building a fence around the Fair, and finally agreed to design one which has gaps that would at least afford some visual continuity for the project.

He would have rather just made it an open field that anyone in Tripoli could use as some kind of pleasure garden. So, I think the only way to resist this colonial preservation impulse is to actually take advantage of the site itself and turn it into something totally useful, relevant, and pleasurable, in a way that enables Tripoli to benefit and very well sustain, as best it can.

AT Yes, especially that the fence should have never been there. When the project is reintegrated with the city, it would become a piece of the people's heritage that they can co-own and be proud of.

FD And it's ironic that abandonment and incompleteness are what have protected the site so far. In a different scenario where the state would have been more active, we may have lost that project a long time ago to more commercially viable developments. Instead, now it has World Heritage in Danger status because of punctual actions by non-governmental bodies, academics, and individuals who care about this project.

I don't think that the government has any capacity to create a strategy for this project at the moment, and it is such punctual interventions that could actually pull it off. Nicolas and Charles's renovation of the Guest House, architecturally and programmatically with the Minjara vocational training center for carpenters of the city, is an example of how I think we can reclaim the functionality and relevance of the Fair, while remaining sensitive to Niemeyer's tremendous design talent and the civic role of architecture.

AT I am agreeing with Farès that "historic preservation is often a project of colonial imaginary", because we are talking about preserving architecture from the modern movement, which acted as a movement of globalisation and was imposing a specific typology and metric for progress as a common culture of modernity. We must not ignore that, in each place, it adapted to the circumstances and the people. Preservation is above all a sustainable action in social and economic terms. The reuse of heritage – in this case, the reuse of modern heritage and the remaining modern structures, while eventually changing their uses and functions – is key for a better and more sustainable future.

In Africa, some iconic buildings recognised by the community, such as the Beira railway station (fig. 7), Luanda's open-air cinemas, and the Obafemi Awolowo University in Nigeria, are undergoing studies for their preservation. The restoration of Palácio Capanema in Rio de Janeiro, dealing profoundly with climate design questions, represents a challenge for the future of the historical preservation of modern architecture and its contribution to innovative methods of passive climate control.

Figure 7. Beira railway station

After a period of great unpopularity, the values of the modern movement have been rediscovered and re-embraced by a new generation of architects, who have reopened the path to learn from modern architecture and create something new from it, continuing the modern tradition evoked by Octavio Paz. Matters such as materials and technology reuse, spatial and functional transformations, as well as updating legislation, are increasingly part of the contemporary agenda. Knowing that many modern architects sought new heights of functionality and changeability, today's challenge is how to deal with heritage in relation to its continuously changing context – physical, economic, and functional, as well as socio-cultural, political, and scientific. Alongside restoration and conservation, renovation and adaptive reuse are starting to "make history", pursuing the idea that "heritage transforms itself with us".

Collaborative Conservation: Revitalising African Modernism

Aziza Chaouni

After the Second World War, many nations of the Global South fought for and gained their independence from Western colonisers that had been exploiting them for over a century. Newly independent states in Southwest Asia, Africa, and the Middle East marked this new chapter by commissioning public architectural works to advance the crafting of new national identities, and to assert their economic and cultural prowess on the international stage. A geographically rooted modernism became a new language and an experimental ground that advanced political, cultural, and aesthetic notions of contemporaneity in the region. In particular, some extraordinary public buildings, complexes, and landscapes were erected, championing passive cooling systems, local materials, and the reinterpretation of vernacular forms and patterns, in addition to a rationalist design approach and an extensive use of exposed concrete.

Despite their significance, buildings emerging from this era remain relatively unknown today, as academic efforts and research funding have been focused mainly on studying the colonial period, especially on the African continent. Revealed first to a wide audience by Udo Kultermann's seminal book *New Architecture in Africa* (1963), postcolonial African architectures have gained a renewed interest through books such as Łukasz Stanek's *Architecture in Global Socialism: Eastern Europe, West Africa, and the Middle East in the Cold War* (2020) and Tom Avermaete and Maxime Zaugg's *Agadir: Building the Modern Afropolis* (2022), as well as exhibitions like the V&A Pavilion at the Biennale Architettura 2023 in Venice entitled *Tropical Modernism: Architecture and Power in West Africa* and the forthcoming 2025 exhibition at MoMA in New York on West African postcolonial modernism, to name a few examples. If a vast amount of research still remains to be covered regarding the genealogy and emergence of this postcolonial architecture, then its evolution, current conditions, threats, use, and future remain all an uncharted territory. This research is even more salient today because of the looming demolition risks threatening to erase landmark modern buildings from our collective memory.

Developing a New Approach for Modern Heritage Rehabilitation in Africa

Since the post-independence period, African modern architectures have evolved dramatically to reflect the contexts and communities that surround and use them. Institutions as well as the public have found ways to formally or informally appropriate each site to suit their needs when the original programmes and operational strategies conceived for these sites have become defunct. The architectural practice of Aziza Chaouni Projects (ACP), based in Fez Morocco, has been working to understand the particular histories of three publicly owned modern complexes in North and West Africa erected during the post-independence era in order to revitalise them through adaptive reuse – working to address public needs, while maintaining their cultural heritage for future generations. Working with limited budgets on large, complex sites, in often fluctuating political contexts, we have developed a peculiar approach that resonates with what this book refers to as "the scaffold". In our work, the term "scaffold" indicates the methodology itself, and the qualities it confers to the public site to be rehabilitated: it allows the modern building(s) and their infrastructure to act as a skeleton, onto which diverse programmes and rehabilitation initiatives, either temporary or long term, could organically attach or find a home. In contexts with shifting political and socio-economic dynamics and limited funds, this approach seems to be the most suitable.

Indeed, this "scaffold" approach offers a framework composed of the elaboration of a conservation management plan that develops an overall vison and orients future usage rehabilitation efforts and maintenance – but that also has a road map for activist efforts aimed to raise awareness of local and international audiences towards the significance of these sites and the importance of their safeguarding. The "scaffold" is designed to be both resilient and realistic, as

Figure 1. Significance and repair matrix for the hotel in the Sidi Harazem Thermal Bath Complex

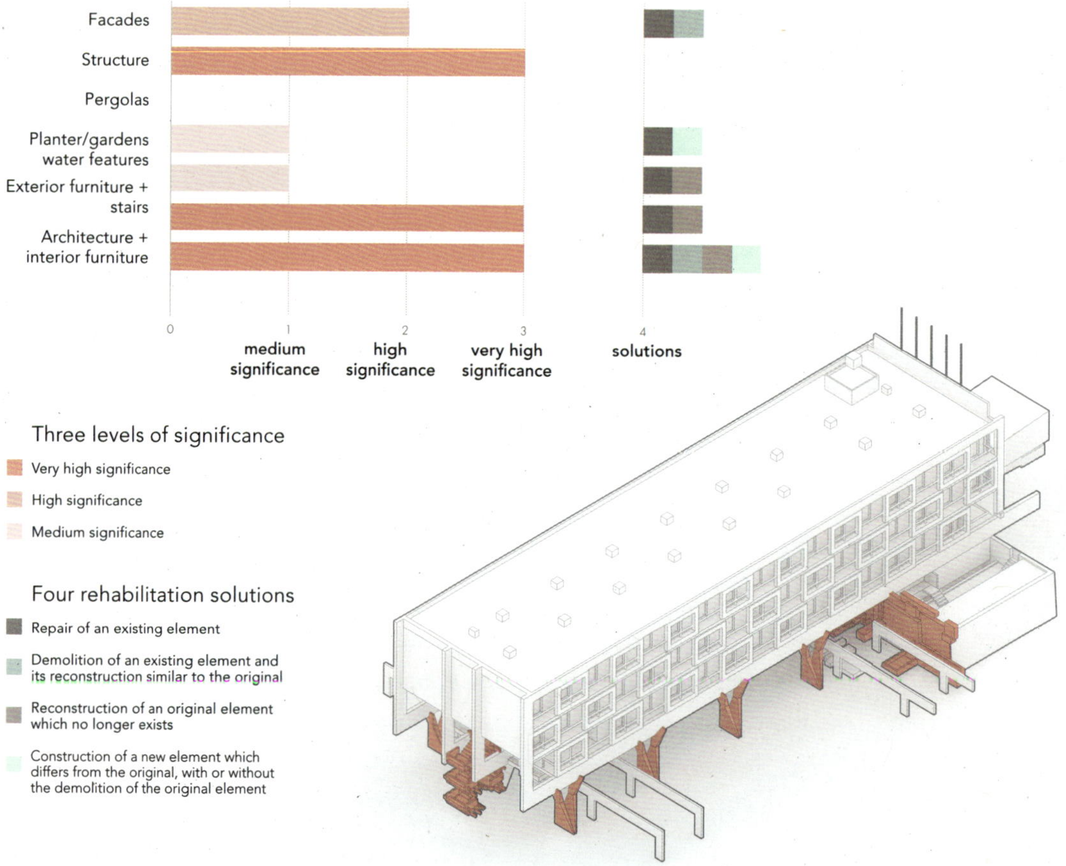

Three levels of significance

- Very high significance
- High significance
- Medium significance

Four rehabilitation solutions

- Repair of an existing element
- Demolition of an existing element and its reconstruction similar to the original
- Reconstruction of an original element which no longer exists
- Construction of a new element which differs from the original, with or without the demolition of the original element

a series of small-scale, low budget, easy-to-implement actions are proposed, each labelled[1] (fig. 1) with a level of urgency based on archival documents demonstrating the architect's original intentions and approach, and the role each item plays in the overall oeuvre integrity and significance matrix.

The goal is to build a solid foundation that could outlive the end of the conservation management plan. The capacity building and awareness which accompany each project comprise Instagram accounts, websites, tour guide training workshops (fig. 2), conferences, and exhibitions (fig. 3). These efforts often generate a long-lasting engagement and appropriation of the site by its users. There is no turning back after the significance of the building/complex is understood, its loss seen as irreversible, and decision makers start being held responsible. For us, the implementation of any of our proposed actions is worthwhile, regardless of scale or budget, as long as it respects the conservation management plan recommendations and overall co-constructed vision.

Most importantly, this "scaffold" approach is co-developed and co-led with local stakeholders, including politicians, managers, and users, who are continuously and genuinely engaged by our team throughout the span of the project. This ensures that they all become advocates for

Figure 3. The exhibition *Sidi Harazem: The Genesis of a Modern Oasis*, curators Aziza Chaouni and Lucy Hofbauer, Rabat, 2019

Figure 2. Architecture guide workshop with local youth of Sidi Harazem, led by Laure Augereau

Figure 4. Sidi Harazem Thermal Bath Complex, postcard

these postcolonial public sites, holding fort against threats and pressures that could comprise their integrity or, worse, erase them. Hence, the core of the "scaffold" as we see it lies in its deployment of a robust collaborative approach. To do so, we develop specific and culturally appropriate tools to enable co-design with site owners, community stakeholders, and young creatives, and to individually address each site's complexities and challenges. These tools help build recognition of the inherent significance and potential of these sites, while reimagining appropriate use that benefits a diverse body of stakeholders.

The ACP team has been involved in the development of conservation management plans of three major modern architectural heritage complexes from the post-independence era in Francophone North and West Africa: the Sidi Harazem Thermal Bath Complex in Morocco, Centre international du commerce extérieur du Sénégal (CICES) in Senegal, and La Maison du Peuple (The House of the People) in Burkina Faso. Located near an oasis where a revered Sufi saint is buried, adjacent to a hot spring, Sidi Harazem was commissioned to the Moroccan-Corsican architect Jean-François Zevaco[2] three years after Morocco's independence in 1959 by the State Pension Fund. The aim was to offer the first tourist destination to Moroccans following best practice tourism standards. As such, it included a large, shaded public plaza with a public spring water fountain, a hotel, bungalows, a public forum called the *ryad* composed of gardens and water bodies, two pools, and a market for vegetables and crafts (fig. 4).

Figure 5. CICES, the Centre international du commerce extérieur du Sénégal by Jean-François Lamoureux and Jean-Louis Marin, Dakar

Figure 6. Le Maison du Peuple by René Faublée, Ouagadougou

The CICES was the result of an international competition launched by post-independence Senegal's first president, the poet and cultural activist Léopold Sédar Senghor, with the ambition to create a state-of-the-art international fair where African nations and others could share technological innovations and knowledge, and nurture collaborations and new ventures facilitated by a special building, which we view as the ancestor of the incubator. Also, Senghor sought a novel, universal African architectural language, shed from Western referents. The young architects Jean-François Lamoureux and Jean-Louis Marin won the competition upon graduating from architecture school and completing their Civil Service in Dakar. They developed a sprawling complex where every form is either a triangle or a derivative of the triangle, beautifully translating Senghor's "asymmetrical parallelism" theory into architecture[3] (fig. 5).

At last, the Maison du Peuple was commissioned to the French Alpine architecture specialist René Faublée[4] by Maurice Yaméogo, the first president of Burkina Faso, then called the Voltaic Democratic Union (UDV). Located in Ouagadougou, La Maison du Parti (known today as La Maison du Peuple) was inaugurated in 1965. It consisted of a 2,500-seat theatre, a hall of honour, two vast pavilions, a technical cabin for radio broadcasting, as well as restaurants and

Figure 7. Hot air exhaust chimneys of Le Maison du Peuple

bars opening onto a large courtyard. The auditorium is passively ventilated by twelve solar chimneys which cap its roof, and whose iconic shapes resemble traditional huts, while its clay-brick-clad facade echoes African patterns (figs. 6 and 7).

All three projects embody different trajectories defined by their socio-political contexts; however, they share several similarities. Morocco, Senegal, and Burkina Faso are all Francophone countries in West Africa with historic, economic, cultural, and diasporic ties to France. Each site had limited available archival documentation. They all represent a form of "Situated Modernism", blending the International Style with local vernacular architecture. As projects from the early era of independence, they served as experimental grounds for crafting new national identities. Today, each site houses activities different from what the architects originally intended, and each has been continuously used.

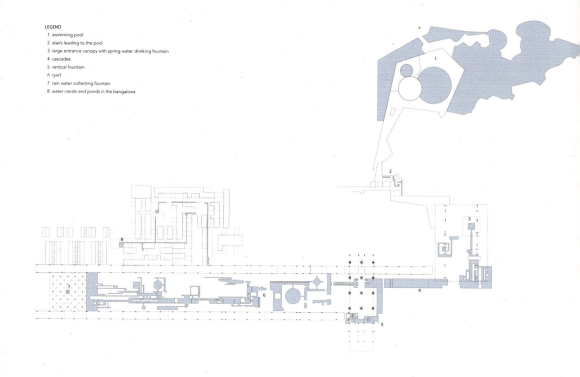

Figure 8. Drawing of the Sidi Harazem Thermal Bath Complex water system

West African Modernism

The emergence of West African modernism and the transnational exchange of ideas during the colonial and post-independence periods have not been thoroughly investigated and are not well understood. The driving factors that may have fostered these exchanges are the colonial professionalisation of the architectural field on the continent (and subsequent reliance on foreign experts), mandatory military or civil service requirements for French nationals that brought them to the African colonies, colonial industrial pipelines and trade, the growth of international development/aid institutions, a global post-war construction boom, a revolution in the use of reinforced concrete, and, perhaps most importantly, a search for aesthetics that represented the progress, development, modernity, and vernacular of each newly independent nation.

Africa was also seen as a space for architectural experimentation,[5] largely free of the bureaucracy and stringent building code of the French system[6] as well as the trauma felt in

Europe after the Second World War. There are many lessons to be learned about the inventive use of local materials in African modernism in which PVC tubes, local stone, mosaics, copper, wood, and textiles, among others, were used inventively. In many instances, locals who received a Western-style education made critical contributions to the early modern movement in West Africa, including Pierre Goudiaby Atepa (Senegal), Cheikh Ngom (Senegal), Demas Nwoko (Nigeria),[7] Abel Isaac Traoré (Burkina Faso), Wango Pierre Sawadogo (Burkina Faso), Elie Azagury (Morocco), and Abdeslem Faraoui (Morocco).[8]

Architectural modernism must also be understood in relation to contemporaneous art movements such as Cubism and Abstract Expressionism, which borrowed from African artisans themselves.[9] Looking beyond ties between France and its former colonies, architects such as René Faublée (Maison du Peuple, Burkina Faso) named the Japanese modern movement as a key inspiration,[10] using Noguchi tables in Maison du Peuple. Although Faublée never visited Japan, his home and office libraries included many books on Japanese art and architecture, representing the increasingly wide networks of architectural exchange in the post-war era. The prolific Jean-François Zevaco was subscribed to the Japanese architecture magazine *Shinkenchiku* (now known as the *Architecture and Urbanism Magazine*). Zevaco drew inspiration from Japanese architecture's elegant wood joinery and seamless integration of architecture with its surrounding landscape elements, including trees, vegetation, and water, both clearly evident in his design for the Sidi Harazem Thermal Bath Station. The overall plan of the water infrastructure in Sidi Harazem, which we thoroughly assembled from partial plans and site surveys, demonstrates Zevaco's mastery at making water a design element *à part entière* of his architecture: it defines circulation paths and weaves itself into the design of all his public spaces (fig. 8). Also, the main interior stair of the hotel elegantly integrates wood, steel, and concrete with joinery displaying definite Japanese undertones.

Understanding the multilayered genealogy of postcolonial modern architecture(s) in Africa help us not only to delineate more appropriate conservation strategies that encapsulate their full significance, but also to challenge the notion that this(these) architecture(s) is a direct transfer of modernism precepts developed in Europe.

Current Use of Modern Heritage in Africa

Today, if several publicly owned modern sites in Africa have been demolished, many others from the post-independence era have been reappropriated and are actively used. In Senegal, CICES has become a green lung for a neighbourhood in overcrowded Dakar, which expanded within the original borders of the site. Maison du Peuple transformed from a legislative assembly hall in Ouagadougou to a popular venue for cultural events and a public square hosting markets and concerts. At the Sidi Harazem Thermal Bath Station in Morocco, local villagers have built their own markets in the absence of adequate commercial infrastructure, while the touristic facilities largely remain empty. These sites have come to answer public needs that are not addressed by authorities with jurisdiction, just as the Rachid Karami International Fair is used as a public green space by some[11] and as an event space a few times a year. The continuous use of modern sites across the African continent discloses their inherent resilience and the crucial social and economic roles that large public facilities can play in rapidly changing and growing African cities.

If there is no universal approach to modern heritage conservation in Africa, our "scaffold" strategy was devised to adapt to diverse situations and buildings. To construct it, new conservation methodologies, different from those common to the Global North, must be developed to address the particular conditions of each site: lost archives, extreme development pressures, mixed public perceptions about modern heritage associated with the colonial era, informal re-appropriation by local actors, the emergence of informal economies, poor infrastructure causing safety hazards, the architecture's monumentality, technical challenges of rehabilitating exposed concrete, changing climatic conditions, economic and operational burdens on public owners, a lack of technical expertise around modern conservation practices, et cetera. Despite these challenges, many of these sites hold a particular nostalgia for the publics that have interacted with them, representing the optimism and identity nation-building of early post-independence eras.

Aziza Chaouni Projects' work often involves building a historical record through the collection of personal memorabilia and oral histories to fill critical knowledge gaps about the past, and to speculate towards future possibilities. The generation of people that can provide first-hand accounts of the development, construction, and early operation of each complex is quickly disappearing, and their histories must be captured quickly. For example, the website of the Sidi Harazem Project[12] showcases testimonies by diverse panels of people who have experienced the genesis and changes of the Thermal Station. Another illustration is the research project West Africa Recorded, commissioned by Lesley Lokko's Venice Biennale 2023 Laboratory of the Future, in which we compiled a short documentary where different voices share their memories of the three modern sites we have been working on.[13]

The other pillar of our approach is building capacity locally in modern heritage conservation through partnerships with communities and academic institutions; empowering a new generation of creatives, designers, and thinkers to explore and build the futures of their cities. By doing so, we have empowered local stakeholders to become leaders in modern heritage preservation.

Figure 9. Sidi Harazem Thermal Bath Complex suspended stairway leading from the hotel to the *ryad*

Figure 10. Public zone of the Sidi Harazem Thermal Bath Complex

Tools for Co-Design and Engagement with Modern Heritage

As a design-based architecture office, we tend to work on all our projects in a collaborative manner hand in hand with the current and future users of our sites. We do so because we believe that we can learn from their knowledge of the site's socio-economic and environmental contexts and its challenges, but also that we can understand their aspirations and needs in this way. In the case of our modern heritage conservation projects in Morocco, Senegal, and Burkina Faso, concertation has proven to be a providential tool beyond getting the buy-in of stakeholders and empowering them to appropriate the site. It has helped alleviate palpable tensions, some with a long history. For instance, in Sidi Harazem, two small villages had existed on the site of the new thermal complex. Their inhabitants were moved to small single-room houses located 4 kilometres away in a newly created village called Skhinat in order to give way to the tabula rasa the new project required. We were able to find three people who have lived this move, which they still describe to this day as traumatic. Once the thermal spring was completed, some of these inhabitants were given small stalls in the new vegetable market and the new craft market. Not all inhabitants benefited. As the complex declined in the 1990s, and the market bungalow and much of the grounds of the hotel closed down, visitor numbers dropped, leaving locals with diminished sources of revenue, with tourism constituting the main source of income for most. In the CICES, land which used to be the parking of the fair was handed to party members who built mid-rises

Figure 11. Workshop results

on it. More of the fair's parcel experienced the same land nibbling over the years. As a result, today the fair suffers massive traffic jams during events. Plus, less land is available for leisure activities for local residents.

Like the Rachid Karami International Fair in Tripoli, where farmland owners were expropriated and under-compensated, Zevaco's gargantuan modern complex and the CICES have crystalised tensions and come to symbolise a legacy of spoilation and social injustice. Acknowledging this part of the site histories while creating a space for respectful discussion around these sensitive topics was an essential component of our concertation efforts. By doing so, we fostered a trustful environment in which every voice could be heard, and concerns raised, with the hope to address them in the final conservation management plan. We made it clear that the conservation management plans will not be able to solve all past unresolved issues, nor answer everyone's needs, but that it could serve as a road map to provide spaces for leisure and work for identified groups while preserving a landmark. By doing so, we ensure that the "scaffold" we are building for the site's conservation is laid upon solid foundations.

The Sidi Harazem Thermal Bath Complex as a Case Study

To identify all stakeholders' needs, the ACP team first identified the stakeholders, then determined which ones are primary and others secondary, delineating which persons would be the most impacted by the rehabilitation of the thermal complex or should benefit from it most. In Sidi Harazem, most participants had little knowledge of Zevaco and the importance of the thermal complex's architecture. Most actually expressed negative feelings towards the complex's concrete architecture, which they described in various ways, such as: old-fashioned, raw, UFO-like, western, un-Moroccan, ugly, in need of demolition or a major recladding, and derelict. However, some participants, especially those managing the hotel and green spaces, shared memories of the complex's past glory and expressed pride and nostalgia for the beauty of its modern architecture (figs. 9 and 10).

We designed six types of workshops targeting different types of participants. All of the workshops began with a brief introduction documented by historical photos and postcards of the complex, highlighting its technological innovations and connections to traditional building typologies and motifs, in addition to a timeline of Zevaco's life and his major buildings in Morocco. Activities in these workshops ranged from games and treasure hunts for children, teaching students how to conduct architectural tours of the complex, an artist residency for young Moroccan artists, to designing inclusive tools for workshops such as pictograms that would enable illiterate members of the community to participate (fig. 11).

The workshops and our numerous formal and informal interviews of various stakeholders resulted in a large amount of nuanced knowledge about the site's current issues and potential futures. We visualised this data to translate the stakeholders' programmatic needs into a master plan for the thermal complex, and shared it one more time for review with stakeholders. This process is largely uncommon on the African continent, where stakeholders, if involved at all, are at best shown final designs for review and do not contribute to the development of their built environment. Our role was to build consensus, while taking into consideration a vast array of variables, such as: the condition of existing buildings, cost estimates for rehabilitation, the significance levels of buildings and landscapes, the socio-economic needs of the most disadvantaged groups, the income-generating programme requirements of the State Pension Fund and the Rural Commune, which both own the complex, the social tensions which would emerge when moving some people during construction to new locations, and so forth.

Building a Cooperative Legacy

Our experience with working in postcolonial heritage buildings and ensembles in Africa has demonstrated that they merge long-standing latent tensions, often connected to the not-so-distant colonial past which the aesthetic of these buildings can echo, from displacements and expropriations common to the inception of modernist projects to intense development pressures, which are particularly predatory in dense urban settings. These tensions can contribute to a contentious context that is unpropitious to their rehabilitation, adding to the challenges that these sites already experience.

The importance of implementing a collaborative approach all throughout the lifespan of the rehabilitation projects is a necessity. It will not only facilitate the process, but also groom a cohort of ambassadors and caretakers of the sites. This task is no small feat. In Africa, this collaborative approach is not yet integrated into the scope of the work of conservation architects, who would need to either advocate for the expanded task list it requires or volunteer to do it. Had we not been the recipient of the Keeping It Modern Initiative grant from the Getty Foundation or working with the US non-governmental organisation World Monuments Fund, we would not have been able to develop and implement this collaborative approach. We are grateful for their support and can already quantify the long-term impact of our joint efforts: in Sidi Harazem, CICES, and Maison du Peuple, not only have we helped construct a resilient framework for rehabilitation work, but, most importantly, we have constituted a solid group of supporters who fully grasp the significance of modern architectural landmarks – from the modest stall owner to the decision maker. Without these buildings and their local supporters, this would have been a slice of our modern collective history that disappeared for good.

1   We provide colour-coded, easy-to-read axonometric drawings and plans highlighting three levels of importance for preservation: very high importance, high importance, and medium importance. Each level can accommodate different degrees of changes: from not all to certain possible adjustments. The Getty Foundation calls this method "the red light", in reference to the three levels of importance (red, yellow, and green).

2   Jean-François Zevaco was born to Corsican parents in Morocco, where he spent most of his life – aside from his years studying architecture in France. He was a French National, yet his closeness to his Corsican roots and to his adopted country Morocco, which inspired him to create a unique architecture in tune with local climate, landscape, and craft, renders him in my eyes the most Moroccan of twentieth-century architects.

3   Léopold Sédar Senghor defines his "asymmetric parallelism" theory, first used in his poetry, as "a diversified repetition of rhythm in time and space", best represented in CICES by the fact that all buildings are triangular but never offer the same spatial experience. As such, the CICES is a unique example of African post-independence modern architecture, which aimed to craft new national identities.

4   René Faublée struggled with fragile health during his lifetime. Upon graduating from the Ecole Parisienne des Beaux-Arts in 1934, he went to seek fresh air in the mountains where he received training under Henry Jacques Le Même. Together with the architect Michel Luyckx, Faublée earned first prize in a ski chalet competition. During this time, he developed his architecture in relation to the vernacular French alpine style, first building a home for his parents in Morzine, France, and then a series of ski chalets.

5   See Jean-Louis Cohen and Monique Eleb, *Casablanca: Colonial Myths and Architectural Ventures* (New York: Monacelli, 2002).

6   Léo Noyer-Duplaix, "Henri Chomette: Africa as a Terrain of Architectural Freedom", in *African Modernism: The Architecture of Independence; Ghana, Senegal, Côte D'Ivoire, Kenya, Zambia,* ed. Manuel Herz et al. (Zurich: Park Books, 2015).

7   Demas Nwoko received training in set design at Le Centre Français du Théâtre in Paris.

8   See, for example, the work of the MAMMA Group related to building an archive of architectural modernism in Morocco: https://mammagroup.org.

9   Carolina Sanmiguel, "African Art: The First Form of Cubism", *The Collector*, 3 October 2020, https://www.thecollector.com/african-art-the-first-form-of-cubism/.

10   From an interview with Michel Faublée, son of the architect Michel Faublée, Paris, January 2023.

11   While visiting the Rachid Karami International Fair on two occasions, we saw visitors using the grounds of the Fair for informal walks or jogging. To gain access, there is a US$20 membership fee per year. The Fair sits empty for most of the year, while the city of Tripoli severely lacks green open spaces.

12   www.sidiharazemstation.com

13   www.modernwestafrica.org

MANUAL/
ANTI-MANUAL

Traduttore, Traditore: Reflections on Collective Restoration
Jozef Wouters

In 2017, as part of the Dream City festival in Tunis, Tunisia, the Belgian scenographer Jozef Wouters took up residence in the historic Dar Baïram Turki building in the Medina of Tunis to propose an artistic project. After talking to neighbours, researchers, and the craftspeople working in the building, he noticed that almost everyone agreed that the building needs restoration. By 2019, Wouters had developed a project that prefigured this restoration, adding layers to the building's historical essence rather than removing them. This approach resulted in a durational installation that featured interactive and performative elements, presented under the name "Soft Layer". The performance of "restoring" Dar Baïram Turki unfolded in both day and night shifts. The day shifts allowed visitors to participate in cleaning a part of the building's courtyard facade, fostering a hands-on connection with its history and physicality. The night shifts were text-based performances that embraced the building's accumulated layers of time, questioning how the architectural space could sustain multiple historical narratives without losing its integrity. Soft Layer is a project that still continues today, having transformed the renovation of Dar Baïram Turki into a script that could be performed on several sites. The contribution that follows incorporates Wouters's reflections on the project via documentations of the process: images from the work in Tunis, extracts from the textual script of the night shift performance, and images of the translation of Soft Layer to the Palermo context in 2021, as well as thoughts on its reiterationin Brussels in 2024.

The making of Soft Layer has been a process that accumulated gradually over a long period of time. I was going to Tunis a few times a year between 2017 and 2019, always intuitively returning to the same building, sitting there in the courtyard with my table and my coffee and my neighbours and the craftspeople who were working there. After a while, I started noticing that the "entire building" – because of the nature of the courtyard specifically – can never be restricted within my field of vision, and that there is nowhere to look that is not the building, even inwards, introspectively, in memories and in imagination. So you could say that this became the core of the whole work (fig. 1).

This is material from the first scene of a performance we wrote as part of our renovation. We had invited people to sit in the courtyard facing the walls and to slowly let themselves become parts of this building. "Have you ever seen an entire building, all of it?" Of course, you can try to go in all the rooms, the first floor, the second floor, and you can try to look inside the ateliers, the storage spaces, everywhere. Still, I haven't seen the entire building at once. It's impossible. And if I could see it all at once, would that even be the building, or its representation? Soft Layer plays along the scales of where the building starts and where it ends, beyond its materiality.

As an architect, you may have that desire, this urge to see the whole building at once. I imagine that when you design a building from scratch, you may get the feeling of a full overview. But how do you quench that desire when the building already exists (fig. 2)?

Figure 1. Excerpt from book *The Soft Layer* (Brussels and Oslo: Varamo Press, 2022)

> Have you ever seen an entire building, all of it?
> All of its walls, rooms, doors, windows.

Figure 2. *What (exactly) are you counting on* (lecture performance, Tunis, 2017)

Figures 3 and 4. Elevation sketch of Dar Baïram Turki (left) and Habib opening a door in Dar Baïram Turki (right)

Model-making in this context becomes a translation of that desire through the manufactured, all-encompassing bird's-eye view. You spend days measuring, scaling, and cutting. It's like you learn the building by heart. But then you glue it all together, and when the model is finished, you realise that you actually want to be inside.

Chance encounters have been crucial throughout this project. I had been invited to come to the Medina of Tunis to walk around and see what inspires me. I always find it slightly problematic: to be an artist shopping for a site, for inspiration, especially in a city that is not mine, and even more so as a European in Tunis.

I met Habib by accident. He was a carpenter who made doors, in an atelier next to a craftsperson making shoes and two others in the corner of Dar Baïram Turki painting tiles. This picture is important for me because it shows the moment that Habib opened the door to a storage space next to his atelier that we would later use as our own. I feel that this act of neighbouring is when the project began (figs. 3 and 4).

"Le futur ne sera pas nostalgique" (The future will not be nostalgic) was the first sentence I embraced as a title for the work. We wrote it over the door of our atelier at Dar Baïram Turki, and it became a sort of commitment for the team. A motto. Preserving this building was not equal to a regression into the past, but rather an opportunity to think about the future. Past and future don't need to be opposites (figs. 5 and 6).

Figures 5 and 6. Screenshot of Jozef Wouters's phone screen (left) and the young Tunisian architects Nour Lemkecher and Balti Kml working inside the atelier (right)

There's an interesting Italian expression, *traduttore, traditore,* which basically means "translator, traitor". Renovation is a form of translation. So were we betraying the building? I think it is correct to assume that the building holds its stories, and our role is to read them and try to translate them. In my view, this is what unites the restorers with the actors: both are busy translating, interpreting, and potentially misunderstanding the script. By investing half our budget into a performance, we created a space where the multitude of different potential stories could be laid out, without the obligation to choose one correct version.

The project consisted of cycles of labour and rest. We were caring for the building and each other. In this first part of the performance, around 120 people were sitting with their faces towards the walls, observing with concentration. Each spectator could only see part of the building, but together, they form a collective gaze that may see it all. In that instant, by focusing on a detail, we mimic the gaze of the restorer, busy with one square centimetre, but in the collective consciousness we might be piecing the whole building together (fig. 7).

The text suggests that what we call "the building" is in fact an abbreviation. It is a collection of impressions and stories, including history, memory, intangible experiences, in addition to its materiality. A stain, for example, is not merely a stain. What story does it tell? Is it intentional? Does it have an author? Or has it happened by accident? These questions have both a poetic and a bureaucratic depth, for Dar Baïram Turki has been listed as an endangered cultural site by UNESCO.

The building is considered one of the most valuable architectural pieces in the Medina of Tunis, built in Hafsid style in the early seventeenth century. The importance of Dar Baïram Turki was broadly recognised. Everyone I had met during my research trips agreed that the building needed to be renovated. This was stunning for me: the unanimous agreement that heritage needs to be restored and preserved. The people I interviewed often seemed to take it almost personally that the building was falling apart. What did they identify with?

Figure 7. Excerpt from the book *The Soft Layer* (Brussels and Oslo: Varamo Press, 2022)

Now pick a stain on the surface of what you are looking at.
It doesn't matter if it is on a wall or a door, it can be small
or big. Just pick a stain and settle your gaze on it.
Look at its shape, its colour, its texture.
When was it added? How did that happen?
Was it added by a person, an animal, a fungus?
Did it happen fast or slow?
Intentionally or by accident?
Is the stain a sign of care or indifference?

FATMA

The more I work here, the less I understand what this building has to do with me. This house was built by men that considered their women as possessions that needed to be locked away from outside eyes. What is it that I am restoring here? What is it that I am keeping alive? If we have to restore the original entrance, are we restoring patriarchy as well? And where will everyone go who is working here now? Will we make them leave like the woman who used to live here but left when the rent became too high?

JOZEF

The woman who had to leave is linked to this plant she left behind. It used to be small, like that little sprout on top of the pillar, which makes me think of a story Fatma invented. She told me this house was first built as a garden and only later transformed into a building. Where the walls are now, there used to be rows of cypresses, the floor was covered with rosemary and thyme, and all the columns you see were cork trees with branches and leaves that produced shade all day. Only afterwards did Bayram Turki decide to replace the plants one by one with stones until it became the building you see now.

FATMA

That story doesn't exist on paper — I haven't had the time to write it down. I made it up while I was cleaning the column and when I saw the little sprout, I had to think of tulips that grow in Turkey, which is where the first owner of this house came from. Those flowers connect to a landscape with hills and rivers that Bayram Turki must have missed when he built this house in Tunis, far from home. He must have been anxious. You can still sense his fear in here. It's cemented inside the high walls without any windows to the world outside.

Figure 8. Excerpt from the book *The Soft Layer* (Brussels and Oslo: Varamo Press, 2022)

In Belgium, my country of origin, it is hard to find heritage that is not already restored, but either way, I feel distant from it because of the political recuperation and national identity politics that encompass it. Compared to the people I was encountering in Tunis, I seemed indifferent to heritage preservation in my country. Over time, I started seeing the complexity of the Tunisian relation as a rich language of nostalgia mixed with a desire for change. I got curious about the many different and personal layers inside the collective desire of restoration.

First of all, I felt the need to learn from this situation, from this collective respect for heritage, and of course from the fear of it being forgotten. What can these stains tell us about this past? Can they be more than just mistakes that need to be cleaned? Maybe not all these stains were signs of indifference? When we work on Dar Baïram Turki, cleaning the stones, are we not also just making more stains? Who has the authority to initiate a renovation (fig. 8)?

What I love about scaffolding, especially in Soft Layer, is that it is a tool that renovators use to touch the building in places where you could otherwise not touch it. Another thing that is interesting about scaffolds is how they are built – very differently than brick walls, for example. While a wall typically needs to be solid on empty ground, a scaffold can weave and embrace the space that is already there. Also, for its solidity, a scaffold needs another building. In this way, scaffolding becomes a language of space that is constantly looking for dialogue with other spaces. Building with scaffolding always means first asking the question that I love so much: What's already there, and how can I weave with it (fig. 9)?

I started using scaffolding in the first place because of a desire to build spaces quickly and cheaply. I have always looked for quick and cheap ways of building to avoid having to deal with the power structures and bureaucratic approvals that seem inherent to architecture. Scaffolding is light, but not only in its weight and materiality. The lightness of scaffolding extends further. When you build scaffolding inside Dar Baïram Turki, everyone can immediately understand that it is a temporary intervention. The materiality of scaffolding helps me to work on spaces without the typical friction and resistance that permanent proposals provoke.

What is special about the specific scaffolding we used in Tunis is that we were able to choose the length of all these pieces, as there was no difference in pricing between custom-made and standardised pieces. In a European context, I wouldn't have even thought of made-to-measure pieces. I would just order second-hand standardised racks and adapt them.

The intention and precision with which we could fit this scaffolding into the existing courtyard was unique. I remember the high level of concentration on the days of construction, how we would slowly try to fit in the blue metal pieces without scratching the stones (fig. 10).

There seems to be a big discrepancy between the position of the National Institute of Patrimony (INP), which considers renovation as a method to go back to the "original" state of the building, and the reality of the care that has been performed for centuries every day by people like Habib and Ridah, who are living with the architecture. I think through the work of cleaning the stones and through the act of being there, we started to realise that the daily manual labour is very much a form of perpetual restoration that is much more vivid than an official decision to formally renovate it. How is cleaning a courtyard every day so different from what we consider restoration (fig. 11)?

The assumption seems to be that restoration is a finite job, done once and well, and that cleaning needs to be repeated over and over again. But after working with Kais and Ahmed and the other restorers day after day, the difference is not so clear. Especially if you consider time in terms of centuries, restoration becomes a perpetual movement that needs to be redone over and over again just as well (fig. 12).

A good way to read a space is to design something that only just fits into it. Then it comes down to centimetres and precision is required. When a group of builders together put up a metal scaffolding that only just fits in the courtyard of a centuries-old palace, then they read the space. Collectively. The scenography engages in a conversation with the space and a conflict always

Figure 9. Excerpt from the book *Moment Before the Wind* (Brussels and Oslo: Varamo Press, 2020)

Figure 10. Team working on restoration during rehearsals

JOZEF
The clean parts are linked to the unclean parts by the work we do every day. That work is linked to the Institut National du Patrimoine and to the Association de Sauvegarde de la Médina and to Unesco, who all have completely different opinions about how to clean this building. One told us we should use sandpaper and rub the stones till they are white and shiny again. The other told us that these stones were never white so we should only clean them with water and lemon juice. The third one told us we better not touch it at all, because whatever we do will be wrong for sure if we don't first carry out a study and then maybe, maybe clean it with a sophisticated laser machine that isn't actually available in Tunis. That's why we asked art historian Kais to join our team and find a compromise, which turned out to be cleaning with toothbrushes, water and a drop of lemon.

Figure 11. Excerpt from the book *The Soft Layer* (Brussels and Oslo: Varamo Press, 2022)

Figure 12. Excerpt from the book *Moment Before the Wind* (Brussels and Oslo: Varamo Press, 2020)

what I later worked on in Tunis. The project *The Soft Layer* (2019), in collaboration with artist Vladimir Miller, was about restoration as a perpetual movement. The performance we made became a ritual that had to be repeated on a daily basis,

After a few months, a participant asked why we put so much work into a space that is going to be demolished at the end anyway. Are all that time and effort necessary for something that won't be left standing? Can't the municipality be per-

Figure 13. Excerpt from the book *Moment Before the Wind* (Brussels and Oslo: Varamo Press, 2020)

Figures 14 and 15. Scenography and performance for *The Soft Layer* in Tunis, 2019

I don't think that the measure of a building – or its renovation for that matter – lies in its permanence. The complexity of such a renovation with all its different techniques and opinions, the unanswerable questions, scarcity of resources, and what-not are definitely more interesting than the actual finished restoration. And as a scenographer, I am focused on finding ways to build and express spaces in such a way that they allow for that complexity to be legible (fig. 13).

Our scaffolding became a structure that is functional as a tool for both parts of our renovation. During the day shift, it helped to reach the upper layers of stone; and at night, it allowed for an audience to gather and observe the performers at the centre (figs. 14 and 15).

I find this shift of focus very interesting, moving from detailed, close-up work – like meticulously cleaning a tiny area with lemon juice and water – to turning back and viewing the entire building as part of a collective perspective. That oscillation between hyper-focus on a detail and collective consciousness is fascinating, and the scaffolding is a tool for that. In all my works, the scaffolding is a means of crafting a communal eye that fosters collective attention that in turn frames a space in which someone can take position.

Aloe vera plants play a central role in the project. During the first year of my residency, I met the tenant on the first floor because of the garden of aloes that she was cultivating in one corner of the courtyard. We did not share a language, but she would make me rub the aloe gel on my skin after a long day's work, and even made me eat some too. When I came back a year later, she was gone. I think the rent had gone up. Her aloe garden was gone too. She had taken all the plants except for one. Maybe she left it for us?

From this one plant we started imagining a fiction in which we would restore her garden as an essential part of the building. We speculated on the future of that one plant inside Dar Baïram Turki that started reproducing and making more and more offspring. In this fiction, she didn't leave the plant by accident. She left it for us to cure the dry skin and the calluses on our hands after long days of sanding the walls. The aloe vera plant became part of the ecology of our restoration and our temporary mythology: it became part of the building.

When I build structures, whether they are in a theatre or outside, I'm very aware of the fact that they are always needing the strength and the solidity of something else, whether it be a roof or a building or stones or earth or sometimes containers of water. To me, this is very meaningful in many ways. It makes you need the space that's already there, and it also makes it impossible to think of your space as an autonomous structure. I see scenography as this: a form of space that is dependent, literally, on the support of another space. Even more than the word ephemeral, which is often used as a way to define my work, I think that the dependency of my spaces is a key aspect (figs. 16 and 17).

> Scenography will always need counterweights. Regardless of the form. The spaces that appear in the theatre will always try to be as light as possible. A stage tree is a hollowed-out tree or an aluminium frame covered in bark. Any excess weight is removed and the bearing capacity decreases. Walls are only painted on the visible side. Steel becomes wood sprayed with a rust spray. Glass becomes plastic. Mirrors become foil. A stone wall becomes a cloth on a wooden frame. In that translation, the sets lose their stability and become dependent on a counterweight in order to remain upright.
>
> Budget is a form of counterweight.
> Attention is a form of counterweight.
> A roof protects a scenography that can't resist water and is therefore a form of counterweight.
> A curator or artistic director who doesn't doubt too much is a counterweight.
> A technician who helps to finish in time is a counterweight.
> Good tools are a counterweight.

Figure 16. Excerpt from the book *Moment Before the Wind* (Brussels and Oslo: Varamo Press, 2020)

Figure 17. Scenography for the restaging of *The Soft Layer* in Palermo, 2021

Recently I have been exploring ways by which Soft Layer can travel and adapt to new sites. In the images here, you see the original pillar created in Tunis on the right, and a translated pillar designed for a Soft Layer interpretation for BETWEEN LAND AND SEA, a programme of original artistic and theatrical productions developed and presented in Palermo, Tunis, and Bremen (figs. 18 and 19).

Palermo and Tunis are only an hour away from each other by plane, and their shores are facing each other on opposite sides of the Mediterranean Sea. We decided to experiment with translating Soft Layer in its complexity on the other side of the Mediterranean with only material from this other side of the sea.

We built a scaffolding structure that evokes the building of the original Soft Layer using sandstone that is very typical for the region of Palermo. As for the tiles visible at the base of this pillar, we collected them every morning at the sea; these tiles have been washed to the shore for decades. The site where we were performing, the Ecomuseo Urbano Mare Memoria Viva, was built on a landfill of old houses destroyed by the earthquake of Palermo. These old houses turned out to have had the same tiles as the ones in Tunis because at the time, Italian tile-makers were the ones tiling the palazzi in Tunisia.

That ritual of perpetual discovery, scaffolding, and care felt meaningful as a practice of looking for and reconstructing Dar Baïram Turki in Palermo. On the night of the opening, I invited four Italian actors to come and do a text reading of the original script inside this new volume of Dar Baïram Turki.

And then, a few months ago, I went even further and restaged the text in Brussels, in the courtyard of my atelier. In one day, we built a quick sketch of Dar Baïram Turki, the minimum, just enough for the Brussels cast of performers to be able to imagine the original building while they read the text. It was remarkable how well it worked. It seemed that, the less of the building we built, the more it appeared inside the collective mind of the spectators. It blows my mind. What does it say about restoration when a building from Tunis can appear in a courtyard in Brussels without anything being transported (fig. 20)?

Figure 19. Detail of scenography for *The Soft Layer* in Tunis, 2019

Figure 18. Detail of scenography for the restaging of *The Soft Layer* in Palermo, 2021

Scaffolds and seats are just a beginning. They don't make the space. They are simply an instrument used to place the eyes of the spectators in a certain position. Only then, in the organized gaze, does the space emerge. A space made of eyes. A visual field that turns, blinks, looks away, and can close down. Scenography orients the gaze, the design is a visual field.

Figure 20. Excerpt from the book *Moment Before the Wind* (Brussels and Oslo: Varamo Press, 2020)

Organic Regeneration: Muharraq as a Resource
Noura Al-Sayeh Holtrop

Meandering around the streets of Muharraq today, through the narrow and organic alleys, one comes across a medley of buildings from different eras that might appear at first as a chaotic mix of styles and construction. Alongside the neat coral-stone buildings with their niche grids – repeating in an almost modernist order – appear buildings from the so-called transitional period, reflecting the arrival of modern materials, and hence larger floor spans, in the city. In between and along the main commercial arteries, which were introduced in the 1980s, are higher buildings of four to five stories in a more anonymous style of glass and concrete that further highlights these incisions within the historic city. More recently, dispersed along a trail that snakes through Muharraq from the southern coast of the island to its northern edge, contemporary interventions have nestled themselves within this urban fabric, in a series of precise infills of open public spaces, restorations, and new additions.

Recent decades have seen a renewed interest in and effort towards historic preservation and urban regeneration across the Arab World, starting in North Africa and the Levant in the early years of the twenty-first century, and more recently in the Gulf states. These efforts, most frequently government-led, often respond to international charters and agreed understandings of the importance of preservation, while presenting local challenges unique to the region and posing many questions. For whom are we conserving? Which part of our heritage is worth preserving and to which national narratives do they correspond? Who decides on what is worthy of preservation? Is there any other ambition beyond an economic one in preservation and regeneration? Is there a wider agenda beyond cultural tourism in the regeneration of historic cities? Have historic city centres become a commodity? Does urban regeneration necessarily lead to gentrification? Is the absence of gentrification a success or a failure?

After decades of rampant urbanisation and modernisation across most of the Arab World and specifically in the Gulf region, efforts to reconnect with and reaffirm a local national identity, in a growingly globalised and homogenised world, have resulted in a mounting interest in vernacular architecture and urban forms, as well as locally nuanced expressions of architecture. This interest is often preoccupied with how architecture can contribute to the making and reaffirmation of a national identity, and its role in creating more cohesive societies, linked by a common national narrative.

Many of the recent urban regeneration projects in the Gulf States, while acknowledging the cultural importance of historic cities and their contribution to the making of a national identity, neglect the fact that they are first and foremost cities that are living and changing organisms. The understanding of the mechanisms and forces that contribute to making a city alive and liveable are paramount to devising successful regeneration processes, just as preserving the material and physical remnants of the city, while neglecting to engage with the communities and actors that make the city, often results, in the long term, in the demise of the preserved.

151

Figure 1. Piercing the pearls, 1967

The Pearling Path project in Bahrain, first ideated in early 2008 by HE Shaikha Mai Al Khalifa, was initiated and conceived in a very different cultural and economic landscape than the one the Gulf finds itself in today. Created at a moment where cultural initiatives were believed to act within and for themselves, the project was mostly removed from the immediate necessity of having to respond to a strict economic agenda. It was rather focused on improving the quality of the urban fabric of the city of Muharraq and on spearheading its urban regeneration – so as to improve both its physical and social networks. While the regeneration efforts also aimed at improving the urban quality of the city, and thus ultimately its real-estate value, it could do so generously and gradually without having the burden of the economic performance of a five-year return on investment plan.

For millennia, pearling and its associated trades shaped the economy and culture of Bahrain's island society. As a centre for pearling, Bahrain was the regional economic hub where pearl

Figure 2. Opening the oysters on board a dhow, 1967

divers and other crew from across the Gulf arrived to test their fate on board the dhows. Even though the pearl collection industry dwindled as a result of many different factors, from the invention of cultured pearls at an industrial level to the financial crisis of 1929 and the discovery of oil in Bahrain in 1932, many of its features and practices survive, and it remains an important component of Bahraini cultural identity. The surviving traces of Bahrain's tangible and intangible pearling heritage are rare testaments to the Gulf's trans-regional, socio-economic connections prior to the discovery of oil (fig. 1).

Indeed, the oyster beds in the north of Bahrain were the centre of a natural pearl fishery that dominated the Persian Gulf from the third century BC until the early twentieth century. Despite the fact that pearl fishing was the main source of wealth for the economy of Bahrain until the 1930s, the oyster beds for which it was known were a shared resource amongst the neighbouring countries, according to an ancestral tribal system that had been commonly practised by these coastal populations for centuries. At the start of each pearling season, dhow boats from countries across the Gulf would sail to the waters surrounding Bahrain to test their luck, sailing from oyster bed to oyster bed during the annual four-month pearling season (fig. 2).

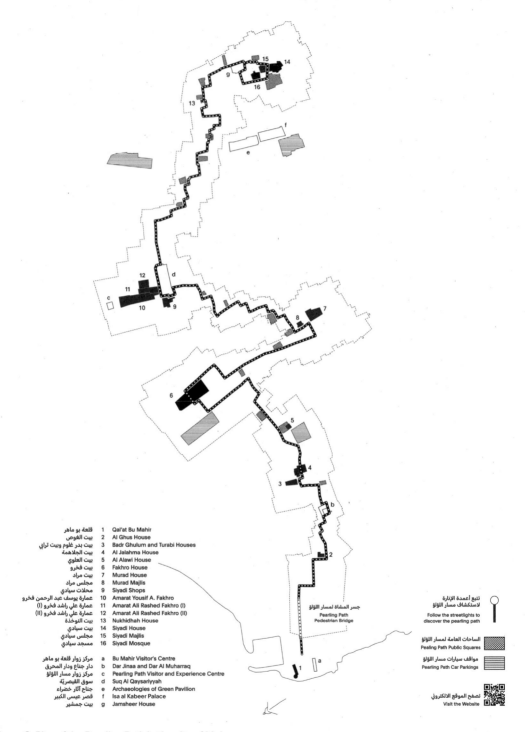

Figure 3. Plan of the Pearling Path in the city of Muharraq

In 2005, the first conservation initiatives in Muharraq were launched by HE Shaikha Mai Al Khalifa through the Shaikh Ebrahim Center for Culture and Research, and in the last ninteen years, they have grown to encompass an urban regeneration project, "Pearling, Testimony of an Island Economy", which is UNESCO World Heritage listed. It includes the conservation of sixteen listed historic properties related to the pearling economy. The project is a work in progress that is constantly adapting itself to the challenges of a changing city, and to reinventing it within its existing footprint. The success of the project can be attributed to its long-term commitment to the improvement of Muharraq, alongside a flexible approach that enables reassessment and changes as it is implemented. Supplementing this approach is an attitude and engagement to the life of the city, reinforced by a government strategy and policies that are developed and implemented to extend the scope of intervention beyond that of a singular project, and beyond the public, into the private and individual realm.

As the path traverses the historical centre of Muharraq, it also offers a cross-section of the many problems affecting these areas; a result of accumulated lack of maintenance, changing demographics of residents, a shift in lifestyle, and the increasing presence of cars within the city. While some problems are specific to Muharraq, others are symptomatic of the neglect that has taken place towards historic urban heritage around the Arab world. The Pearling Path was designed through its punctual interventions that cross through the historic quarters of Muharraq as a catalyst for the rehabilitation of the Old City (fig. 3).

In order to spearhead this rehabilitation, the scope of the project was widened beyond the conservation and rehabilitation of the World Heritage–inscribed properties to include comprehensive urban and architectural initiatives that would together preserve the historic features of the city, while propagating it into a sustainable future vision that would build on, rather than threaten, the historic assets of the city. A comprehensive conservation study of the city was undertaken following which several urban rehabilitation initiatives were launched. The site was also widened to include further public squares, the facade upgrade of 400 houses along the path, two visitor centres, and four multi-storey parking structures aimed at alleviating the mobility problems of the historic city.

From the onset of the project, one of the ambitions has been to avoid any unnecessary expropriations. Whenever possible, agreements have been made with the owners of the properties to reach an understanding of a shared use of the building. The Murad Majlis, for example, has been renovated through the Pearling Path project as one of the sixteen properties but continues to be used by the family as a majlis and is open to the public two days a week. Similarly, the Fakhro House is still owned by the Fakhro family and is open to the public as part of the Pearling Path, while a part of the exhibition featured in the house is focused on the history and

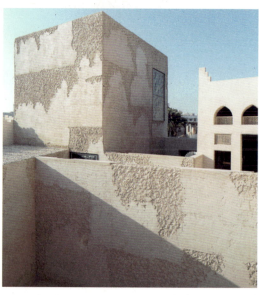

Figure 5. Siyadi Pearl Museum

Figure 4. Rehabilitation of Suq Al Qayssareyah by Anne Holtrop

contribution of the family to pearling and the modern history of Bahrain. The upgrade of the 400 facades along the path were similarly done through an agreement with each of the owners, which guarantees that the initial investment in upgrading the facades will be protected and maintained by them. Beyond the physical conservation and rehabilitation of the historic structures, these agreements guarantee that the intangible heritage of ownership, and link of the owners to the city, is preserved. The project is not only designed for the community; it was made with the community (fig. 4).

The project also includes the construction of additional cultural infrastructure for Muharraq, enhancing the surviving traces of its tangible and intangible pearling heritage. It navigates the challenges in reviving the memory of pearling through a culturally led development approach that binds the physical makings of the city and its identity. Acknowledging that the city is a living and contemporary social space influences, in turn, the way in which you perceive and understand the addition of new structures as opportunities for the construction of contemporary civic buildings that represent the values, technological capabilities, and challenges of our societies today (fig. 5).

Figure 6. Aerial view of parking D by Christian Kerez

This understanding allows us to build a multi-storey parking structure that need not conform to formal clichés such as a wind tower or historic screened openings but can demonstrate technical know-how in construction and structural prowess (fig. 6). In the same way, a visitor centre can offer a scale of shading and monumentality that did not previously exist in the city (fig. 7). All these new additions to the historic city of Muharraq add to the complexity of the urban fabric and to the different historical layers of development. By being radically different from one another, these additions enhance the authenticity and uniqueness of each era of construction, thus creating a coherent whole – a living city that can be understood and read through its different historical layers, while being linked by a common DNA informing the relationship between its architecture and its local context, climate, and resources.

Figure 7. Visitor Centre by Valerio Olgiati

It is often believed that the making of a whole – especially in the context of historic cities – needs to be made by sameness and harmonious aesthetics, with the old being authentic and the new attempting to resemble the old. The creation of sameness by approach and attitude, rather than visuals, gives rise to a living historic city that shares common values instead of appearances, and thus can create a coherent community. In the case of the Pearling Path, a focus on the creation of open public spaces and an emphasis on the importance of the void serve to promote a city that enhances social cohesion and interactions in order to foster greater engagement and appropriation of the city, which more than buildings is made by the people who inhabit them.

· The Pearling Path offers a methodology beyond the current prevailing trends in programming and approaching historic structures. By considering heritage, as an opportunity to rethink the present and not solely as a means of profiting from history, it affords the possibility to imagine different futures. In a country and region where the investment in public spaces and infrastructure for the community has often been neglected or privatised within gated communities and developments, this avenue heralds an intervention that takes the opposite approach (fig. 8).

158

Figure 8. Dar Al Muharraaq by OFFICE Kersten Geers David Van Severen

Practice as Context
Civil Architecture

There's a basic epistemological crisis that happens to every architect sorting a bookshelf in the Middle East.[1] Imagine three shelves with three books. The first shelf holds Rifat Chadirji's *Concepts and Influences,* the second has Al Farabi's *Opinions of the People of the Ideal City,* and the third holds Robert Venturi's *Complexity and Contradiction in Architecture.* One can choose to consolidate the first two, putting Chadirji and Al Farabi together under a geographical commonality, as books by Middle Eastern authors;[2] or to place the Chadirji and Venturi books together, being that they are both architecture monographs.[3] One might even put all three together on a single shelf under "Theories of Architecture" and arrange them chronologically.[4] The simplest solution would be to keep the library as it is, with each book occupying its own shelf and distinct category, avoiding the crisis of organising knowledge by theme. The problem for an architect based in the region, however, is not simply the organisation of these books, but rather the crisis caused after one has placed them together. Setting the books side by side reveals the gaps between them, suggesting that there are books unwritten, missing from the shelf.

Rifling through Arab architecture monographs from the mid-twentieth century reveals an interesting correlation between architectural practices and how architects perceive the monograph as a tool for communicating their work and for filling in the missing literature on the region. The monographs of Rifat Chadirji, Mohammed Makiya, and Hassan Fathy, for example, are less a pure survey of architectural work and more "books of everything". These monographs cover both built and unbuilt work – as is the norm – but also precedents, contextual notes, some historiography, and a position statement typically made against international practices operating in their context. Chadirji's first chapter tackles everything from how culture is disseminated, to a history of the architectural profession after industrialisation, to a theory of aesthetic collapse – all within twenty or so pages.

Other contemporary architects would write their treatises in similar fashion, although more constrained in scope, on architecture in the city. Robert Venturi's "gentle manifesto" for architectural form in *Complexity and Contradiction in Architecture* spans several centuries of architectural history, moving between Bernini and Grimsthorpe, Lutyens and Le Corbusier, to reach Moretti and Aalto. Similarly, Rem Koolhaas's *Delirious New York* is not a theory of everything, but it provides the model for the twentieth-century global city or financial capital, and the forms of architecture that populate it. These books do not construct sprawling theories of everything; they form a set of architectural precedents and a lineage to position one's work within. As books, they set up an architectural trajectory that culminates in the author's work rather than a primordial soup of ideas, materials, contexts, and philosophies which generate buildings (as, perhaps, in the case of Chadirji).

It is within this lineage – loose as it may be – that we distinguish between architecture as a profession and Architecture as a discipline or body of knowledge – working between both, in an effort to produce a Civil Architecture. We are interested in this way of thinking of a monograph: less as a survey of works and more of a loose theory of everything with architecture as its medium. For one, we find that in our context it links the idea of a monograph to a larger body of treatises written in the region, like Ibn Wahshiyya's *Nabatean Agriculture* or Ibn Khaldun's *Muqaddimah* – books which are centred on one topic and emanate outwards, claiming territory as they test the bounds of their discipline, profession, and knowledge.[5] They also unpin architecture from its tendency to sequester itself within disciplinary bounds, expanding further to claim a position within a general regional outlook. These treatises suggest a totalising way of understanding the world circumscribed within a single publication. The tendency to produce such books has largely fallen out of fashion, as they are unwieldy and take too long to get past the exposition to the architectural drawings. Most contemporary practices in the region have either defaulted to the strict monographic catalogue (similar to 2G or El Croquis) or the edited volume, collating varied thoughts into a single all-encompassing grab bag of positions – a multivalent theory of something specific described in general (say landscape, or modernism) as in the case of *Al Manakh*.[6]

We find ourselves enraptured with the "everything-monograph" way of producing publications, precisely because it represents the impossible task of shoehorning the sum total of one's knowledge into a single format – ordering all thoughts, causalities, and theories into one way of seeing the world. More important than the impossibility of the task is the fact that in doing so one addresses the very reason why these books emerged in twentieth-century Iraq and Egypt: because these architects needed to produce some way of correlating their problematic existence as local consultants in newly independent client states paying for foreign expertise.[7] The resulting books searched for modes of practice, looked for alternative ways of producing architecture as a way of existing and contesting a client state value system which privileged their competitors. Economics aside, on an even more existential level, the effort to produce a book of everything generates a set of values, conditions, and contexts for appraising architectural work – sets up a sequence from context to building that renders all imported architecture as aberrant urban behaviour.

As practitioners based in the Middle East and SWANA regions, we operate in the space between the commercially driven architecture market and the risk-averse bureaucracies that commission the built environment. This is true of architecture globally, but the commitment to branding the future, progressive, and utopian modern visions in this part of the world has meant that the prospect of dreaming "other" architectures is constantly contradicting the pragmatic banality of its implementation. The brand-new utopian policy is contrasted with the lack of critical discourse (from internal and external architects), and as a result there is a dissonance between the architectural ambitions and the architectural reality of the Gulf. The dubious notion of the future as used in Gulf Futurism, or tabula rasa, has been a way of promoting visions of

Between East and West: A Gulf, the companion to the Kuwait Pavilion at the 2016 Venice Biennale. The pavilion was an exercise in re-spatialising the Gulf as a body of water through its islands. The publication is a collection of essays, documents, photographs, and mappings which retell the story of the Arabian Gulf, and of projects interpreting the history and present of the region for a future built around the sharing of the body of water, rather than its negation due to foreign conflict.

architecture that are unsustainable, overly idealistic, or simply just marketing ploys. We try not to think of the future as a trajectory or vector to reach, and instead pin our aspirational intents on a kind of optimal present or long present. We think of practice as a thing that must generate its own context, and our work has been a recursive operation of research, arguments, and theoretical frameworks which in turn produce architecture.

It is in the context of the Gulf – promoting visions for 2030, 2050, and further, while also projecting them abroad for global buy-in – that we feel the need for practices that produce not only design solutions, but also the metrics and value systems by which to appraise design work. This form of architectural practice as a civil service runs counter to an otherwise self-interested short-term architectural ecosystem.

We describe our practice as "interested in buildings and books about them", an exercise that began with our remediation of *The Gulf* in the Kuwait Pavilion at the 2016 Venice Biennale – and continues to the present.

Two Thousand Years of Non-Urban History began as an investigation of formal planning methods in the Arabian Peninsula. We began with frustration with the idea that cities and towns were unplanned, and that all of the architectural and urban typologies that we could find documented were ad hoc accumulations of courtyard homes. The project eventually formed into a triptych composed of fish traps, farm plots, water infrastructure, and desert kites. Together, these devices or early architectures form a narrative around planning and collective resource management that runs counter to the idea of the ad hoc Arab city. The publication acted as a primer for all the ideas about collective planning, sustainability, and resource management that the literature on the architecture of the Gulf had omitted.

1. FARMING SUPPLY ROOM & MECHANICAL ROOM
2. CAFE
3. EXERCISE EQUIPMENT
4, 8, 10. SHOPS
5. FEMALE WC
6. MALE WC
7. ELECTRICAL ROOM
9. PLAYGROUND
11. AMPHITHEATRE
12. AGRICULTURAL MUSEUM
13. EVENT SPACE/PUBLIC PLAZA/FOOD TRUCK AREA
14. MOSQUE

Drawings from *Two Thousand Years of Non-Urban History* served as the inspiration for the landscape proposal in the Abu Makhrouq Public Park Competition, redeploying the traditional farm plots of Riyadh into a design for a productive public park in the city.

The project that followed the Kuwait Pavilion was *Two Thousand Years of Non-Urban History,* a primer on landscape and ecology which moved towards the mainland of the Gulf, covering notions of formal planning from fish traps to water channels to desert kites.

To us, the relationship between books and buildings is one of scale and immediacy. The former is more immediate – although still the product of a one-to-three year process – and easily distributed, while the latter is perhaps more permanent but also experienced over longer durations. A book can encompass the totality of the world, not in the sense that it can or should be encyclopaedic, but in the sense that a book's ideas can be scalable. And when it articulates the questions it poses in their entirety, a book can become a model of things much larger than itself.

A T-shirt as archive can reframe our relationship to the colonial buildings of a previous century.[8]

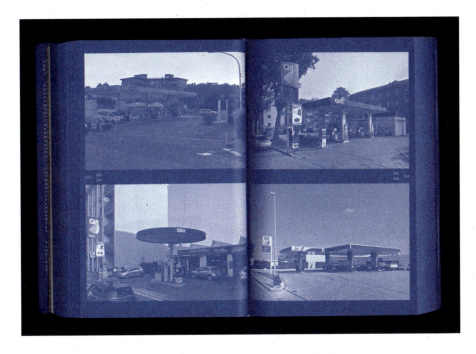

Petrol stations in Europe can tell us all we need to know about client states, decolonisation, and balance of trade and architecture as a unit of national sentiment.[9]

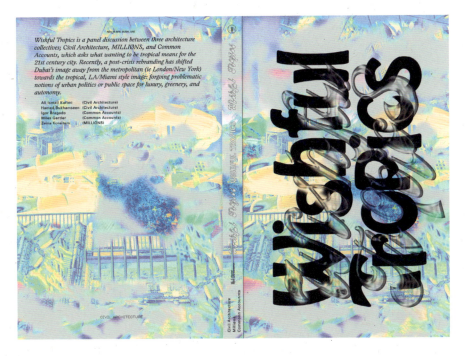

A book of lectures and discussions asks what fantasies drive the way we understand our context, and to whom we project those fantasies, and onto what we project them.[10]

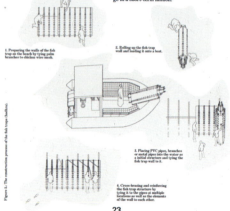

Fish traps in the Gulf can tell us everything we need to know about the borders of landscapes, the definition of edge conditions, their formalisation and eradication.

Both buildings and books act as ways of containing the world and provide a way of rethinking it. The practices that resonate with us establish their own parameters and objectives; they generate their own worlds of ideas and connections, from which architecture inevitably emerges fully formed as autochthonous assemblages of matter. Their buildings and texts are self-referential, holding within them the entirety of the world they project beyond their limits.

    Ultimately, for us, it is the working on the perception and conceptualisation of the built environment that is the most resilient form of architectural intervention – and that can occur in the space of construction as well as in the space of text. Each project or publication can be a synecdoche – a world in miniature – and when brought together they become like ships in a bottle, extrapolated to provide a view of the ocean – or perhaps plants in cloches, indicating rainforests and deserts and tropics, and thus a world beyond the glass.

168

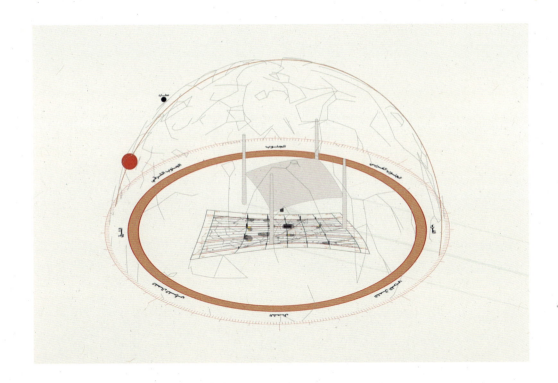

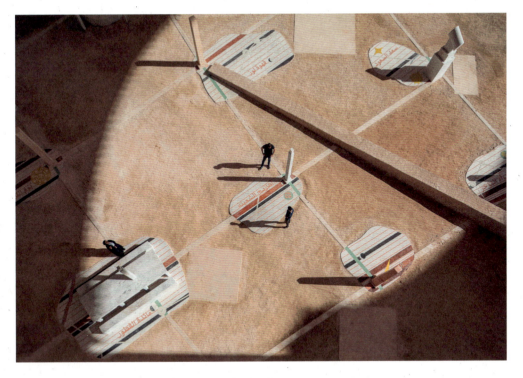

A Sun Path for Jeddah (top) or a 1:1 roof model (bottom) in Doha can tell us about the cosmos and the seasons we inhabit.[11]

We see buildings as publications with lives of their own, and books as miniature buildings – both didactic instruments for sensing and rethinking the world.

1 The term Middle East is used here because it is the category that persists in most library catalogues.

2 Al Farabi wrote in Arabic but was born in Khorasan; alternatively, the section could be Arab Cities or Islamic Architecture.

3 Appropriate also because Venturi wrote Chadirji's foreword.

4 The Harvard Library has them organised under: Architecture – Middle East, Architecture – Composition, Philosophy, Arab, respectively.

5 Ibn Wahshiyya's *The Nabatean Agriculture* is a tenth-century book of techniques for agriculture in the Arabian Peninsula, which includes notes on architecture, astronomy, and agronomy. Ibn Khaldun's *Muqaddimah* or *Prolegomena* is a fourteenth-century work on historiography and social theory, explaining the rise and fall of civilisations.

6 *Al Manakh*, edited by Rem Koolhaas, Ole Bouman, and Mitra Khoubrou, is a publication by AMO, the research arm of the Office for Metropolitan Architecture (OMA). Published in 2007 by Archis in Amsterdam, *Al Manakh* analyses the rapid growth of the Gulf, and specifically Dubai, in the first decade of the twenty-first century.

7 For Makiya and Chadirji, it was a response to having major commissions being assigned to modern firms like TAC, Frank Lloyd Wright, and Le Corbusier. Having grown up in Mandatory Iraq and having studied abroad, both architects returned to the country looking to establish a local architectural discourse as part of the larger nation-building project of a newly independent Iraq. This search for a modern architectural language saw both practices develop in different directions, while also attempting to compete with British and American architects. They would play a part in the commissioning of these architects, through their roles as the Dean of the University of Baghdad's Architecture Department in Makiya's case, and the Councillor to the Mayor of Baghdad in Chadirji's.

8 *Objects for a Painless Past*, a small exhibition in Muharraq accompanied by a T-shirt catalogue. The exhibition documented – in models and in T-shirts – a set of buildings constructed by the British during Bahrain's protectorate period. Collectively, these buildings (many of which still exist) constitute a crucial, if contested, part of Bahrain's architectural history, being that they were built during what was effectively a colonial period on the island. By having the publication as a T-shirt, it allowed the buildings and their documentation to exist as a personal artefact, worn by attendees, rather than as a neutral body of knowledge on a shelf or exhibition space.

9 The volume *Foreign Architecture / Domestic Policy* examined the five thousand Q8 petrol stations that Kuwait owns across Europe. These stations are more than investments in propagating the oil economy; they are also vehicles of foreign policy. The stations act as embassies for Kuwaiti diplomacy broadcasting the state's prowess and identity. The book charts the evolution of these stations from Kuwait's acquisition of the Gulf's stations in Italy to the rebranding of the company into what would eventually become one of the main actors in the liberation of Kuwait during the Gulf War.

10 The *Alserkal Ecology Reader* is a compilation of three lectures held in 2018 and 2019 in relation to Civil Architecture's summer residency at Alserkal Arts Foundation in Dubai. The lectures are centred on architecture's relationship to ecology, landscape, and life in the Gulf. Civil Architecture invited interlocutors from the region and abroad to discuss larger trends in the discipline and their connection to the context of Dubai.

11 *Sun Path*, 1444 in Jeddah tracked the movement of the sun throughout the Hajj Terminal designed by Skidmore, Owings & Merrill. Obelisks marked the different hours, weeks, and months of the exhibition, acting as a live calendar throughout the Islamic Arts Biennale. In Doha, we presented a 1:1 reproduction of a roof from a small house designed for a garden in Bahrain. Titled *House between Two Trees*, the roof was a formal response to the trees the house was sited between and to the process of caring for the garden.

ADDITIONS/ MATERIALITY

Stone Matters
Elias and Yousef Anastas

More than 200,000 Palestinian construction workers commute every day to Israeli territories for work.[1] They are paid four to five times more than in any Palestinian territory. Only half of them have official circulation permits delivered by the occupation authorities to cross checkpoints and work. The rest are sneakily allowed in and literally picked up in trucks by Israeli contractors waiting on the other side. They pick and choose from what is effectively an exploitative marketplace of workers.[2]

A typical journey starts with queuing lines at 3 a.m. waiting for checkpoints to open at 5 a.m., working until 3.30 p.m., and arriving back home around 8 p.m. At the age of thirty-five, these men are exhausted, and in the eyes of Israelis they have become expendable. The average age of Palestinian workers in Israel is twenty-eight years old.[3] Capitalistic exploitation associated with the harsh conditions of a humiliating occupation probably best describe the contemporary framework in which this construction labour evolves.

In consequence, the Palestinian side suffers from a clear shortage of construction labour. The contemporary formalisation of Palestine's labour crisis is evidently linked to the current occupation's exploitation systems. However, the history of architectural practices ever since the British Mandate, from one side, and global shifts in materials for construction, from the other, are aligned with the evolution of a complete disregard for the value of labour, the use of stone in architecture in Palestine, and politics of supremacy.

Stone Matters is a project by AAU ANASTAS that looks at ways of using stone in contemporary architecture to emancipate it from imposed policies of domination and to suggest new economical logics in construction, a valuing labour, and shifting perspectives on heritage. It builds upon ongoing, experimentation-based research into the potential for including structural stone in the language of contemporary architecture, and for combining traditional craftsmanship and materials with innovative construction techniques.

In 1918, the British military general Edmund Henry Hynman Allenby ordered Sir William McLean to put together an urban master plan for Jerusalem. One of the bylaws states that all buildings within the walls of the old city should be built out of stone: "The external walls of all buildings shall be constructed of stone."[4]

In 1919, Sir Ronald Storrs invited Charles Ashbee to oversee the master plan and create for that purpose the Pro-Jerusalem Society. In 1936, the bylaw was extended outside the boundaries of the old city. At the same time, global developments in concrete and steel in architecture began progressively affecting the building methods. Under the pressure of developers, the law was modified in 1944: "The external walls and columns of houses and the face of any wall abutting on a road shall be faced with natural, square dressed stone."[5]

Officially, the 1918 bylaw was set to create a unified built environment in Jerusalem. However, it has resulted in defining imaginary boundaries to the city: everything that was not built out of stone was considered out of Jerusalem. This was specifically used in the post-1967 annexation strategies for Zionist housing operations around Jerusalem where stone was used to inscribe their establishments in the imaginary as part of Jerusalem's boundaries.[6] De facto, the use of the material became a political tool for reclaiming and annexing territories. The material progressively stopped being used as a structural massive material but was instead seen as a covering of concrete structures. To dissimulate the fakeness of its construction even more, some typologies of stone – called *dustor* – were produced specifically at angles of buildings to hide the edge of stones where one can specifically differentiate a clad structure from a solid stone construction.[7] Some buildings were even erected in zones beyond the area defined by the bylaw, yet still using stone as a way of influencing the body of Jerusalem.

After the Oslo Accords were signed in 1993, the bylaw became part of the urban law in a large majority of Palestinian cities. There are mainly three periods to distinguish in the production of stone that relate to policies adopted by the different ruling bodies in Palestine, and that affect the labour and artisanship entities in the region. The first period includes buildings constructed before 1918, where stone is used as a natural material for structural and climatic purposes. Its thickness in construction varies from 50 to 80 centimetres. Unlike in neighbouring countries, stone construction and vaulting in Palestine are not reserved for noble buildings or palaces but are completely inscribed in common domestic architecture.[8] Stone is a material chosen for its natural properties, its availability, and the historic presence of a skilled labour.

The second period is a transitional one referring to the modern era of architecture in Palestine. Stone elements are relatively thick, around 30 centimetres, and are used in walls with concrete. Stones have a dressed facade and a rougher interior that enhances the adherence to the body of concrete. This hybrid wall still uses stone as a structural material and is typical of buildings proper to modern architecture in Palestine. And finally, the third period is identified as a serious shift in the use of the material. Stone elements are standardised and only used as cladding for panels with a thickness of 2, 3, or 5 centimetres. They are used to clad concrete structures. This period marks the progressive loss of architectural references in Palestine, a progressive loss of know-how about stone masonry and, ultimately, about the occupation-inflicted humiliating commodification crisis of construction labour.

The contemporary architecture in Palestinian cities is heavily influenced by the 1918 bylaw. Worldwide domination of concrete and steel structures associated with a requirement of stone covering has reduced the possibilities of construction methods and techniques to a unique process. Buildings in Palestinian cities all look alike and create an urban fabric that is shaped by real-estate developers. With hindsight, it is puzzling that a city built out of a noble material such as stone suddenly becomes sadly monotonous.

The quality of construction labour has known a parallel impoverishment. While construction workers' main objectives are to work for a better wage on the Israeli side, the building techniques in Palestine got stalled. There are no apparent or notable developments in the ways of building, even in concrete. All structures are built with manual timber formwork assembled by hand on site, and regular-grade concrete is poured on site. The unique way of making – resulting partially from a systematic use of stone exclusively as a cladding material – gave away architecture to developers that do not value labour. Workers' wages are low and stagnant, and, as such, contractors are not keen on developing new technologies for building. In other words, in the current cost-on-investment logic that prevails, contractors prefer to keep wages low and extend construction durations instead of raising wages and introducing faster construction techniques.

Yet, the use of stone is key in the economy of the Palestinian construction world: it is the only fully available and usable material that is independent from the occupation's stranglehold. Stone quarries are distributed across two main areas, in the south and in the north of the West Bank. The Oslo Accords define zones within the West Bank (Palestinian territories):

Area A: Palestinian land under Palestinian control

Area B: Palestinian land under Palestinian civil control and Israeli security control

Area C: Palestinian land under Israeli control

Quarries are, for the most part, situated in Area C.[9] Palestine is the twelfth exporter of stone worldwide.[10] The quarries feed the Palestinian, Israeli, and international markets. In Israel, there are only a few quarries for two main reasons. First, the land is by default state owned and, as such, a quarry project is economically viable only if considerably big, which requires large-scale investments. And second, the law for environmental protection is strict enough for quarries not to be profitable projects, especially when Area C quarries are being over-exploited a few kilometres away. Area C – specifically areas where stone quarries are present – is intentionally left off the radar by Israeli authorities in terms of pollution, landscape disasters, and dust diseases in neighbouring villages. In fact, Area C is even purposely allowed to wildly quarry to fulfil the needs of a growing market.

The issue of stone in Palestine today is intertwined with political, ecological, and social problems that are directly linked to the labour crisis in terms of know-how, wages, and dependency on the occupation domination system. Stone Matters aims at challenging the way we use stone and the architecture it creates, and it values a new form of labour that is centred around resources, both intellectual and physical, that are completely independent. Stone Matters formalises into a series of experimentation and architectural projects built with structural stone.

Buildings erected before 1917 are protected by Palestinian law. Buildings constructed after 1917 can be demolished even if their architectural and historical interests may seem relevant. This is the case for a series of buildings built between the 1930s and the 1960s using the hybrid structural walls mentioned above (stone plus concrete). These structures truly represent an era of architectural modernism in Palestine. In the last decade, a great number of buildings were demolished by developers to be replaced with commercial projects.[11]

The recent interest in stone construction globally is linked to the sustainable nature of the material. Sustainability policies have been built around prevailing construction materials such as concrete and steel. The use of these materials has been progressively associated with a form of consumerism and short-term, profit-based economies that were dominant in the second half of the twentieth century. As a result, buildings are not meant to last beyond a couple of decades.

Stone Matters positions itself (and contemporary architecture) in a much more expansive history. In one of our experimentations, we collected stones from a demolished building and created an architectural component out of salvaged elements. *Amoud* is a column made of collected stone architectural ruins.[12] The different stone elements come from various periods and illustrate different techniques of construction (fig. 1). This addresses the question of the possibilities

Figure 1. Detail of *Amoud* at the *Hangar Exhibition* in 2019 at Amman Design Week

Figure 2. *Qamt* circular lintel bench at the Victoria and Albert Museum in London

of reusing stone as a structural material, as well as the finite resource that it embodies and its consequent effect on the natural landscape. On a more global note, the approach seeks to integrate salvaged building components in contemporary architecture.

Modern societies value the heritage of historic structures but do not look at building structures for future heritage. In that context, sustainability is put in direct contradiction with durability. This opposition is associated with the paradigmatic shift in material use, history of techniques, and construction logics and economies. The main argument that prevails in contemporary times for not using solid materials and/or traditional techniques of construction is related to initial costs and investments highlighting the lack of long-term financing of buildings.[13] Yet, an elemental analysis of building components reveals that if the entire life-cycle assessment of a material is taken into account, and provided that quarries are regionally available, solid stone construction is more economical than concrete for instance.[14] In that sense, the embodied carbon footprint of stone structures addresses an urgent global energy consumption matter, with the building industry being responsible for more than 40 per cent.[15]

By deeply inspecting stone's planetary echoes, Stone Matters highlights local and global exchange techniques and traces unseen analogies between architectural forms and dwelling rituals across borders. *Qamt* is a prototype that sits at the intersection between form and function, where we experimented with systems of lintels inspired by stereotomy – the process of cutting stones – found in Jerusalem to create a public circular lintel bench (fig. 2).

Figures 3 and 4. Construction documentation of el-Atlal project in Jericho

In addition to these excavations into historic nuances, techniques, and networked impacts of stone, Stone Matters relies on novel computational simulation and fabrication techniques, divorcing the material from its archaic connotations. This is evident in our work on the el-Atlal art residency in Jericho, where we designed a self-supporting canopy made of 300 individually cut and mutually supporting stone pieces, modelling radical morphologies towards a rooted and sophisticated urbanism without dispensing local craftspeople (figs. 3 and 4).

Our latest prototype, *Tiamat*,[16] positions itself at the intersection of different realms, with the aim of opening up new families of possible structures made out of stone. The structure brings together intrinsic geometrical properties of surfaces morphing Gothic architecture, the desert sand formations, and stereotomy to transform Bethlehem limestone into a powerful organism setting new standards for contemporary architecture (figs. 5–8).

Figures 5, 6, and 7. Clockwise: *Tiamat* construction documentation, diagram of principal moment lines, interior view

Figure 8. *Tiamat* installation view at the *Arab Design Now* exhibition in Doha, 2024

From quarrymen, who are literally sommeliers of mountains, to stonemasons, Palestine has an opportunity to bring to the world a new way of thinking architecture. It is a model based on the long-term financing of buildings that is aligned with the way stone structures are historically implemented: relying on a continuous feed of information from design to mounting. Stone structures call for a renewed relationship to construction labour, one that would reconcile our ability to understand our history and be able to foresee our heritage, one where sustainability is not exclusively measured with alienated criteria, one that is able to resist supremacist systems of domination and aspire to build political aspirations through architecture.

1   Steven Scheer, Ari Rabinovitch, and Ali Sawafta, "Loss of Palestinian workers at Israeli building sites leaves hole on both sides", Reuters, 22 March 2024, https://www.reuters.com/world/middle-east/loss-palestinian-workers-israeli-building-sites-leaves-hole-both-sides-2024-03-21/.

2   Leila Farsakh, Palestinian *Labour Migration to Israel: Labour, Land and Occupation* (London: Routledge, 2005); Andrew Ross, *Stone Men: The Palestinians Who Built Israel* (London: Verso Books, 2019).

3   I. f. P. Studies, "Palestinian Labor in Israel: A Fluctuating Market Subject to Israel's Interests", *Interactive Encyclopedia of the Palestine Question*, https://www.palquest.org/en/highlight/33700/palestinian-labor-israel.

4   William McLean, City of Jerusalem Town Planning Scheme, 1918.

5   Ibid.

6   Eyal Weizman, *Hollow Land: Israel's Architecture of Occupation* (London: Verso Books, 2007).

7   Ibid.

8   Susan Slyomovics, *The Object of Memory: Arab and Jew Narrate the Palestinian Village* (Philadelphia: University of Pennsylvania Press, 1998); Tawfiq Canaan, *The Palestinian Arab House: Its Architecture and Folklore* (Jerusalem: Syrian Orphanage Press, 1933); Halvor Moxnes, ed., *Constructing Early Christian families: Family as Social Reality and Metaphor* (London: Routledge, 1997); Friedrich Ragette, *Traditional Domestic Architecture of the Arab Region* (Fellbach: Edition Axel Menges, 2003).

9   "Israeli stone quarrying in the Occupied Palestinian Territory", *Global Atlas of Environmental Justice*, 14 October 2021, https://ejatlas.org/conflict/israeli-stone-quarrying-in-the-occupied-palestinian-territory.

10 International Trade Centre, *The State of Palestine National Export Strategy: Stones and Marble Sector Export Strategy 2014–2018*, 2018, https://paltrade.org/uploads/1608048895879360691.pdf.

11 Tessa Fox, "Ramallah construction boom threatens city's architectural heritage", *The Guardian*, 6 November 2018, https://www.theguardian.com/cities/2018/nov/06/ramallah-construction-boom-threatens-citys-architectural-heritage.

12 Commissioned by Amman Design Week in 2019, *Amoud* was part of the *Hangar Exhibition* curated by Noura Al-Sayeh Holtrop.

13 Luisa María Gil-Martin, María José González-López, Alejandro Grindlay, Armando Segura-Naya, Mark A. Aschheim, and Enrique Hernández-Montes, "Toward the production of future heritage structures: Considering durability in building performance and sustainability – A philosophical and historical overview", *International Journal of Sustainable Built Environment* 1, no. 2 (2012), pp. 269–73.

14 Dimitra Ioannidou, Stefano Zerbi, and Guillaume Habert, "When more is better: Comparative LCA of wall systems with stone", *Building and Environment* 82 (2014), pp. 628–39.

15 Barnabas Calder, *Architecture from Prehistory to Climate Emergency* (London: Pelican Books, 2021).

16 Commissioned for Design Doha biennial's *Arab Design Now* exhibition in 2024, curated by Rana Beiruti.

Small Touches, Big Hopes: Renovating an Icon of Global Modern Architecture in Tripoli, Lebanon
Sibel Bozdoğan

In May 2005, the cover image of *The New York Times Magazine* showed the cardboard model of a modern building protected by a glass bell jar, with the polemical caption: "Is it Time for the Preservation of Modernism?". It was a whimsical image that nevertheless captured the profound tension between modern architecture and the very idea of preservation. What does it mean to preserve an architecture whose theoretical premises are rooted in the avant-garde modernist notions of change, transience, and impermanence? Can "modern" be a "heritage" or a "period style" just like the historical styles it once set out to reject? What exactly is the "original" to be preserved when most modern buildings and complexes are added on and transformed several times along the way? If preservation is a memory project, what is to be remembered and what is allowed to be forgotten? Is it about restoring the original modernist object (as, for example, in the precise reconstruction of the Barcelona Pavilion, the inviolable Miesian glass box to which nothing can be added or subtracted), or an acknowledgement of modern architecture as a "living heritage" that is as much about its present and future uses as it is about the initial design (fig. 1)?[1]

Figure 1. Barcelona Pavilion by Ludwig Mies van der Rohe

Figure 2. Overview of the Rachid Karami International Fair in Tripoli

EAST Architecture Studio's renovation of the Niemeyer Guest House in Tripoli offers us a provocative case to ponder some of these questions. With deliberately modest and minimalist interventions respectful of the conceptual integrity of the original structure, it presents not only a successful adaptive reuse of an iconic modernist building by a legendary Brazilian architect, but also promises to be a catalyst towards the preservation of the rest of the badly ageing structures of the entire Rachid Karami International Fair ensemble that it belongs to – arguably one of the most iconic, if unfinished and long-neglected heritage sites of post-war global modern architecture (fig. 2). As my title "Small Touches, Big Hopes" suggests, this renovation gives "less is more" a whole new meaning, and it is these two aspects of the project that I seek to unpack in this essay: namely, its specific approach to renovation through restrained, tentative, and reversible interventions; and its larger symbolism in highlighting the historical legacy of twentieth-century modernist architecture in the Middle East, projecting hope at a time when hope is in short supply in the region.

"Small Touches": Calibrating Permanence and Ephemerality

> The characteristic approach of the piecemeal engineer is this. Even though he may perhaps cherish some ideals which concern society "as a whole" . . . he does not believe in the method of re-designing it as a whole. Whatever his ends, he tries to achieve them by small adjustments and re-adjustments which can be continually improved upon. . . . he will make his way, step by step, carefully comparing the results expected with the results achieved, and always on the look-out for the unavoidable unwanted consequences of any reform.[2]

Philosopher Karl Popper's ideas of piecemeal social change through "conjectures and refutations" offers a good analogy for EAST Architecture Studio's philosophy of "scaffolding" – a strategy of piecemeal and potentially reversible renovation. The architects Charles Kettaneh and Nicolas Fayad employ "scaffolding" as an evocative metaphor that conceptualises renovation as merely one iteration in a longer generative process, rather than an end in itself. Just like a scaffold is removed after construction is complete, the renovation is conceptualised as being temporary

Figure 3. Inside the Niemeyer Guest House

and tentative, accepting any possible reversal or even removal of some of its own interventions as may be needed for future reprogramming of the building and/or the fairgrounds as a whole. While giving the first order of priority and urgency to rehabilitating the structural problems, such as the material wear-and-tear and crumbling finishes of Niemeyer's original building, the new additions – mainly, glass partitions with thin metal frames to accommodate the new programming – make a point of touching very lightly (or not at all) wherever they meet the floor or the ceiling structure, thus visually highlighting a sense of removability and ephemerality (fig. 3). It is as if the renovation were merely suggesting *the possibility* of reoccupation of an abandoned modernist ruin, without prescribing anything more at this time.

This Popperian incremental approach, both out of necessity (budget constraints) but also out of conviction (in the inevitability of change), is also a compelling meditation on the dilemmas of "preserving the modern" that I already alluded to in the beginning. All the good work and accomplishments to date of Docomomo, Getty, and other institutions notwithstanding, the idea of heritage preservation still sits uncomfortably with a modernism whose own foundational discourse celebrates transience, ephemerality, and impermanence as modern values par excellence. Ideas to incorporate change and obsolescence into design as an inevitable part of the natural life cycle of a building have captured many imaginations in twentieth-century architectural theory – from Cedric Price's mantra of "indeterminacy" to the Japanese Metabolists' belief

Figures 4 and 5. Former Manama post office, originally from 1937, was encased behind a concrete portico and steel facade in the 1980s (top) and the Rehabilitation of Manama Post Office by Anne Holtrop, 2019 (bottom)

Figure 6. The Flying Saucer in Sharjah, built in 1978 in the Brutalist style, originally served as a café, restaurant, newsstand, and gift shop. Its purpose evolved multiple times starting in 1988.

in an architecture of renewable, impermanent parts to be replaced periodically.[3] The Rachid Karami International Fair differs from those in its heavy presence as a monument, of course, but the Niemeyer Guest House renovation still invites us to contemplate how renovation, too, can be informed by such ideas – how it can seek to incorporate reversibility to anticipate the future, while also affirming the *heritage value* of Niemeyer's building to celebrate the past.

Given the historical importance and international stature of Oscar Niemeyer, the heritage value of the Guest House and the larger fairgrounds has never really been in doubt. Indeed, the long period of disuse and neglect (from the onset of the Lebanese Civil War in 1975 to the Fair's recent "emergency nomination" as an endangered UNESCO World Heritage Site in 2023) can possibly be seen as a blessing in disguise – preserving the entire ensemble more or less in its "original", albeit unfinished and deteriorating state, largely unburdened by subsequent uses.[4] With the exception of one minor alteration to Niemeyer's original concept (the enclosing of the facades of the Grand Couverture) and another more detrimental post-Civil War intervention (the conversion of the collective housing on the southeast end of the site into the now abandoned Quality Inn Hotel), the most iconic structures of the ensemble, including the Guest House, have remained unaltered, ageing, and empty.

By contrast, many other post-war modernist structures in the region were transformed beyond recognition over time, necessitating a thorough "clean-up" of accumulated clutter in order to reveal the "original" in which the heritage value resides. For example, two other renovation/ adaptive reuse projects shortlisted in the 2022 Aga Khan Award for Architecture Cycle have had to tackle such accumulated baggage of a building's afterlife. The first project, the Manama Post Office Building in Bahrain (2019), has necessitated the removal of a prior conversion from the 1960s – an entire precast concrete facade that enveloped the original early twentieth-century Customs Building underneath (figs. 4 and 5). Likewise, the "Flying Saucer" Rehabilitation in Sharjah (2020), a free-standing concrete shallow dome and star-shaped canopy grid propped up with V-shaped supports (fig. 6), has had to strip off all traces of the structure's subsequent uses as a supermarket and fast-food restaurant in the 1980s, in order to reveal the formal purity of the original structure dating from 1975.

It is, without doubt, a formidable challenge to tackle a monumental site like the Rachid Karami International Fair which, after Brasília, is the single largest signature project by Niemeyer, who was always vocal about his commitment to "form" before function. "I am in favour of almost unlimited plastic freedom . . .", he wrote in 1960, "a freedom that is not slavishly subordinate to

Figure 7. On the grounds of the Rachid Karami International Fair

Figure 8. Inside the Niemeyer Guest House

the reasons of any given technique or of functionalism, but which makes an appeal to the imagination, to things that are new and beautiful, capable of arousing surprise and emotion by their very newness and creativeness."[5] In the case of the Fair in Tripoli, these "new and beautiful things" include the 640-metre-long, boomerang-shaped Grande Couverture, the Lebanese Pavilion with its pointed arches and reflecting pools, the thin-shell domed Experimental Theater, the underground Space Museum with its Helipad, and the Outdoor Theater with its ceremonial ramp and framing arch, collectively making up a modern composition of bold, concrete sculptural forms spread over the site (fig. 7).

In comparison with the formal exuberance of these other structures, however, the Guest House is a rather "tame" rectangular building occupying the farthest northwest corner of this ensemble – a large introverted concrete box lit only from roof openings. Finding it in a materially decaying but otherwise unfinished or unused state was, in a way, an opportunity for EAST Architecture Studio to focus on the urgent task of rehabilitating the structural weaknesses and material ageing of the original building, rather than having to remove additions and alterations. That they have introduced a brand-new use with specific programmatic requirements (workshop, library, exhibition space for Minjara, which is a vocational training centre for local carpenters) while successfully preserving Niemeyer's imprint on the building testifies to the amount of research, analysis, and meticulous detailing involved. For example, with careful respect for the original spirit of Niemeyer's Carioca School of Brazilian modernism (that has flourished mostly around Rio de Janeiro), Kettaneh and Fayad chose to paint the concrete rather than leave it exposed (in the manner of the Paulista School of João Batista Vilanova Artigas). Also, they have used the materials, colours, and textures of what could easily have been a Roberto Burle Marx landscaping (the gravel surface and fountain grass berms of the courtyard) (fig. 8). Niemeyer's ghost is clearly still there, but the building has moved on.

The renovation work in only one half of a single building within a vast modernist complex of different iconic structures across a 72 hectare area is undoubtedly more of a symbolic gesture than the ultimate comprehensive preservation of a major World Heritage Site. Nevertheless, as a pilot project, it succeeds in setting meaningful standards of material refinement, incremental approach, and public programming to offer guidelines for the preservation of the larger Fair ensemble. Philosophically, it lays bare the absurdity of "total design" as opposed to careful "piecemeal engineering" (to use the Popperian terms again) in very large projects of this scale and significance. It rules out, for example, once and for all, any large commercial development projects like the "Middle Eastern Disneyland" proposal of 2001 (which was successfully rejected as a result of campaigns by Lebanese architects, preservationists, intellectuals, and the public). Programmatically, by giving the Minjara a centre of work, display, learning, and exchange among stakeholders aiming to reinvigorate Tripoli's declining wood industry, it shows the social and economic benefits of adaptive reuse that prioritises spaces of production (rather than just consumption) and public access (rather than privatised spaces). The biggest symbolic significance of the project, however, extends far beyond Tripoli and even Lebanon. It offers a glimmer of hope towards registering, saving, and repurposing other comparable iconic modernist buildings and complexes in the region, which were themselves generators of optimism when they were first built. It draws attention to this rich legacy of modern architecture in the Middle East, which tends to be forgotten in the midst of current regional turmoil.

"Big Hopes": Reclaiming Architectural Legacies of Optimism

> [In countries like Turkey, Brazil and India, to name just a few, or Lebanon, for that matter] modernist ruins are not just ruins; they are allegories that narrate the paradoxical crossing of "newness" and "nationhood."[6]

Theories and historiography of modern architectures of the Global South have produced a vast body of scholarship in the last two decades or so, articulating the need for what the Indian art historian Partha Mitter has compellingly called "de-centering modernism" – that is, reconceptualising modernism as plural, heterogeneous, and worldwide, hence the property of everyone rather than of a privileged Western "centre".[7] Contrary to the representation of modern architecture in the "non-Western world" as an alien and imported discourse unsuitable to local cultures, this perspective urges a fresh look at this modernist heritage as the expression of these countries' own national aspirations for participation in a larger international conversation about modernity across the ideological divides of what are known as the First, Second, and Third Worlds. Rather than thinking of Chandigarh primarily as a Le Corbusier masterpiece, for example, or the Tripoli International Fair as exclusively the legacy of Oscar Niemeyer (who is said to have distanced himself from the project after 1975), it casts such modernist projects as *co-productions,* in this case with their Indian and Lebanese interlocutors respectively. It invites us to think of them as products of many cross-cultural exchanges of expertise, innovative on-site technological adaptations, and localisations of knowledge. Above all, it reframes the historical significance of these modern buildings and complexes as primary sites of national pride, local agency, and societal optimism.

Given the larger-than-life fame of their designers, Chandigarh and the Tripoli International Fair are particularly provocative case studies for reconceptualising the history of global modern architecture as "histories of co-production". While much of traditional historiography has focused only on the international designers of these grand projects as the primary agents who introduced modernism to these countries from the outside (Le Corbusier with Jane Drew and Maxwell Fry in the former, and Oscar Niemeyer in the latter), in reality it was a myriad of local actors (politicians, designers, builders, and the public) who initiated and "owned" these projects, shaped them along the way with numerous two-way exchanges and negotiations with the international designers, and ultimately built them as home-grown modern architectures. This question of "authorship" was raised by Maristella Casciato when Chandigarh was nominated for the UNESCO World Heritage List (approved in 2016). Drawing attention to the 30,000-person, all-native Indian workforce involved, she asked: "What is being discussed [in this nomination]: the capital's buildings or a living city, which owes its character, its spaces, its materials and, if you want, its defects to other authors, not only to a single Franco-Swiss maestro?"[8] Similarly, talking about the formative role of the project on the nine Indian architects (including his own father), as well as countless technicians and local builders who worked with Le Corbusier (and who, never even once, thought of the project as "foreign"), Vikram Prakash wrote: "Origins are not ends, and therefore, are not the only ways of deriving identity and ownership. There are other equally valid ways such as adoption, participation and appropriation. Postcolonial histories and practices of modernisms need not apologize for their modernity. One does not need to 'Indianize' them; they were/are Indian always."[9]

Similar histories of co-production and local agency can be written for the Rachid Karami International Fair as well, where Niemeyer only authored the initial architectural design, visiting Tripoli for two months in 1962 and again during construction, but never saw it completed. It was local construction and development firms (like Dar Al Handasah of Shaer & Partners and Nazih Taleb & Partners, among others) that carried out the project. The 2023 Emergency Nomination report for UNESCO World Heritage Listing states: "The close collaboration between Oscar Niemeyer and the Lebanese engineers and contractors who prepared the technical studies, the execution drawings, the tender documents and supervised the construction, was a remarkable example of technical exchange between different continents: [the latter] gained valuable experience with sophisticated reinforced concrete structures of large spans and concrete shells, while a new generation of Lebanese architects were inspired by Niemeyer's 'Brazilian modernism'."[10] The afterlife of the project was also shaped by local initiatives and subsequent uses, sometimes diverging from Niemeyer's design – such as when the southern part of the Grand Canopy was enclosed following the recommendations of Dar Al Handasah in 1997. Its "Brazilian" origins notwithstanding, the Fair was primarily a "Lebanese" modern enterprise, nationally produced and proudly embraced.

Sadly, it is the dark aftermath of such optimistic beginnings that is another commonality between Chandigarh and the Tripoli Fair, both sites embroiled in histories of conflict and communal violence. The former, not given over to the Sikh community of Punjab as initially promised, has been at the centre of Sikh grievances for much of the 1980s. In the first decade of the twenty-first century, it was described as "a beleaguered site . . . emerging from a prolonged political siege, cordoned off by layers of barbed wire and backed-up by sandbags and the military".[11] The International Fair in Tripoli, too, ". . . due to its strategic location at the city entrance and its proximity to all main transportation arteries",[12] was occupied by different armed forces and militias during the Lebanese Civil War, and the Grand Canopy of the main exhibition wing was used as a shelter for tanks and military equipment.

I will suggest that the largely parallel histories of these two iconic projects inspire us to carry the *co-production* perspective one step further. Now that the masters are dead, dreams are shattered, and the concrete is crumbling, can renovation, too, be a co-production? Rather than a restoration of the original object and its authorial uniqueness (thereby rendering the renovators invisible), can it be a practice that shares the authorship, contributes to the original, and advances it for contemporary uses and changed conditions (thereby turning the renovators into co-designers)? To this rhetorical question, EAST Architecture Studio answers in the affirmative. With their interventions, they co-produce Niemeyer's project one more time, in the same way that it was co-produced by the Lebanese teams who built it in the first place. Who can say that there will not be other co-productions and re-productions in an open-ended, indeterminate future?

Figure 9. View of the Hall of Nations by Raj Rewal, 1972

This cultural shift towards de-centring modernism and writing its history as one of co-production has been more internationally visible in the cases of postcolonial Southeast Asia and Sub-Saharan Africa, as shown for example by two recent exhibitions at The Museum of Modern Art in New York (2022) and the Victoria and Albert Museum in London (2024), respectively.[13] In both events, post-war "tropical modernisms" of these regions of the Global South are highlighted as architectures of post-independence optimism, along with a renewed appreciation of concrete – that much-maligned material of post-war architecture, now viewed as a contextually appropriate material in terms of the available resources and local labour conditions in poorer countries.[14] International trade fairs and exhibition spaces feature particularly prominently in these recent celebrations of global modern architecture as sites of performative modernity, not just for experimenting with the bold formal possibilities of concrete as the modern material par excellence, but also for projecting faith in the country's future, just like the Rachid Karami International Fair project sought to do in Lebanon. For example, included in both exhibitions are buildings like Raj Rawal's Hall of Nations in India with its monumental concrete 3D space frame (a remarkable structure inaugurated with national pride in 1972 and ruthlessly demolished in 2017), or the

Accra International Trade Fair in Ghana with its large circular roof canopy covering the exhibition stands of African countries (fig. 9), not unlike Niemeyer's Grande Couverture of the Tripoli Fair (fig. 10), both designs dating from 1962.[15] In comparison with this international interest in Southeast Asian and African modernisms, the Middle East (a region burdened by its more complex post-Ottoman Empire histories, current political conflicts, and the anti-secular agendas of political Islam) has largely lagged behind, at least until relatively recently when new publications and exhibitions began to appear.[16]

The Fair is a more internationally known project of course (due in no small measure to the fame of Oscar Niemeyer), but other precedents in the region also carry the legacy of the grand social and urban ambitions that such modernist projects once held. İzmir International Fair in Turkey, built in the 1930s in a large urban park as the showcase of the new republic's modern aspirations, still exists as a public space of recreation, albeit transformed dramatically with very few traces of the original structures remaining. Damascus International Fair is another example, initially conceived in 1950 for the promotion of trade and economic development but also intended for public use as a park – a landscape of leisure and recreation with exhibition pavilions lined along the river, interspaced with a series of fountains and cascades of water. A recent article narrates how in its heyday it flourished as a popular public space in modern continuity with the tradition of *sayran* (people promenading and occupying outdoor spaces for picnics, music, and

Figure 10. View of the Lebanese Pavilion at the Rachid Karami International Fair

Figure 11. Derelict textile factory in Sümerbank in Kayseri

singing).[17] The site was abandoned in 2003 and today "most buildings have disappeared and the site looks almost empty, with only a few structures and trees still standing . . . Its future use as a permanent site or open space remains unknown."[18] Across the Middle East, several such abandoned large public sites, industrial complexes, and once vibrant fairgrounds stand as modern ruins, testifying to the "cycles of collapsing progress", as the title of a major art exhibition held in the Tripoli Fair expressed it in 2018.[19]

Now that the initial excitement of nation-building is long gone and the buildings themselves are at least half a century old, the formidable challenges of ageing structures, obsolete programmes, crumbling concrete, and rusting metal are everywhere in the region from Turkey to the Levant and the Gulf, awaiting innovative strategies of renovation and adaptive reuse. One recent example from Turkey, comparable to the Guest House renovation in scale and refinement, reaffirms the feasibility, realism, and strategic foresightedness of piecemeal "emergency renovation/adaptive reuse", beginning with individual buildings to save them from further decay, while also setting standards for the rest of the complex. The early republic's legendary textile industrial complex / factory town of Sümerbank in Kayseri (designed by a Soviet team led by Ivan Nikolaev, an associate of Moshei Ginzburg and other Constructivists and built in 1933-35) was decommissioned in 1999 and left abandoned in a derelict, partly vandalised state (figs.11-13). After the site's transfer to Abdullah Gül University in 2012, a "Restoration and Adaptive Reuse Master Plan" was proposed, designating individual pieces of the complex to be renovated and

198

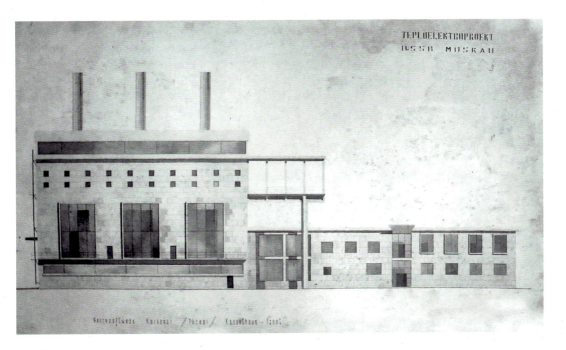

Figures 12 and 13. Original drawing of the electricity power plant at Sümerbank Textile Factory, Kayseri, 1933-35 (top); electricity power plant after renovation as Abdullah Gül University Information Center / Museum by Emre Arolat Associates, 2013-16 (bottom)

Figure 14. Passenger port warehouses along the Galata embankment

reintegrated in a piecemeal fashion, beginning with Emre Arolat Associates' conversion of the original electricity and steam power plant into the new Library / Information Center. Like EAST Architecture Studio, EAA sought to strike a careful balancing act between the needs of the new programme and the preservation of the spatial integrity and material traces of the original industrial building (such as keeping the patina on the surfaces, incorporating original elements like ash pits and smokestacks, etc). Unlike the Guest House renovation, however, the EAA interventions were not intended to be reversible to accommodate possible future changes; and the development of the rest of the campus has been intermittent and fraught with uncertainties.[20]

Another high-profile conversion and adaptive reuse project from the country of Turkey, the temporary Istanbul Modern Museum (2004), more closely echoes EAST Architecture Studio's idea of renovation as a process, rather than an end product. On the eve of Turkey's application for full EU membership, one of the empty warehouses of the passenger port along the Galata embankments was hastily converted by Tabanlıoğlu Architects into a contemporary art museum (figs. 14 and 15).[21] The conversion by Tabanlıoğlu was functional but minimal, simply adding removable exhibition panels and lighting systems, as well as a gift shop and restaurant separated by transparent partitions and a terrace extending towards the spectacular view of the Bosporus. The warehouse was a non-descript steel-frame structure (unlike an iconic Niemeyer concrete building); however, like the Guest House renovation, the project was conceived as a more ephemeral conversion of temporary interventions. It was meant only as the urgently

Figure 15. Renovation of passenger warehouses by Tabanlıoğlu Architects

needed "seed" or initiator of the larger Galataport Istanbul development project, which included several buildings along the shore to be rehabilitated and reprogrammed for a vast promenade of commercial, cultural, and public uses. After almost two decades of contentious urban politics involving multiple actors (the government, contractors, developers, designers, preservationists, and the public), the museum was completely redesigned by Renzo Piano and inaugurated in 2023 along with the rest of the Galataport development (fig. 16). The modest temporary conversion gave way to a brand new starchitecture.

By selecting the Niemeyer Guest House renovation project for the 2022 Aga Khan Award for Architecture, the Master Jury (of which I was a member) sought to draw attention to the predicament of modern heritage in the Muslim world. This is a heritage that needs to be reclaimed as a physical register – not of earlier dynastic histories that typically come to mind when "historic preservation" is mentioned in Islamic countries, but rather of more recent histories marked by transformative efforts to industrialise, urbanise, and modernise these societies. It was a plea for the recognition of modern architectures and sites as the built legacies of the brief but exciting moments of optimism for these countries, partaking in the promise of a modern, rational,

Figure 16. Istanbul Modern Museum by Renzo Piano Building Workshop

scientific worldview that was shared across the ideological divides of the Cold War, as well as among the Non-Aligned nations of the Global South.

The fact that many countries of the Middle East are at the centennials of their establishment as modern republics (Turkey celebrated the 100th year of the republic in 2023 and Lebanon's anniversary is approaching in 2026) offers a symbolic opportunity for the reclamation of this legacy, not as museum pieces, but as a "living heritage" bearing the optimism of the past and the possibilities of an uncertain present. It is no coincidence that numerous commentators use the word "hope" in association with the Fair in Tripoli. Beginning with the presidency of Fouad Chehab in 1958, leading to the commissioning of the fairgrounds to Oscar Niemeyer in 1962, and reaching its tragic end with the onset of the Civil War in 1975, this is "the post-independence *golden age* of modern Lebanon"[22] (George Arbid), and the Fair is its symbolic "*dream* project" (Wassim Naghi).[23] With the "small touches" of the Niemeyer Guest House renovation, we are reminded anew of the site's big potential to connect Lebanon's bygone era of optimism with her troubled present. Beyond the admirable quality, refinement, and restraint of its renovation work, the Guest House's much bigger symbolic significance rests precisely in this inspiration it provides to turn a modest renovation project into a larger commitment to – and excitement about – an architectural legacy symbolic of better times in the region and the world at large.

1 On this idea of the modern movement as "living heritage", see Maristella Casciato and Emilie d'Orgeix, *Modern Architectures: The Rise of a Heritage* (Wavre: Mardaga Editions, 2012).

2 Karl Popper, *The Poverty of Historicism* (1957; repr., New York: Routledge Classics, 2002), p. 61.

3 Hence, it is even more ironic that huge, if ultimately unsuccessful campaigns were launched to protect Cedric Price's Kentish Town Interaction Center in London (1972) and Kisho Kurakawa's Nakagin Capsule Tower in Tokyo (1972) from demolition. Both were demolished, in 2003 and 2022 respectively.

4 When one considers the historical predicament of the Rachid Karami International Fair (from the abandonment of the project with the onset of the Lebanese Civil War in 1975 to its recent "emergency nomination" as an endangered UNESCO World Heritage Site in 2023), one is overwhelmed by the sheer number of official reports, successive preservation plans, academic discussions, media coverage, brand-new development proposals, and several decisions and reversals along the way. These are covered extensively in "Emergency Nomination of the Rachid Karami International Fair, Tripoli, Lebanon", the seventy-three-page nominating report of the Lebanese Ministry of Culture for UNESCO listing.

5 Oscar Niemeyer, "Form and Function in Architecture" (1959), in *Architecture Culture 1943–1968: A Documentary Anthology*, ed. Joan Ockman with Edward Eigen (New York: Rizzoli, 1993), pp. 308–13. The original was published in *Módulo 21* (December 1960), pp. 2–7.

6 Dilip Parameshwar Gaonkar, *Alternative Modernities* (Durham, NC: Duke University Press, 2001), p. 22.

7 Partha Mitter, "De-Centering Modernism: Art History and the Avant-garde from the Periphery", *The Art Bulletin* 9, no. 4 (December 2008), pp. 531–48. In addition to Mitter's seminal essay, see Vikram Prakash, Maristella Casciato, and Daniel Coslett, eds., *Rethinking Global Modernism* (London: Routledge, 2022).

8 Maristella Casciato, "Authorship and Heritage Issues", in Casciato and d'Orgeix, *Modern Architectures*, p. 50.

9 Vikramaditya Prakash, *Chandigarh's Le Corbusier: The Struggle for Modernity in Postcolonial India* (Seattle: University of Washington Press, 2002), p. 25.

10 "Emergency Nomination of the Rachid Karami International Fair, Tripoli, Lebanon" (see note 4), p. 4.

11 Prakash, *Chandigarh's Le Corbusier*, p. 152.

12 "Emergency Nomination of the Rachid Karami International Fair, Tripoli, Lebanon" (see note 4), p. 30.

13 *The Project of Independence: Architectures of Decolonization in South Asia, 1947–1985* at MoMA, New York, in 2022 and *Tropical Modernism* at the Victoria and Albert Museum, London, in 2024.

14 See especially Martino Stierli, "The Politics of Concrete", in Prakash et al., *Rethinking Global Modernism*, pp. 275–89, and Adrian Forty, "Cement and Multiculturalism", in *Transculturation: Cities, Spaces and Architectures in Latin America*, ed. Felipe Hernández, Mark Millington, and Iain Borden (Leiden: Brill, 2005), pp. 144–54.

15 See Łukasz Stanek, *Architecture in Global Socialism* (Princeton: Princeton University Press, 2020), p. 31.

16 For the Arab world, for example, we can cite important recent contributions like George Arbid and Philip Oswalt, eds., *Designing Modernity: Architecture in the Arab World 1945–1973* (Berlin: Jovis, 2022); and Mohamed Elshahed curated *Cairo Modern*, Center for Architecture, New York, 1 October 2021 to 12 March 2022.

17 Rafee Hakky and Wael Samhouri, "A Modern Public City Space: Damascus International Fair and Its Monument 1950s–1960s", in Arbid and Oswalt, *Designing Modernity*, pp. 227–43.

18 Hakky and Samhouri, "A Modern Public City Space", p. 231.

19 See Lemma Shehadi, "Too little Too Late? The Battle to Save Tripoli's Futuristic Fairground", *The Guardian*, 3 January 2019.

20 Another master plan was developed, and the Fire Station was renovated by Burak Asiliskender and Nilüfer Baturay Yöney (also co-chairs of the Turkish Docomomo Chapter).

21 The original port facilities and warehouses, built in 1958–60, had already been vacated in 1988 when the passenger port was no longer in operation.

22 George Arbid, "Hope on the Horizon", in Arbid and Oswalt, *Designing Modernity*, p. 119.

23 Wassim Naghi, "Rachid Karimi International Fair in Tripoli", Knowledge and Innovation Center (KIC) Architectural Design Project Competition Brief, 2019, Appendix B, p. 46.

Activating Heritage
Nader Tehrani in Conversation with Nicolas Fayad

In this dialogue, Nicolas Fayad invites Nader Tehrani to discuss cultural continuity and authorship in the translation between heritage craft and contemporary architecture, and to speak to the architectural project as a site of learning and knowledge exchange. This conversation invokes moments from the Niemeyer Guest House renovation as well as examples from Tehrani's practice to highlight humility as a key ingredient in adaptive reuse projects, bracing existing buildings and their cultural ecosystems for the future.

Figure 1. Niemeyer Guest House workshop view after the renovation

Reflections on "Conceptual Craft"

Nicolas Fayad To start off this conversation, it would be interesting to link what you call "conceptual craft" to preservation, and to emphasise the impact that preservation has on cultural identity, craft, and creativity. First, through cultural continuity, where conceptual craft in itself involves innovative interpretations or reinterpretations of traditional or, as in the case of the Niemeyer Guest House, more recent building techniques, material applications, and processes that bridge the gap between past and present (fig. 1).

Similarly, when looking at modern heritage preservation and how it seeks to conserve culture, or cultural artefacts and traditional ways of conceiving architecture, we see that these practices are very much rooted in the historical craftsmanship of the times in which these buildings were built. And to recognise the significance of these practices is important, but also the interpretation of them as a place where the conceptual craft comes in to foster a sense of continuity, especially for the particular building or the intervention in itself.

Second, through dealing with conceptual craft as an innovative practice that still embraces tradition. And then third, by examining how heritage preservation – or, more specifically, modern heritage preservation – can contribute to the construction of narratives of identity and belonging. For these reasons, we can't talk about conceptual craft in isolation, but always in the context of the project as a practice of contextual modern heritage preservation where there is a shared commitment to simultaneously honouring and reinterpreting past techniques, and to fostering creativity and innovation.

Nader Tehrani From my perspective, the culture of craft is more often associated with techniques, traditions, and rituals, which are not, in the first instance, intellectually motivated. They're actually filial. They are handed down, from one generation to the next over ages, and potentially not interrogated; maybe transformed in subtle ways, they become a marker of identity.

The advent of architecture as a discipline within the Western world introduces a couple of key challenges to the culture of craft. First, by separating the métier of the architect from that of the builder, it posits the drawing as a key protagonist; but in doing so, it also separates the architect from the site of construction where the detail can be seen as the consummation of a design idea. But second, it also recognises the discipline as a discourse that is able to reflect on itself, comment on its own devices, and even imagine architecture as a critical act. And so there's a rupture that happens between architecture and the guilds.

The agency of representation, indicated by this historical transition, suggests an intellectual project, something not readily evident in the transfer of craft over the ages. Of course, this idea was challenged by Bernard Rudofsky in his *Architecture Without Architects* exhibition at MoMA in 1964–65, if only to demonstrate an engrained self-consciousness in the organic evolution of architecture in informal ways. Still, what I am after in this confrontation between traditional and conceptual craft is the framing of ideas in a state of self-consciousness. I'm rejecting the idea of craft as a naturalised phenomenon through mere inheritance: that, in some way, the discipline needs to be articulated.

All of this is to say that in the context of the Niemeyer project, Nicolas, I think that you brought in an intellectual craft – a conceptual surplus; indeed, not only did you engage the guild-based economies and their structure in Lebanon, but you also transcended them.

There are elements within the existing building that you work with, things that you elevate by detailing them in a particular way. They bring our attention to the capacity of everyday details to transcend the terms of their expected functions – you heighten them to a point of tension, and this I find very interesting. One recognises that you are working with local trades – mediating, as it were, on the one hand, but then one realises that you adopt their means and methods in your own working out of details to absorb their mentality within your design studio – all this to develop a curiously inventive reflected ceiling plan, a smart of way of integrating the interiors with exteriors.

The question of means and methods is central to this discussion because the advanced state of economic development in the West has resulted in the compartmentalisation of labour and the alienation of the architect from acts of building. In a strict sense, what architects do is represent through drawings, while labourers fabricate the various forms of representation that architects draw: the implication being that the limits of architectural power are contained within "design intent", with the builders left with relative freedom to build as they wish. Thus, if an architect had a precise idea about the assembly protocols of a system, that would not necessarily be within their legal reach.

Of course, the counterpoint to this argument is that architects don't actually always know everything about material behaviour and construction systems. They have a general knowledge of them, and once they delve deeper, it's often because they are learning something from trades and labourers, digging deeper into the very means and methods. And it's in that transaction that we find the inflection point of invention.

I'll give you an example. If a basket weaver is trained to make the same basket over and over, they will transmit that knowledge to their next of kin, with limited levels of transformation over decades. Sometimes it requires a prompt from a protagonist who is external to that craft in order to challenge the limits of its techniques. Consider this: How did Frank Gehry's Cross Check Arm Chair made of bent maple evolve as an idea? My hypothesis is that it required lateral thinking on his part, delving not only into the mid-century technologies of the Eames duo, but also incorporating techniques of basket-weaving, albeit at an entirely different scale than its intended conventions – which produces the ingenuity of that piece of furniture.

We can think of this as the productive site of knowledge exchange, where an architect builds on known conventions, by deftly altering the scale of a known technique. In turn, this is also a prompt to the craftsperson to realise the most radical eventuality of their means and methods – by allowing it to be cast onto a different context in which they conventionally operate.

Building as Mediation

NF I would say that the starting point for this is to admit and understand that architecture is not just about creating the physical structure, but also about potentially facilitating relationships between stakeholders, reconciling differences, and maybe engaging with different perspectives. Here we can speak to the mediation between the built and the natural, where architecture exists within a larger context, including the natural environment that surrounds it. The idea arises that renovation or reconciliation projects can perhaps serve as mediators between these different contexts, harmonising the built form with its immediate natural surroundings and the distinct fabric around it through thoughtful design and integration strategies (fig. 2).

NT I think your project mediates at many levels, and I am particularly interested in how you articulate the differences between your intervention and the presumed ideal envisioned by Niemeyer as an original condition. From the perspective of the landscape, you freeze certain things that only time could have unleashed onto the building – the overgrowth of trees and weeds, for

Figure 2. Niemeyer Guest House exterior view after the renovation

instance. Though unintended in the original plan, they offer alternative interpretations of what preservation could mean to us at this time, producing a new dialogue between architecture, landscape, and a form of modern archaeology for which there is no easy categorisation.

Now to be clear, I am not sure which stakeholders you needed to work with to make this happen, be they landscape architects, archaeologists, or other players, but even if these were invented conditions, they suggest the presence of other voices that you insert within your own work to cultivate these conditions of mediation.

NF This reference to archaeology or modern archaeology resonates well with a quote I came across from Mark Wigley: "Preservation itself is a forward-thinking celebration of life, that it is a way of looking at something that seems to be fading or gone and incubating new life within it. Preservation is always suspended between life and death – calling on us to get smarter, faster, deeper, longer, sharper, and I would say more tender." This quote is an excerpt from Wigley's introduction to Rem Koolhaas's publication *Preservation Is Overtaking Us* (from the series *Columbia Books on Architecture and the City*, 2014).

Working with an existing building requires the highest level of empathy. It is an act of conciliation, an exercise of optimism and reinterpretation. Following this thinking, and instead of fixating on Niemeyer's idealised original vision, I have attempted to courageously hold on to the transformative effects of time. By selectively or purposely preserving or even highlighting some elements that bear the marks of temporal evolution, the design process becomes an invitation to alternative interpretations that challenge conventional notions of architectural authenticity. Just as Wigley suggests, preservation hovers delicately between life and death, serving as a catalyst for renewal and regeneration. It forces us to deepen our intellectual judgement, to comprehend, to delve further into the layers of history, to extend our vision beyond the immediate horizon, and above all, to infuse the design process with tenderness and empathy.

The Project as a Site of Knowledge Exchange

NF There are a few things that we could talk about here in the context of the exchange of knowledge in this project in particular. One aspect is that we thought about it as a means of raising awareness and of highlighting the cultural significance of the building by revealing and buttressing the cultural identities and histories that are embedded within the site. It was also an opportunity to engage in a dialogue about the relationship of the site with the local community.

In this context, I opt to refer to cultural significance as knowledge exchange, where we must first establish a personal stance with regard to the relevance of the past. In contrast to earlier stages of modernisation in the Western world, during which architects often saw the past as an obstacle to growth, our project embraces a simultaneous engagement with historical traditions and future possibilities. We recognise that both past and future exert a constant influence on our present reality, echoing the sentiment famously articulated by Stephen Hawking that "the past, like the future, is indefinite and exists only as a spectrum of possibilities".

I realise that contemporary training in the formal norms of conservation faces a unique challenge in navigating a trajectory that moves both backward into history and forward into the future. Our society's profound fascination with the past sometimes obscures our vision of the future and hinders our ability to fully grasp and accept present realities. Consequently, we find ourselves compelled to question conventional approaches to conservation, which often prioritise adherence to formal norms and overlook the dynamic interplay between past, present, and future.

At the heart of our proposal lies a fundamental inquiry into what we choose to preserve and for whom. This prompts us to consider whether conservation serves merely as a tool for regulating the pace of change or if it embodies deeper functions within society. Is conservation solely about preserving memories and fostering nostalgia, both of which are vital for societal well-being? Or does it involve expert judgments about what constitutes our collective heritage and aesthetic preferences? Undoubtedly, these questions carry significant political implications.

Navigating the delicate balance between preserving architectural illusions of continuity and recognising new significances is a challenging task. We are tempted to believe that the creation or preservation of architecture is fundamentally informed by interpretations of cultural significance. Therefore, it becomes imperative to redefine the notion of significance in both architectural and conservation discourse. This entails a careful process of inventing and negotiating the uses, associations, and meanings of historic environments, ensuring that they remain relevant and useful to contemporary society while safeguarding them for future generations.

NT There's a distinction between architecture as a process versus architecture as an "object". What you are describing, Nicolas, allows the process of conception and delivery to become the story itself – and this, despite all of the virtues of the formal precision in your own work.

At NADAAA, we have also seized upon opportunities for the exchange of knowledge, not always just from collaborators, but sometimes also from one project to the next. In the case of Georgia Tech's Hinman Research Building and the University of Melbourne's Melbourne School of Design, the idea of "levity" is transported from one project to the other, even when the two buildings are manifest in fundamentally distinct ways. There is no material knowledge transfer. There is no trade protocol transfer. There's no technical transfer, just a conceptual transfer through this question: If there's value in turning a building upside down, what would that be? Beyond the phenomena of levity and its sense of wonder, flexibility is achieved for both projects, allowing them to be programmed in accordance with a variety of events that columns would have otherwise interrupted; by extension, it also afforded services under the floor, enabling electrical connections to be wired for those very functions.

The Hinman Research Building was commissioned to rehabilitate its high-bay research space into a flexible studio hall for the College of Architecture at Georgia Tech. The original space was spanned by trusses, paired with a gantry crane that serviced the entire space. We suggested that everything be suspended from the truss system, while repurposing the crane to suspend an additional studio space, ensuring that nothing touches the ground except the bottom of the stairs – and thus maintaining the flexibility of the ground (figs. 3 and 4).

The Melbourne School of Design in Australia had constraints that were fundamentally different from the Hinman Building, its main challenge being that it could not afford a dedicated studio space. Our real contribution to that building was the way in which we extracted square footage from the net to gross area to form a more generous circulation space, reprogrammed as a vertical studio hall, filled with "hot-desks". In turn, this allowed us to utilise a suspended structure, housing three rooms as dedicated studios for visiting critics (figs. 5 and 6).

That is a direct transportation of the suspended studio from one project to the other, but in a completely different guise – a distinct expression of the same strategy. The transfer of knowledge allows one to build up on ideas, to overturn them, or even fix their mistakes, but in essence

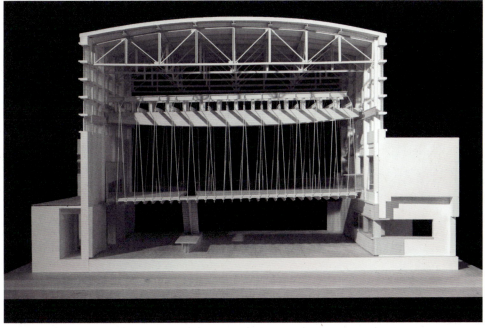

Figures 3 and 4. College of Architecture at Georgia Tech: studio hall by NADAA (top), and sectional model of the studio hall by NADAA (bottom)

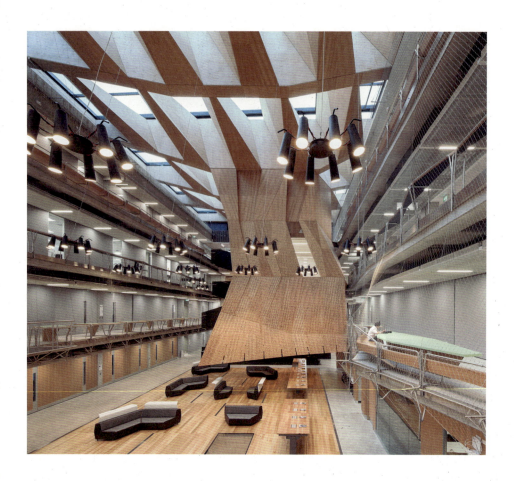

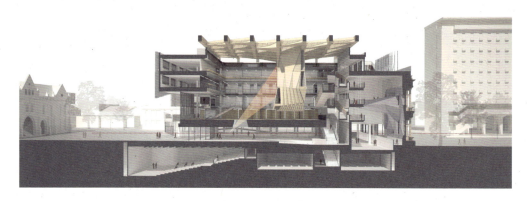

Figures 5 and 6. The Melbourne School of Design by NADAA (top), and sectional perspective of The Melbourne School of Design by NADAA (bottom)

it describes the design process as a cultural practice whereby buildings speak to histories and discourses outside of the immediate reach of the commission, and a larger cultural conversation is established.

Notes on Shared Authorship

NT In the current climate, there are many commercial and political reasons why inclusion is touted as the new foundation of a good practice, but the reality is that many historic practices were substantially diverse; they just didn't acknowledge it. There are few modern "masters" (those considered the canons of the twentieth century) who didn't come with either partners or key collaborators, often women of notable cultural presence, who were marginalised in terms of their credits. Think here of Lilly Reich, Charlotte Perriand, and Anne Tyng, among others.

The reality is that design is a complex practice that requires involved processes. Process and critical thinking go hand in hand to come up with the types of invention, wonder, and uncanniness that not only address the functional mandates imposed on architecture, but indeed transcend them towards a state of poetics, revelation, or whatever it is that brings the environment to a state of awareness.

NF I'd like to start positioning authorship with a quote by the Spanish sculptor Eduardo Chillida from his 1998 lecture at the International Conference on Sculpture, Trinity College, Dublin: "I work to learn; I value the act of knowing more than I value knowledge itself. I think I should dare to do what I do not know how to do. I should dare to search, to imagine where I cannot see, and to long to recognize what I cannot perceive."

I believe that designing space is designing an experience – which, in the best case, can lead to happiness. This, in my opinion, is the utmost goal of architecture. But again, with the renovation of the Niemeyer Guest House, a different challenge arises, which is a tension between contemporary and historical buildings since the beginning of modernity and conservationists believing it was important to stay true to the origin and techniques and materials when working with historical sites, for example, where others have meant to make a statement on contemporary possibilities (fig. 7).

So how do you renovate without disruption? And how do we intervene without hiding? There's currently so much change and a lot more complexity, and I'm curious how architecture could reveal exactly how its own systems work and what they're made of.

These inquiries are situated within the broader context of producing site-specific architectural manifestos. However, rather than serving as mere historical investigations, they represent a critical examination predicated on the idea that site-specific manifestos, particularly the study of existing buildings, remain potent tools for tracing design narratives in contemporary discourse. The process of uncovering insights while studying a specific structure, such as the Niemeyer Guest House, becomes an act of "rewriting", engaging in a dialogue that simultaneously interrogates the building's original, perhaps irrecoverable purpose alongside its current or potential future functions. Moreover, it prompts reflection on the inherent relationships within this dialogue, thereby delineating an urban scenario that extends beyond the confines of the individual structure to encompass the broader context of the fair or event it serves.

This approach emphasises the importance of understanding the complementarity between the urban environment and the architectural scale. By recognising the interplay between these realms, punctual interventions emerge as powerful tools for deciphering the intrinsic qualities of site-specific settings. These settings, often characterised by layers of history and complexity, offer valuable insights into urban taxonomies and social systems. Through such investigations,

Figure 7. Niemeyer Guest House lateral courtyard view before the renovation

Figure 8. Niemeyer Guest House exterior view before the renovation

architects and urban planners gain a deeper understanding of how interventions at the architectural scale can resonate within larger urban contexts, shaping narratives that are responsive to the dynamic interplay between past, present, and future.

It's important to account for the creative dimension in conservation projects that enable critical dialogues to be created between the old and the new, asking questions such as what does conservation practice mean for architects and designers? How do we evolve a critical practice of conservation which facilitates the simultaneous validity or maybe the level of fidelity that we have for the past while still incorporating contemporary aspirations (fig. 8)?

I think this is the challenge and the beauty of it. And these interests are shaping me as an architect and shaping us as a practice that is trying to establish itself with an architecture that is the architecture of the interior almost. The renovation of the Niemeyer Guest House, which really mostly is an interior renovation, was one of our first commissions. And it became a way to experiment, to maybe investigate concepts, test some spatial ideas, and take decisions that not only are the result of a diligent research process, as I have described it thoroughly in the past, but sometimes are also deliberate or unconsciously driven by some personal design ethos or sensibilities. It's too soon to say if they were successful or not, but we use these opportunities in our early careers as a means or a method to possibly cultivate architectural thinking that goes on to hopefully inform other projects that we're working on across other scales (fig. 9).

Figure 9. Niemeyer Guest House exterior view before the renovation

NT What's interesting about adaptive reuse and renovation projects in the context of an emerging practice is that they are commonly one's first commissions – deemed in some way a testing ground. By extension, they often test the young designer in ways for which they have not been amply cultivated. It is no secret that most design programmes reward authorship and the design of new "objects" in ways that overlook the significance of historic buildings, environments, and artefacts.

But, of course, what is precisely interesting about these renovations and adaptive reuse projects is the degree to which they test our understanding of fraught histories, complex authorships, the design as a consequence of a process (not just an object conceived as an ideal), the impurities and compromises that were made, and how all of that might inform a strategy today. Determining one's own role in inheriting that history is a moment of reckoning – and, if to respect it, then how exactly that respect may be manifest – whether in emulation, differentiation, or a complex interrogation of it. Whatever it is, the projection of new work onto an older relic is more involved than we are often taught.

I imagine your project as a response to this complexity, a critique of the objecthood as an ideal, in combination with an invitation to mediation – mediation not as liability, but as the very

216

asset that culture brings into an intellectual formation. Your intervention works within the physical and cultural frame of this building, compromising neither it, nor the ethic you bring to it on your own terms.

You also evoke another tension between how we think of architecture as objects versus spaces. Curiously, in the context of pedagogy and my engagement with students, no matter my emphasis on the spatiality, their de facto priorities revert back to objects, things they can see ... somehow icons are an easier witness to their ideas. They hardly ever see the spaces in between. I'm constantly looking for ways to illustrate, to embody what it means to allow them to see the counterpoint to the object, the negative space, as it were. When one is drawing a building, for example, one commonly centres it on the page. One rarely places it at the edge of the paper. But the reality is that any given project is almost always at the edge of something more important, which makes for interesting urban conditions, or spatial conditions that offer distinct hierarchies.

On Heritage, Humility, and Continuity

NF In one of our previous conversations, you mentioned beautifully that "maybe one of the most satisfying things in a project like the Niemeyer Guest House renovation is to learn a different language, establish constraints that are external to oneself, if only to discover a modesty that speaks to history, that imagines a space that preceded oneself by decades or outlasts oneself by decades."

Certainly, one of the most gratifying aspects of working with an existing building is the opportunity to immerse oneself in a different language – not merely linguistic or formal, but a construct that talks to history, context, and limitations. Exploring narratives and boundaries imposed by external forces – whether they stem from historical, cultural, or environmental contexts – unveils the intricate layers within the built environment. Establishing constraints that transcend our subjective preferences compels us to confront our own biases and limitations and helps us to develop a sense of humility and broader perspective. It reminds us that our design processes and methodologies are not developed in isolation but are intricately intertwined with a larger temporal and spatial context. Envisioning spaces that predate or will outlast our own existence – as you have described – serves as an emotional reminder of the interconnection between past, present, and future (fig. 10).

We become custodians of a legacy that stretches far beyond our individual lifetimes, and we assume a profound responsibility to honour and safeguard the stories and memories encapsulated within the built environment. This process of engaging with history and conceptualising spaces that transcend temporal boundaries is a truly enriching experience. It challenges us to transcend self-interest, embracing complexity and ambiguity, and contributing meaningfully to the ongoing dialogue between past, present, and future. Through this journey, we not only shape physical structures but also nurture a collective consciousness that reverberates across generations.

NT Thank you! You articulated this so thoroughly and so beautifully that I'm hard pressed to add on to that. I do think that the circumstances that lead to this humility sometimes revolve around understanding societies and communities that are alien to oneself, independent of architecture.

It's just about understanding cultures and traditions that are different. And secondly, they also emerge out of reconstituting architecture not as a centre, but as a periphery to the urbanism that constitutes the whole of people's daily lives – effectively the city as the space of engagement.

Figure 10. View of the Lebanese Pavilion at the Rachid Karami International Fair

And so, architecture is never an end in itself, but an actor on a larger stage. And sometimes it is meant to play a supporting role, in dialogue with other conceptual visions in need of architectural translation. We really got this sense when we were working with Carol Terry, the Rhode Island School of Design head librarian. She had been working on a vision for that library for twenty-five years before she had the budget to build it. And we were only there at the very end to manifest that vision into some kind of architectural terms.

And though that did not lessen the architectural vision, it nonetheless made it beholden to an idea that has been worked on for decades prior. What was critical was that her ideas were in need of "architecturalisation" – into spatial, formal, and material terms: not something immediate, obvious, or singular, but rather a circling around of ideas to adapt them to the space and circumstances we inherited.

For Carol, this process required a dexterity to understand that her ideas come in a myriad of forms. In the first instance, they came through her words and associated images, but eventually they also came through specific architectural terms that required testing and play. That's where the humility gets played out between another person's vision and yourself.

NF Thank you, Nader, for sharing this meaningful example. Ending here with this idea of architecture and humility; much of the architecture of our time, along with its associated publicity that attempts to convince us of its genius, often exudes self-satisfaction and authority. These architectural attempts seem more focused on dominating the foreground rather than providing a supportive background conducive to human activity, perception, and interaction. Our age seems to have lost the virtues of architectural restraint, and modesty. However, genuine artistic creations continue to hover delicately between certainty and uncertainty, faith and doubt. As we stand at the threshold of this century's second quarter, architectural culture would need to foster constructive tensions, balancing cultural realism with artistic idealism, determination with discretion, and ambition with humility.

CULTURE

Life amid Ruins
Costica Bradatan in Conversation with Raafat Majzoub

In this conversation, Raafat Majzoub invites Costica Bradatan to discuss failure in lieu of architecture's role as a narrator of civilisation and to unpack preservation as a grounding human instinct. Ruins are inspected as humbling reminders of people's proximity to nothingness, offering an intimate contrast to the detached "bird's-eye view" typically adopted in architectural imagining. The conversation highlights the paradox of ruins – how they, while signalling collapse, are simultaneously brimming with potential, and how abandoned buildings, though failed in purpose, inspire new avenues for imagination and creativity.

Raafat Majzoub I am curious about your perspective on ruins. They seem to be closely connected to failure and humility, topics you engage with in depth in your latest book, *In Praise of Failure: Four Lessons in Humility*.[1] Failure in the sense of languages becoming ruins after their utility dies off, buildings becoming ruins for lack of management or maintenance, ideologies becoming ruins for the depletion of stamina.

Costica Bradatan Ruins seem indeed closely connected to failure and humility, but perhaps in a manner even more dramatic than the one you suggest. The sight of ruins, as you point out, may evoke poor management or even a complete failure of maintenance. It is almost common sense: bringing something into existence is only one half of the process; the other half is *keeping* it in existence, which makes it, I imagine, a process of continuous creation.

Yet the presence of ruins signals something deeper, more serious, and more devastating: the fundamental precariousness of all things human, the eventual ruination of everything that comes from our labour, the "vanity of it all". No matter how much care we take of something, how much time and effort we invest in its maintenance, it will eventually "fall into ruin". Ruins are our destiny.

In this sense, ruins remind us of just how close to nothingness we always are. They are part of this world, and yet they evoke another. They are a border marker – literally, the boundary stone – that separates two realms: existence and non-existence. And in that respect, they are fascinating objects to study. They signify the nothingness in the proximity of which all things human exist, and to which they will return eventually.

RM And what about humility?

CB That's precisely where humility comes in. For this encounter with ruins as harbingers of nothingness brings us "down to earth". A fitting phrase if we consider that in English (as in other modern European languages) "humility" comes from the Latin *humilitas*, with its root in *humus* – "earth" or "ground". And much is to be learned from this downwards journey of ours: as we are brought down, we are given the chance to wake up, and to see ourselves, and indeed everything else, with new eyes. People – especially architects – tend to praise "the bird's-eye view" and various "perspectives from above" for what they can reveal. Yet that's nothing compared to the "perspective from below", from where you could get access to the intimacy of things, to a level of detail and a richness of insight that no "bird's-eye view" could ever offer. One of the film directors I love most is Yasujirō Ozu. His stylistic signature is the low-angle static shot: his camera looks at the world not from the perspective of a person standing up, as in the case of most directors, but from that of someone sitting on a tatami mat. That's the working method and the point of view of humility itself.

My point here is that being as close to the ground as possible, being brought "down to earth", a feeling that ruins tend to instil in us, can truly make us wiser because it puts us "in our place". Ruins, then, could be said to "ground" us. Which is why, for all their whiff of nothingness, or maybe precisely because of it, we should preserve them whenever we can.

RM Could you speak, then, about the concept of preservation? Reading your work, I might assume that it could hint at the failure to imagine the future, but I wonder if we could also think of it as a technology to calibrate it. The two perspectives may also mean the same thing, but I'd love it if you would expand your thoughts on preservation.

CB Before I do that, Raafat, I think we owe our readers an explanation. I, for one, owe them a confession. The fact is that I have no expertise in architecture. That doesn't prevent me from being fascinated with it, just as my general ignorance of aerodynamics doesn't diminish my fascination with flying. And the thought occurred to me that, by inviting someone to contribute to this volume who is such a complete innocent, you showed remarkable audacity, didn't you? In fact, your audacity was so striking that there was something endearing about it. That's how I came to think that the only way for me to match your audacious invitation was to do something equally audacious: to accept it. And here I am speaking at length of something I don't know much about. You can't top that.

To get to your question now: we want to "preserve" something, no matter how ruinous its current state, because it gives us a certain sense of "grounding". Restoring an old building and giving it a new lifeline is like lowering an anchor into the past: it keeps us in place, settled, rooted. We do that all the time, no matter the costs and the technical difficulties, no matter how inconvenient the whole thing may be. We do it because that's where life is: in the past. And we always tend to stick to life.

RM Hah! Well, thank you for humouring me . . . but what do you mean by "life is in the past"?

CB Of course, life is in the past – where else? Just take a walk in a new neighbourhood, around some recent development (there are plenty of them these days). There is, you must admit, something unmistakably lifeless that comes from all that novelty, something shallow and uninviting, and we don't want to spend more time there than we have to. No matter how faux-antique those buildings are made to look, how "classical" their styles, we know that life is elsewhere. Life – real, authentic "lived life" – is where the old buildings, the old churches and mosques and temples, the ancient piazzas are. That's why, when we visit Athens or Rome, Istanbul or Cairo, Beijing or Kyoto, we always feel attracted to their ancient quarters, no matter how ruinous, primitive, or precarious they may look, and we rarely go to visit the new developments. You will say that there is nothing much to see in the new neighbourhoods, that all look the same. And that's precisely the point. We are spontaneously attracted to the humanity stored in the old stones. Not merely because they are old (there are rocks in nature that are even older, but we don't feel any particular attraction to them), but because human history – long stretches of it – happened in their presence, and they not just mirrored our existence along centuries, but somehow absorbed it. We know instinctively that, for all their ruinous appearance, there is more potency in them than we can find in the latest edifices.

RM Isn't this a bit paradoxical?

CB It certainly is. Indeed, this must be one of the most beautiful paradoxes we are dealing with here: ruins are harbingers of nothingness, and yet they are brimming with life and potential. In that respect, they express, accurately, something essential about the human condition: as human beings, we occupy a place on the edge of existence, one foot already dangling over the abyss. We, too, are nothing much, yet brimming with life at the same time.

RM In your conversation with Robert Zaretsky, about George Steiner's *The Idea of Europe*,[2] you ask, "What kind of thing is Europe if we can find part of it in the Himalayas?" Here, you were reflecting on the city of Shimla, India: "The architecture is there, and so are the theater and the art galleries." As the present volume focuses on the renovation of a building in an abandoned modernist fair by a Brazilian architect in Lebanon as part of its post-independence, nation-building strategy that never really launched, it makes me wonder about your thoughts on how public artefacts – buildings, for example – create and enforce collective mythologies, and what happens ontologically when these artefacts fail.

CB Everything we accomplish, as I noted earlier, once it has run its course, "falls into ruins". All things human end in failure. But then there is a class of things – like the Rachid Karami International Fair, projected by Oscar Niemeyer – that *begin* with failure, things that fail to launch, as you put it. Philosophically, I find the situation fascinating. It is as though they refuse to come into existence. In the book you mentioned earlier, *In Praise of Failure,* in the chapter where I discuss

E. M. Cioran, I touch on a Romanian phrase that he was very fond of: *n-a fost să fie*. It translates, roughly, as "it wasn't (meant) to be", but the way in which the phrase is normally used in Romanian suggests something forbidding, predestinarian, "set in stone". When something *nu e să fie*, then no matter what you do, no matter how hard you try and how many times, you just cannot bring it into existence. One cannot change destiny. Certain things (a European city in the Himalayas, for example) just aren't meant to be, and their failure to launch probably tells us an important story about the limits of what we can – and especially what we cannot – do. Oscar Niemeyer's project to build a futurist fair in Tripoli, for all intents and purposes, seemed to be one of those things as well. It never quite launched. The burning question now is: What is this restauration project doing here? Is this a resurrection from the dead of Niemeyer's project or something else? Are you just trying to finish a building or to challenge destiny?

RM There's something spiritual in your answer here. It may be interesting to speak about secular spirituality within the conceptualisation of the mortality of buildings within a city. Abandoned buildings, although possibly charged with traumatic events, usually stimulate the imagination because they are devoid of function. I would be curious to have your thoughts on that.

CB I find abandoned buildings fascinating. They are obvious sites of failure – devastating failure, sometimes – living reminders that something hasn't worked out as planned. And yet there is something open and indefinite, even inviting and creative, about them. Even though they failed as *something*, if not because of that, they can now be turned into nearly *anything*. There is sometimes almost no relationship between the purpose for which the building was originally designed and its new function, for which it's been redesigned. I happened to stay recently in a hotel in Łódź – one of the most imaginative hotels I've ever stayed in – that used to be a textile factory, and a rather oppressive one at that. It would have been so much easier to tear down those bloody walls and to build a brand-new hotel instead. And yet, again, people wanted to stick to the "lived life" stored in those old industrial structures. For some reason, they wanted to prolong its story – or, indeed, to "re-cycle" it. For stories, too, get recycled all the time.

RM What happens to meaning when stories get recycled?

CB I guess the meaning gets rejuvenated.

RM This being said, what does it really mean to say that a building has failed, if it has not been taught or designed to die? In that sense, architecture's denial of time/reality is an interesting provocation. I think you speak about this in the epilogue of *In Praise of Failure*, where you talk about people that accept that life may not have an overall meaning, and yet they don't kill themselves because they feel like their stories haven't run their course.

CB I was talking there about how important stories and storytelling are in our lives. We need a story to wake up in the morning and we need a story to go through the day. We need stories for everything we do. Indeed, we need stories more than we need food – it's stories that keep us alive, more than anything else. You are now suggesting that the same applies to buildings: we can't really tear down a building while its story is still unfolding. The hotel where I stayed in Łódź is just another chapter in the story of the old textile factory that somehow refuses to come to an end. I like that. But keep in mind: it's always us who are in charge of these stories – they are *our* stories, not the buildings'. By repurposing an abandoned building, by redesigning an old structure, we only show how much we need stories and how dependent on storytelling we are – not as individuals this time, but as communities. Architecture is always a collective story.

RM In the present volume, we identify the Niemeyer Guest House renovation as a scaffold, rather than as a static renovation. This metaphor allows us to explore the complexity of authorship and transience in recent heritage renovation projects. The "void" you describe in "Born Again in a Second Language",[3] where the author writes in a language that is not her mother tongue (you say: "It is as though, for a moment, as she passes through the void – the narrow crack between languages, where there are no words to hold on to and nothing can be named – the self of the writer is not any more"), is reminiscent of this scaffold. It also illustrates the platform that abandoned buildings provide in imagining beyond the single authorship of the architect. Could you reflect on that comparison and elaborate on what we learn about collective stories, connected identities, and shared characters from such authorship?

CB I appreciate the Buddhist undertones of your question: the implication that the self is a dubious thing, if it exists at all. In the essay from which you quoted, I was talking about one and the same person, who, by changing languages, adopts different selves, each language with its own self, as it were. As a result, the very idea of self is undermined. In the case you mention, however, for all the similarities you notice, the situation is slightly different: the same project passes through different phases and regimes of authorship, changing hands and selves as it goes – those who commissioned the project, Oscar Niemeyer himself (the original designer), the renovators, the carpenters, the community within which this occurs, the place (Tripoli) where all this happens, and to some extent even Brazil, from where the original architect came. There is an obvious sense of fluidity in all this. Not only because modernity is "liquid", as someone said, but above all because architecture, by its nature, is fluid.

RM Some would argue that architecture can be the opposite of fluidity.

CB Yes, they would argue. But Hagia Sophia is an example I'd use to illustrate what I mean. It has been an Orthodox cathedral, a Catholic one (during the Fourth Crusade), a mosque, a museum, then a mosque again (while still serving as a museum), a masterpiece of public art, and a major tourist attraction. It was designed by two Greek geometers, commissioned by a Roman Christian emperor, repurposed (as a mosque) by an Ottoman Sultan, repurposed again (as a museum) by a Turkish secular leader (Atatürk), then repurposed yet again (as a mosque-cum-museum) by another Turkish leader, though one not exactly secular (Erdoğan). Different communities have woven their collective life around this building: Byzantine and Ottoman, Christian and Muslim, religious and secular, traditional and modern. Within its walls, at different times, Greek was spoken, and so was Latin, Venetian, Arabic, and Turkish – Ottoman and then modern Turkish. Now, in the age of global tourism, Hagia Sophia speaks the language of Babel itself, while still serving as a mosque. Can you think of anything more fluid?

RM It's interesting that you bring up Babel as a by-product of preservation practices. It makes me think of this fluidity rather as an ocean of crashing waves. Babel was a punishment for humans challenging their finite destiny, which you touched upon earlier, by destroying their ability to communicate. Would you like to reflect on this further in the context of translation at a collective and identitarian level?

CB It's hard to overstate the importance of Babel as one of our foundational myths. The story is about one of the best things that ever happened to us. Before the mythical event, we only spoke one language, which must have made communication easy, smooth, and boring to death. Like two computers talking to each other. Have you seen anything more atrociously monotonous? This kills the soul. Then God decided to "confuse the language of the whole world" (Genesis 11:9). As a result, a wide variety of local tongues appeared, and, along with them, a host of other necessary things: translators and translations, lexicons and dictionaries, interpreters and interpretations, hermeneuts and hermeneutics, schools of foreign languages and of foreign cultures, anthropology and ethnography, linguistics and semiotics, professional spies and schools of spying, writing in codes, code makers and code breakers. You must admit, because of an architectural failure, the world became, all of a sudden, a much more interesting place.

Indeed, in the wake of this crisis, something novel and refreshing emerged: a mode of expression that was all about nuance and irony and subversion, which betrayed a mode of thinking that was sceptical, provisional, and above all humble. That's, in fact, how the humanities were born: in the aftermath of Babel. Before that we didn't need them. Communication between humans is never simple, and we need the humanities precisely to make it even more complex, more nuanced, more fecund. This may be the thing that will save us in the long run, for the human mind thrives not on computer-like monotony, but on ambiguity and equivocation, on double entendre and sophistry – on the blunders and embarrassments, the errors and misunderstandings, we continuously fall prey to, and then the painful efforts we make to correct them.

The collapse of Babel, then, was truly a blessing. That's why I take the multiplication of languages that the myth talks about as the prize with which God rewarded humans for their daring, and not at all as a form of punishment.

1   Costica Bradatan, *In Praise of Failure: Four Lessons in Humility* (Cambridge, MA: Harvard University Press, 2023).

2   Costica Bradatan and Robert Zaretsky, "The Idea of Europe", *Los Angeles Review of Books*, 12 August 2015, https://lareviewofbooks.org/article/the-idea-of-europe/.

3   Costica Bradatan, "Born Again in a Second Language", *Opinionator*, 4 August 2013, archive.nytimes.com/opinionator. blogs.nytimes.com/2013/08/04/born-again-in-a-second-language/.

Convened by Buildings and by Building Alike
Sumayya Vally

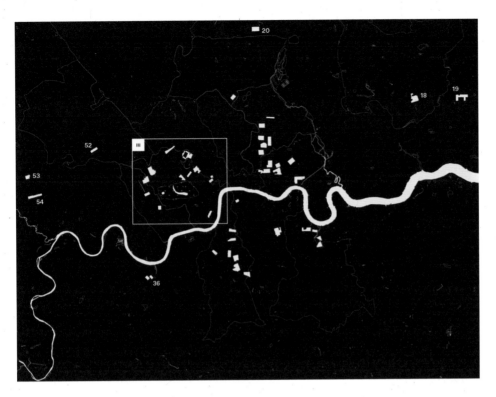

Figure 1. Index of places. This map represents places that inspired the design of the Serpentine Pavilion 2021, which is based on past and present places of meeting, organising, and belonging across several London neighbourhoods significant to diasporic and cross-cultural communities. Responding to the historical erasure and scarcity of informal community spaces across the city, the Pavilion references and pays homage to existing and erased places that have held communities over time and continue to do so today.

What I find very intriguing about cities is that many of the spaces that host key moments in their cultural transformations are very small, and tend to – on the scale of history – become invisible. As Counterspace, our main drive in working on what would become a very visible Serpentine Pavilion in London has been to build support by bringing these otherwise disparate spaces together (fig. 1). In a way, one could think of the project as a cultural scaffold, both present and transient, taking root across time and place to situate media, thinkers, work, and programmes from different realms and from across the city into the same platform.

We were really immersed, for example, in the story of Claudia Jones, born in Trinidad, in how she came to London via New York and was the founding editor of the newspaper *West Indian Gazette*. She set up the office above a small barber shop in Brixton. That tiny little space meant so much for a whole generation and community, for whom it created a sense of belonging and a place for people to identify with – through the stories that she published – because people saw their own image in that way.

Many other spaces that are very small have also been key in creating important cultural movements, like the Mangrove in Notting Hill, which was the unofficial headquarters of the Notting Hill Carnival; the Four Aces Club in Dalston, which was the first venue in the UK to play music by Black artists; and Centerprise, which was a very important hub for Black and queer publishing and literature. I read a lot of these books that were published in the 1970s at Centerprise. It was really interesting to discover their importance, and that there had previously been no voice present for so many people in these communities.

I'd like for my work to become a conduit for fragments of the past, and for the archive to embody future awareness and seeds for further research and collaborations. The Serpentine Pavilion's decentralised methodology is comprised of parts determined by forces beyond ourselves. Being a response to – and a celebration of – a tapestry of stories and voices, this project reconfigured my role to something more akin to a co-author, allowing other voices and stories to help shape the structure and its "limbs".

Figure 2. Serpentine Pavilion 2021 by Sumayya Vally, Counterspace

Figure 3. Four Aces Club, Dalston Lane, 1986. The Four Aces Club was a pioneering music space. Established in 1966, it was one of the first venues in the United Kingdom to play music by Black artists.

In the simplest terms, my Serpentine Pavilion is a circular form carved into the ground made up of forms that articulate different scales of gathering and different scales of intimacy (fig. 2). Some of them are about one-to-one interaction, some are about a group discussion, some are about sitting on the floor and having a meal. All of them have been inspired by either looking at photographs in the archive of gathering spaces that have been erased, or by walking through London and taking photos of everyday gathering spaces.

Each area is effectively inspired by a neighbourhood, but, by extension, references similar conditions across London and beyond. Each piece is a slice of floor, wall, and ceiling. It represents an order of architecture not measured and separated into its constituent elements in terms of construction or the categories of two-dimensional projection (floors are flat things, walls are upright, etc.), but defined by the way we convene in them and are convened by and in them.

It is formed from an intersection, superimposition, and abstraction of imprints of elements drawn from places of gathering specific to migrant and peripheral communities across London. What I've tried to transfer is some of the atmosphere of what that space feels like.

The very nature of this Pavilion was fragmented, with pieces located in different neighbourhoods across the city – a means to take the Pavilion back out into London and root it in the spaces that inspired it (fig. 3). That logic came from thinking about diasporas, and thinking about things

Figure 4. The Fazl Mosque, also known as The London Mosque, is the first purpose-built mosque in London. It opened in 1926.

that root themselves or uproot themselves from one place and travel to another place and then take on the conditions of that other, new place.

Through this Pavilion and with the Serpentine Gallery, we also established the fellowship programme Support Structures for Support Structures, which is geared towards artists and collectives working at the intersection of art, spatial politics, and community practice. Its intent is to nurture the practice of individuals and collectives that hold space for communities to gather across London. Year for year, it builds and grows a deeper network of bodies of knowledge that are coming from places of difference, so that we can seed and see different pathways and other worlds. These initiatives have extended the legacy of what would otherwise have been a temporary structure, by making tangible impact in various spaces throughout the city.

The references that the Pavilion hybridises are cross-cultural and diasporic, offering a statement on the power of spaces to cross-pollinate culture (figs. 4 and 5). The forms in the Serpentine Pavilion are all inspired by these references. It draws on and honours past and present places of meeting, organising, and belonging across several London neighbourhoods of significance to diasporic and cross-cultural communities. Responding to the historical erasure and scarcity of informal community spaces across the city, the Pavilion references and pays homage to existing and erased places that have helped communities over time and continue to do so today.

Figure 5. The first carnival organised by Claudia Jones known as the Caribbean Carnival or the West Indian Gazette Carnival was held indoors at St. Pancras Town Hall on 30 January 1959. It would not be until 1964 that the carnival would move outside onto the streets of Notting Hill.

At the research level, and throughout this project, I was interested in how people have started to construct belonging and a sense of home in London. I was also exploring the idea of an exchange, or a mutation between host and home. Much of the research for this Pavilion involved spending time in archives and investigating spaces and neighbourhoods with histories of migration where important parts of history are being slowly forgotten. The archive of these elements is not just in the formal archives; it is on the street too, and in the ways people transfer culture and identity in everyday life and rituals as everyday forms of resistance.

This includes the first radical Black publishing houses, the first venues to play Black music, the first West Indian restaurants in London, the first mosques and places of worship, streets, sidewalks, porch steps that were traversed during significant protests, carnivals, and festivals as

Figure 6. For over thirty years, Jagonari Women's Centre offered crucial support and education for local women and represented part of the wider collective action of the Bengali community in Tower Hamlets. The building for the Centre was designed by the London-based feminist architects' practice Matrix.

Figure 7. Roti Kitchen is a restaurant in West London specialising in Caribbean and Indian roti.

Figure 8. Ridley Road Market. Ridley Road has been home to the market in the heart of Dalston since the late 1880s. The market consists of around 150 stalls offering a diverse range of international produce.

important forms of cultural production and gathering (fig. 6). By mapping these different places, the Pavilion can be seen as a compass, as a navigation device that provides not only direction, but also access. This allowed me the profound opportunity to explore the role of architecture in expanding, and indeed excavating, the cultural domain.

It was important for me to fold these places and their stories into the structure, to give recognition to the many fabrics that make up the city itself, and in doing so, to allow those rituals and practices to enter a space not traditionally cognisant of these points of difference. The forms in the Pavilion are all inspired by everyday rituals of gathering, everyday forms of resistance and being in a city, from street iftars, restaurants, and moments of street performance (figs. 7 and 8). Throughout the summer during which the Pavilion lived, in 2021, we launched a set of initiatives, to host these same kinds of rituals – celebrations of gathering and belonging in various forms.

The Serpentine Pavilion itself became host to a specially commissioned sound programme "Listening to the City", which featured work by artists including Ain Bailey and Jay Bernard. The programme engaged with a set of sonic landscapes from selected London neighbourhoods,

Figure 9. Fragment of the Serpentine Pavilion 2021 for The Tabernacle.

Figure 10. Notting Hill Carnival, 1979. Sound System on Portobello Road under the Westway.

paying attention to existing and lost spaces of gathering and belonging, with particular relevance to migrant communities across the city. The programme extended into other parts of the city as well.

"Sound System Sundays", curated by the artist Alvaro Barrington and the CEO of Notting Hill Carnival, Matthew Philip, was a live programme that featured six sound systems, each playing an exclusive set for two hours on a Sunday during the summer. "Sound System Sundays" was hosted at the Tabernacle in Notting Hill, home to one of the fragments of the Pavilion (figs. 9 and 10). This fragment offers an additional seating area for people to enjoy and share a meal from the Tabernacle restaurant. Additionally, it can be used as a stage for small performances.

Valence Library, another fragment location, also became home to the Becontree Broadcasting Station, which was launched as part of the Serpentine Pavilion and "Listening to the City" – featuring a selection of tracks, archival recordings, and sound works that create alternative ways of experiencing changing cities through collective listening. Brian Eno and Joe Namy presented a variety of music, sound archives, and broadcasts, so as to create alternative narratives of the city and unravel layers of sonic histories.

Spaces of gathering need to be valued. They are sacred. Discourse, dialogues, and publishing are all integral forms of practice too; and they are part of the fabric we have to work with in bringing people together and sharing beliefs – ideas as spaces to share and to differ. Architecture is about constructing spaces *and* situations. That involves the built realm, but there are other ways to understand it, too. Ritual, atmosphere, and even forms of dress are essential parts of how a space is constructed. I've always been very interested in how we can work with those other ingredients and in the construction of situations beyond just what is built.

This is important because these ingredients of home and belonging are not only forces of cultural production in and of themselves; they also evolve culture by virtue of the languages they transmit and allow a continuous cycle – we shape our spaces, and they are in dialogue with us and shape us.

The Mangrove restaurant on All Saints Road in Notting Hill, London – opened by Frank Crichlow in 1968 – provided, for example, some field notes towards what institutions can be:

The presence of "home" food: recipes, languages, and sounds, space for people to meet outside of traditional institutional atmospheres, barbeque smoke, opportunities for chance engagements with others (fig. 11).

Figure 11. The Mangrove was a Caribbean restaurant which was opened in 1968 by the Trinidadian community activist and civil rights campaigner Frank Crichlow. It was a meeting place for the Black community in the area, as well as for white radicals, artists, authors, and musicians. It functioned as the unofficial headquarters for the Notting Hill Carnival. It was repeatedly raided by the police on grounds of drug possession, despite a lack of evidence. The Mangrove Restaurant became the focus of a Black Power march and protest against police victimisation and attempts by the police and the council to shut it down.

Figure 12. View of the Serpentine Gallery from the inside of the pavilion

Figure 13. Fragment of the Serpentine Pavilion 2021 for New Beacon Books

In the same year, the British Black Panthers were founded – bringing together Black and Asian activists. The Mangrove was instrumental in attracting a constellation of thinkers, activists, and creatives – it became the unofficial headquarters of the Notting Hill Carnival, where artists, musicians, and organisers living in Notting Hill began to express and celebrate their presence in West London's streets.

Architecture has a profound role to play in expanding the cultural domain by simply listening to the contexts within which we work. This Pavilion has been a case study for that approach, but it remains and has always been a core principle of my practice.

The fragmented nature of the Pavilion opens it up to interpretation and reinterpretation, imagination and reimagination. It is conceived in five pieces, taking place all over in London – the Tabernacle, New Beacon Books, The Albany, Valence House, and Kensington Gardens (fig. 12).

Each piece is a small public offering: a shelf, a stage, a seat, a podium, and a table. They are seeds for collaboration between the Serpentine and the places that house them, extending beyond the structure's short lifetime. A shelf at New Beacon Books holds in its form traces of its surrounding streets. It houses literature from the African diaspora and a space for a person to sit and read in solitude or to an intimate audience (fig. 13).

Figure 14. Fragment of the Serpentine Pavilion 2021 for The Albany

Figure 15. Fragment of the Serpentine Pavilion 2021 for Valence Library

A stage for the Tabernacle draws on its continued celebration of song, sound, and street food. A seat at The Albany is an offering of rest, meeting, and organising (fig. 14). A podium at Valence Library draws on the Serpentine Civic team's legacy of collaboration in the London Borough of Barking and Dagenham, and it has now become home to a radio station (a very important form of public space) and its listening sessions (fig. 15).

I was inspired by intangible public spaces – radio and otherwise – and this also spurred on some of our programming throughout that summer. Radio Freedom,[1] broadcasting in South Africa, Tanzania, Zambia, Ethiopia, Angola, Madagascar, was a force in bringing people together and sharing culture from the "underground". It has always been a point of reflection on shifting, digital, scaleless, clandestine public spaces. In "A History of South African Underground Radio", Chris A. Smith writes:

> The static broke. A sonorous, unmistakably South African voice, all clipped cadences and martial rolling "r"s, announced what listeners undoubtedly already knew: "This is Radio Freedom."
>
> At seven p.m. sharp, seven nights a week, during the darkest days of apartheid, an incendiary radio broadcast beamed out from Lusaka, Zambia. . . . Hundreds of miles and two countries to the south, people gathered in matchbox homes in Johannesburg's industrial townships . . . hunched over shortwave radios, straining to hear through clouds of static. They listened with the lights off, making sure that nobody had followed them . . . there were informers everywhere.[2]

Figure 16. Serpentine Pavilion, 2021

Alongside news, the pirate radio propaganda arm of the African National Congress and uMkhonto weSizwe[3] held community space for connecting diverse struggle movements from the 1960s to the 1990s. It became a place of access and connection for South Africans to hear music from exiled South African musicians like Dollar Brand, Dudu Pukwana, and Miriam Makeba.

In honouring the history and architecture of sound systems in the UK, "Sound System Sundays" and "Listening to the City" became vital components of the Serpentine programme – and provided another means to extend access across the city.

The launch of the Becontree Broadcasting Station at Valence Library included a residency, with Joseph Namy becoming the inaugural artist-in-residence. Namy often works collaboratively and across mediums – in sound, performance, photography, text, video, and installation – with projects that focus on the social constructs of music and organised sound, such as the pageantry and geopolitics of opera, the noise laws and gender dynamics of bass, the colours and tones of militarisation, the migration patterns of instruments and songs, and the complexities of translation in all this.

242

These programmes created collaborations between the Serpentine Gallery in Kensington Gardens and community arts institutions across London. So the building became a communication device between places (fig. 16). The message of that way of working originated from thinking about diasporic logics and reflecting on how people have moved across places.

While these fragments have clear functional use, they were conceptualised as intentionally incomplete pieces to be filled in or imagined around. This method – of not being overly prescriptive – suggests a power of imagination, which we wanted to encourage and watch unfold.

Through this typology, we are reminded again of the importance of listening. In this scenario, the research drew on spaces that were important for migrant communities when they first moved to London, thinking about some of the first mosques, churches, synagogues, and marketplaces where people would be able to find traditional ingredients for recipes, or some of the first venues to play Black music in London. The questions arose: What offerings could these spaces make to the present day? And what would that look like in built form?

This method of working points directly to our collective role; and to the responsibility that architects have in working towards systemic change. To listen deeply to, and to seed and support different networks and bodies of knowledge in the arts, and beyond. The voices that have come together around the making of this Pavilion have done so far beyond what I could ever have imagined. We are convened by buildings and by building alike.

In the same way that the idea of home is owned, shared, and transmitted through community, so too does the Pavilion exist through those who have inspired and come together to build something that belongs to them. The making of a building does not end with the completion of construction. Building is also a verb, and it is through living, breathing, and sharing space that the building is continuously completed.

1   Radio Freedom was the radio arm of the African National Congress during South Africa's apartheid years.

2   Chris A. Smith, "Radio Freedom: A History of South African Underground Radio", *South African History Online*, 20 December 2013, https://www.sahistory.org.za/archive/radio-freedom-history-south-african-underground-radio-chris-smith.

3   Translated from the Zulu language as "Spear of Africa", the uMkhonto weSizwe was the guerrilla wing of the African National Congress during apartheid. The faction was formed when peaceful negotiations with the government were proving unsuccessful and combat seemed to be the only logical conclusion.

Architecture as Archive
Marco Costantini

Architecture, far beyond a mere artistic expression or functional solution, is a living archive of human history. Through its forms, materials, and visual language, it narrates stories about the societies that created it and the eras that shaped it. As the architect Alexandra Pacescu aptly notes, it can be considered a true archive of the values, sentiments, traditions, and transformations that societies undergo at different times.[1] It constitutes the archaeological layers of a communal way of life and remains the silent witness to humanity's evolution and change.

Lebanon possesses an architectural archive particularly rich in historical, social, and cultural lessons. Its architecture reflects the profound political shifts that have shaped the country and its two main cities, Beirut and Tripoli.

The current consideration of this unique and specific heritage must nonetheless take into account both the period in which it originated and the vision guiding its preservation today. So while the preservation and archival safeguarding project of the Corm Tower in Beirut, conceived in 1928 by Charles Corm, and that of the Rachid Karami International Fair in Tripoli, designed by the Brazilian architect Oscar Niemeyer, particularly his Guest House, differ in terms of form, they can be used as case studies to explore the idea of making buildings themselves an archive.

The eras in which they were erected are vastly different. The Corm Tower was built during the period of the French Mandate (fig. 1). Defeated at the end of the First World War, the

Figure 1. Offices of Charles Corm & Cie Headquarters with assembly sheds in the front, ca. 1930

Figure 2. Exterior of the Corm Building as restored in 2024

Ottoman Empire gave way to France, which established a mandate in Lebanon, as well as in neighbouring Syria. In 1920, Beirut was proclaimed the capital of Greater Lebanon, and it became the place where all major political decisions for the Levant States would be made. Under French influence, the city saw its former Ottoman projects modernised and supplemented by new developments, including the creation of Place de l'Étoile and Place al-Bourj, now known as Martyrs' Square. This transformation was in line with French urban reforms, such as those carried out by Baron Haussmann in Paris, aimed at modernising the city and improving traffic flow.

Under the French Mandate, Beirut underwent a transformation according to a Western model, breaking away from the traditional Arab-Muslim urban fabric. The urban development plans conceived by French urban planners, notably those of the Danger Brothers in 1932 and Michel Écochard in 1943, reflect a radical overhaul of the city, disregarding pre-existing urban structures. This approach reflects a denial of identity and imposition of colonial urbanism.

The Rachid Karami International Fair in Tripoli, on the other hand, was conceived in 1962 and falls within the period of Lebanon's "Golden Age", from 1943 to 1975. Lebanon gained independence in 1943 after twenty-five years under the French Mandate. Beirut then became a major regional metropolis, attracting a flow of population and capital. Economic development was fuelled by trade, industry, regional oil capital deposits in banks, and foreign investments. This growth led to an expansion of Beirut, with the emergence of new urban centres, such as the Hamra district in the western part of the city. However, it was Tripoli, not Beirut, that was chosen to host the site of the International Fair.

The chosen city and architectural style of these two examples are rich indicators and testimonies of historical lessons. The objectives behind the construction of these buildings also serve as vehicles for understanding the political and economic situation of the country, which differed in the two respective periods to which they belong. In a conversation with the Corm brothers in Beirut, David Corm reflects that their "father always saw architecture not just as buildings but as stories carved in stone and steel. The tower is a testament to his ambition and love for Beirut."[2]

The recent opening of the Charles Corm Cultural Foundation on the outskirts of Achrafieh and Badaro, established in the former headquarters of the family business from the 1930s, exemplifies a successful renovation accompanied by a functional reorientation, while preserving the original architectural integrity (fig. 2). This project was spearheaded by David Corm (b. 1937) and Hiram Corm (b. 1938), the sons of Charles Corm (1894–1963), a Lebanese poet and entrepreneur, himself the son of the painter Daoud Corm (1852–1930).

In 1913, Charles founded La Maison d'Art with his father, pioneering in the sale of artistic items as well as typewriters and cameras. After the First World War, with Lebanon now a French Mandate, Corm engaged in supplying Beirut, while also launching Les Tréteaux Libanais, a theatre troupe whose light comedies subtly evoked the country's social and economic reality. Simultaneously, he worked to promote the emerging Lebanon as a land of culture and humanism by founding the *Phoenician Review* in 1919.

Despite his numerous cultural activities, Corm also had to support himself and became a representative for Ford automobiles in the Levant, which holds significant importance for our analysis (fig. 3). Indeed, during his trip to the United States in 1912, he was fascinated by the

Figure 3. Charles Corm & Cie Headquarters, Place Assour, Beirut, ca. 1921

Figure 4. Ground floor showroom furnished with chairs by Ludwig Mies van der Rohe

automobiles crisscrossing the city, as well as by the modern architecture of the time, particularly the early Art Deco buildings, which he drew inspiration from in 1928 for the construction of his tower in Beirut.

In 1934, at the age of forty, he abandoned his commercial activities to devote himself to writing and married Samia Baroudy, Miss Lebanon 1935, with whom he had four children: David, Hiram, Virginie, and Madeleine. By the end of the 1930s, he had transformed his white tower into the residence for his family.

Imagined in 1928 by Corm himself, the tower, the tallest in Beirut until 1967, was clearly intended as a nod to the American skyscrapers of the time. One recognises the stacking of decreasingly sized parallelepipeds with a triangular pediment similar to that of the Empire State Building, which would be inaugurated two years later. Its initial purpose was to house the Ford agency and its administration (fig. 4). Many cars were assembled in the courtyard, now transformed into a garden. David and Hiram Corm remind us today that many signs of this industrial past remain inside, such as car headlights used as light fixtures, tubular-steel railings, or shelves for spare parts turned into libraries (figs. 5 and 6). Design would also be prominent when the place became the family residence. The precise inventory of the Corm family's belongings

Figure 5. Library in the lifetime of Charles Corm, 1950s

Figure 6. Ludwig Mies van der Rohe chairs and side tables, Youssef Howayek's sculptures, and Ford headlights as lighting

includes invoices from Maison Saddier et Fils of Paris, as well as references to several lighting fixtures signed by Robj and Daum, and lamps and furniture by Etienne Kohlmann.[3] All this attests to Charles Corm's certain tastes, but also to his belonging to his era, to its architecture, and to its design.

Today, the foundation is the custodian of the invaluable documentary heritage bequeathed by Charles Corm throughout his life. "The logic of archiving has been [present] since the beginning. Every letter was duplicated on the typewriter and they had a copy," says Hiram. This treasure trove encompasses a variety of historical documents, such as reports from the King–Crane Commission, a rich correspondence between Corm and the intellectuals of his time, and an impressive collection related to the activities of the Ford agency at the dawn of the automotive era in the region. Furthermore, these archives include the author's library, which was once one of the country's most significant private libraries, housing novels, poetry collections, essays, and art books, as well as a multitude of periodicals and newspapers from the era (fig. 7).

From an architectural standpoint, the recent restoration primarily returned the structures and interior spaces to their original state. These spaces have undergone several phases of use, ranging from industrial to residential, ultimately adopting a cultural purpose. Only an elevator has been added, without compromising the coherence of the initial project. The garden, on the other hand, has undergone a significant transformation, having originally housed automobile assembly workshops.

This recent repurposing of the Corm Tower reflects the principle articulated by Hiram Corm, that of "building the future by drawing from the past". By emphasising the importance of respecting the past as a source of inspiration rather than perpetuating it, he demonstrates an openness to innovative ideas, shared with his brother.

This perspective aligns well with the idea that this architecture serves both as an archive and a platform for discussing its history and future. Despite Lebanon's modest size, the diversity of architectural experiments that have taken place there offers a cultural immersion as one walks its streets.

The Art Deco architecture of the tower also expresses the vision of its patron and his commitment to his business and country. Charles Corm deliberately chose an American style to establish his industry in the Middle East, thereby highlighting his expansionist ambition and openness to the world. This decision demonstrates his singular and daring character, also illustrated in the choice of furniture that must harmonise perfectly with the building, thus reflecting the taste of an era but also a taste committed to a then bright future.

Thus, the Corm Tower fulfils a plurality of functions, merging two identities into one organism. As the only Art Deco skyscraper in Lebanon, it serves as a witness to a bygone era. Together

Figure 7. Library on the first floor in 2024 with a 1923 Ford Model T with the original Ludwig Mies van der Rohe furniture and Ford headlights as lighting in the background

with seminal projects such as the Rachid Karami International Fair in Tripoli, and especially through sensitive renovation methods like those employed to revive the Niemeyer Guest House, it underscores that architecture, as a physical manifestation of a society's aspirations, constraints, and values, can transcend its functional aspect to become a living archive. This perspective transforms the superficial appreciation of buildings to encompass a deeper understanding of their role as guardians of human history. Architecture and the entirety of built cultural structures then act as a reservoir of historical information linked to belief systems, social stratifications, or technological advancements of their construction era. Contemporary architecture is no exception to this, capturing the challenges, concerns, and advancements of current society, whether it be environmental sustainability, social inclusion, or technological innovation.

A genuine awareness of architectural heritage in Lebanon only emerged in the early 1960s. Until then, the issue remained secondary to the need to renovate the political system and local urban planning.[4] Geographer Eric Verdeil sees three important factors in this paradigm shift: the development of tourism, significant publications, and the creation of the Association for the

Protection of Sites and Ancient Dwellings (ASPAD).[5] The latter was founded in 1965 at the initiative of various individuals from prominent Greek Orthodox and Sunni families, such as Lady Sursock Cochrane, Assem Salam, and Mitri Nammar, the latter two both architects.

From this moment on, the preservation of architectural heritage and the understanding of its conception take on crucial importance for several reasons. Firstly, it maintains a tangible link to our past, preserving knowledge and traditions for future generations. Secondly, it fosters a sense of cultural identity and historical continuity within communities. Finally, it stimulates a new form of cultural and economic tourism specific to the expanding interest in architectural heritage and its societal implications.

Considering architecture as an archive requires a critical and contextual reading. Therefore, in-depth analysis is necessary to understand the underlying meanings and implications of each structure. This critical approach allows for questioning dominant historical narratives, recognising marginalised voices, and promoting a representation often more accurate of human history.

However, interpreting architecture as an archive is not without challenges. Buildings can be subject to multiple, sometimes contradictory interpretations. Moreover, human interventions, such as restorations, renovations, or even intentional destructions, can alter the original meaning of a building. "Each addition to an old structure should be like a new chapter in a book – complementary, yet capable of standing on its own," explains Hiram. Thus, the redevelopment of the Corm Tower with the addition of an elevator and the transformation of the Niemeyer Guest House into a carpentry workshop have not completely frozen these architectures in time.

The important ethical question raised by Alexandra Pacescu is how to determine a way to add new layers to something that is already complete and coherent without losing or deteriorating its meaning: "Addition is not only a matter of architectural language, although it is crucial, but also a question of ethics of added value, both in terms of concept and function."[6] The Corm Tower, as Hiram and David Corm have well reminded us, has lived three distinct lives: that of a commercial space, that of a private residence, and finally, today, that of a cultural institution. This necessitates a cautious and multidisciplinary approach necessary to unravel the complex layers of meaning and symbolism contained within this unique architectural structure.

The Corm Tower in Beirut and the Niemeyer Guest House in Tripoli ultimately act as witnesses and guardians of human history, capturing the different evolutions of Lebanon over time and the personal ones of those who are their custodians. By considering them as an archive, we are encouraged to promote their preservation and critical interpretation. It is by considering this mixed state of function and archive that architecture, as a reflection and agent of historical change, continues to enrich our understanding of the world and our place within it.

A final but crucial element in considering architecture as an archive involves looking in two distinct directions. On the one hand, through different historical, political, and cultural contexts. On the other hand, through the eyes of residents, activists, and professionals.[7]

Thus, recent examples such as the Niemeyer Guest House of the Rachid Karami International Fair in Tripoli, the Corm Tower in Beirut, and, before them, the Barakat House in Beirut as well, located at the intersection of Damascus Street and Independence Avenue, on the former demarcation line, testify to the crucial role that architecture plays in the collective memory of a nation and the importance of preserving its most striking witnesses. Modern or premodern, all of these architectures are the shared heritage of all Lebanese because they were conceived as constitutive elements of the urban landscape. In Lebanon and elsewhere in the world, many constructions await to be saved from oblivion and/or ruin. Research initiated on contemporary architectural heritage should then reveal many yet unknown aspects about our time. As David Corm so eloquently puts it, "it's not just about preserving buildings; it's about maintaining a connection to our past and ensuring that future generations understand where they come from."

1   Alexandra Pacescu, "Architecture as Archive: The Ethics of Adding New Layers", in *Research through architecture*, International Conference on Architecture Research, 2015, https://www.researchgate.net/publication/279713006_architecture_as_archive_-_the_ethics_of_adding_new_layers.

2   All quotes originate from a conversation with David and Hiram Corm, 22 March 2024.

3   Thank you to David and Hiram for sending several reproductions of the inventories of the Charles Corm Foundation. This should be studied carefully to trace the institutional history of the Corm House, but also the underlying issues that it entails.

4   Sophie Brones, *Beyrouth dans ses ruines* (Marseille: Editions Parenthèses, 2020), p. 34.

5   Eric Verdeil, "Années soixante: le patrimoine n'est pas encore un article d'importation au Liban", *Lettre d'information de l'Observatoire de recherche sur Beyrouth et la reconstruction* 14 (2001), pp. 28–32.

6   Pacescu, "Architecture as Archive".

7   Brones, *Beyrouth dans ses ruines*, p. 146.

SPECULATIVE FUTURES

MetaNiemeyer
Charles Kettaneh

A common trait in architectural production in the twenty-first century, and arguably since the 1990s, is the use of the computer as a tool. As early as the 1950s, two decades before construction works started on the Rachid Karami International Fair in Tripoli, Lebanon, Douglas T. Ross, a researcher at the Massachusetts Institute of Technology (MIT), introduced the term computer-aided design (CAD). Also at MIT, in 1963, the exact same year that Oscar Niemeyer was commissioned to design the Fair, Ivan Sutherland created a CAD software known as Sketchpad while working on his PhD thesis.[1]

Whether a coincidence or not, the end of one of the last great "isms" of architecture almost overlaps with the advent of the personal computer (PC) in the late 1970s, which marks the starting point of its own exponential age of digitalism – its ramifications encapsulating many aspects of our lives today. What is poignant in the context of the uncovering and archiving of modern relics such as the Tripoli Fair is that their historical proximity and overlap with the digital age, as well as their influence on contemporary canons and methods of construction, make it almost frustrating that they are not part of the computer era altogether. The latter would have made archiving, at least, a less challenging task.

The Tripoli Fair – whose construction was halted in 1975 due to the Lebanese Civil War that lasted until 1990 – is an even more severe case of a disjointed timeline, as one reflects on the presence of these extraordinary concrete structures in the vacuum of the city. It is not only the physical attributes of the Fair that make it look like the "Other" in the city of Tripoli, but also the fact that it was never fully completed, was never used in its original intent, was a bunker during the Civil War, was then fenced in and purposely detached from the city, never reintegrated and always debated, thus transforming it into a subject of socio-political altercation, crystallising the numerous divisions of an entire population. This unborn monument has, however, been the subject of many emotions; and its future use – if any – has captured the imagination of generations of artists, planners, and architects, as well as Tripolitans, who hope that, one day, these square meters will be given back to them.

The above details merely a few of the many reasons which make the Tripoli Fair such a complex topic. It is precisely this complexity that allows it to be ripe for further exploration, particularly by dislocating it, at least conceptually, in a space akin to a laboratory – in a state of weightlessness visible for everyone to see, dissect, and analyse. The internet.

Very soon after the personal computer, the internet arrived – a novel way of accessing and sharing information that has revolutionised, still today, the way humans interact. The internet has allowed free access to everyone and everything, and it has to some degree democratised information, speech, and knowledge, to name a few. It is worth highlighting here that while the internet has been a driving force of globalism, it also acts as an enabler of many other movements.

Even though the monopoly held by large corporations over data exchanged through the internet is today a serious topic open to critique (mainly of neoliberalism), the possibilities offered through that medium are actually the most exciting aspect deserving of attention, particularly in the context of architectural production. Possibilities that very often lie at the intersection of the physical and digital, in the interstitial space that bridges both worlds in a unique way that can only be appreciated by the human conscience.

Architecture as a Digital Practice

The widespread availability of personal computers facilitated the transition of the "digital", from theoretical concept to practical application, blurring the boundaries between both realms. As technology advanced rapidly, architects pioneered new methodologies, utilising digital tools to speculate about the future of architecture, cities, and our interactions with both. In parallel to this technological shift, a liberal and globalist wave, perhaps facilitated by the end of the Cold War, acted as a catalyst for the global adoption of this technology.

Mario Carpo, in his essay "A Short but Believable History of the Digital Turn in Architecture", depicts in words – but also through an interesting graph (credited to Mark Garcia and Steven Hutt) – how "computational tools" emerged to become prevalent in architectural design, tracing back its recent history and extracting the different "waves" of its evolution.[2]

This highlights the emergence of the first theories around artificial intelligence and machine learning, with fields such as "cybernetics" that arose in the 1950s with early systems that looked at automatic input/output from machines. From Marvin Minsky's conference paper "Steps Toward Artificial Intelligence" in 1961 to Nicholas Negroponte's essay "Toward a Theory of Architecture Machines" in 1969, these ideas flourished for about two decades.

The era between 1970 and 1990, with a "peak" in 1980, marks a period known as the "winter of artificial intelligence" (coincidentally, this time also encapsulates the Lebanese Civil War, and the stalling of construction works at the Tripoli Fair). It was only in 1990 that the rise of computation in architectural design was to go fully exponential, helped by the rise in personal computers (PC) and in AutoCAD, the most successful and commercial version of computer-aided design software to run on a PC, developed by Autodesk.

From the 1990s until today, a succession of "waves" that intersect and interact with each other have also overlapped with two "meta waves" to create this complex chronological construct of digital genres that define contemporary computational design in architecture. Such genres include Folding and Blob as part of the Emergence and Self-Organisational wave, with works by Peter Eisenman, Frank Gehry, or Greg Lynn. Other genres include Robotic Assembly and Gaming with a reference to Jose Sanchez's Gamescapes studio (2013). The genres and

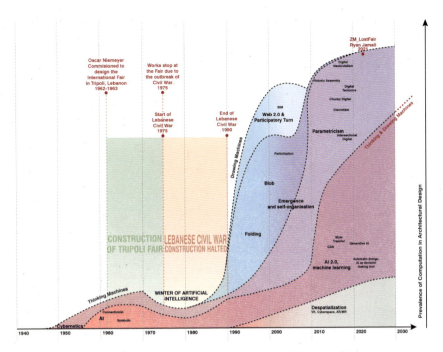

Figure 1. "Prevalence of Computation in Architectural Design with Tripoli Fair Overlay" by the author. The works at the Tripoli Fair were halted during the same time as "the winter of artificial intelligence", though for very different reasons. One could have hoped that, in the 1990s, the Fair would have shared a similar fate as computation in architectural design: exponential growth and development.

waves are numerous, and they truly encapsulate all the possibilities, trends, and usage of the computer as a tool since its inception.

The aforementioned graph also notes differentiation between the computer as a tool for "drawing" and as a tool for "thinking". From 1990 to 2010, there is a clear dominance of the former, while from 2010 onwards, the waves of using machines for "thinking" start overlapping and taking on importance. While the graph was drawn in 2023 and takes generative AI (DALL-E, Midjourney) into consideration, it doesn't speculate on a complete takeover of the computer as a machine for both drawing and thinking, although the latter seems to be the writing on the wall (fig. 1).

Hacking the Fair

Ryan Jamali, a Tripolitan artist and designer, is one of many of the city's natives who have a perilous, complicated, and curious relationship with the Fair. Struggling to freely enter the Fair growing up, Jamali has grappled with the site's inaccessibility, "governed by the country's resource gatekeepers". He recalls sneaking into the Fair with his friends to ride bicycles, and noticing the danger posed by the collapsing structures damaged by war, the passing of time, and lack of maintenance.[3]

Figure 2. Initial scene of ZM_LostFair, where the player attempts to escape an apocalyptic world outside of the Fair by breaking into it. We can see the side entrance canopy as well as the "Great Arch" in the background.

Years later, during a Covid lockdown – when the Tripoli Fair could have been a timely and much-needed outlet for the city's residents – Ryan Jamali decided to "hack" the Fair, designing an access point liberated from obstacles imposed on him, his friends, and family. Inspired by the works of Anthony Dunne and Jose Sanchez,[4] Jamali introduced participatory design methodologies to re-define the role of architecture in fostering inclusivity and in addressing societal challenges.

Through "speculative archaeology", design, and critical thinking, Jamali modified the popular online game Call of Duty by digitally modelling the entire fairgrounds within the game itself, reimagining and importing this cultural asset into an open-source virtual platform. He had initially titled the new game ZM_LostFair, with ZM standing for "zombie mode", the mode in which one can create one's own game and rules on top of the basic Call of Duty platform. Accessing the otherwise neglected and fenced-in site through an online portal enabled Jamali to rewrite the rules of the game and override the basic power-imbalance reality of the city. Instead of asking for permission to engage, the game is written to promote and encourage access, expansion, and collaboration (fig. 2).

Rather than building an analogue archive of the photography, sketches, pieces, interviews, and multiple data points he had collected about the Fair, Ryan Jamali gamified them, proposing a deeper exploration of the digital realm as a conduit for social interaction and collective creation. Jamali's game, accessible online and outside of the legislative parameters of Lebanon, is not intended only as a site of play; it also uses gaming as a conduit to empower communities and to shape the city for the better. Jamali particularly relates to the concept of "digital social life", spending years on gaming platforms or web networks and befriending people "differently" in the digital realm.

As an alternate reality game (ARG) anchored in the Tripoli Fair, ZM_LostFair would necessitate a hybrid digital and in-person playing experience, inviting gamers to physically engage with the fair by linking geotagged information and narratives inside of it, aiming to engage a collaborative local and international online community to "uncover" the Fair and reappropriate it, via a hunt for clues much like an Easter egg hunt. The nature of these clues would vary – from photography to an online database of documents incriminating politicians, like the Panama Papers (figs. 3 and 4).

Figures 3 and 4. Leaked documents spilled on the floor in ZM_LostFair. They are part of the "Easter Egg hunt" meant to engage the community in uncovering "real world" clues in order to advance in the game.

Though Ryan Jamali initially started the project "just to have fun" with a close circle of friends and family, it is the engagement and responses of the wider community (through the ARG) that convinced him to pursue this further. A lot of the Lebanese diaspora still care about the country deeply, so being able to connect remotely on a subject of interest has made them feel included in the process. They did the research, found the hints, and felt that they were active participants in the story "because without the viewer the project wouldn't exist".

Collective Reclamation as Democracy

Ryan Jamali envisions his project as a potential prototype for instigating debate and experiments worldwide, inciting similar projects in other regions. He highlights the project's alignment with digital activism and resistance, aiming to leverage the game as a tool for social, political, and creative revolution. By hacking the access to the Tripoli Fair through a digital portal, itself potentially richer than its physical counterpart, Jamali has "democratised" the Fair in a way never done before.

ZM_LostFair exemplifies how creative computation tools can be used in architectural design. The game – as an existing online platform, Call of Duty – leverages the open-source possibilities of the internet to connect the people in the Fair virtually. This new Fair is crafted through community involvement, using other open-source forums such as Reddit.

The digital version of the Fair is a distortion of the physical one (fig. 5). But rather than thinking of it as a false "digital twin", it can be understood as one of many possible digital siblings or a "meta" (as in the self-referential version) of itself. This is true for Jamali's modelling of the Fair that was based on "speculative archaeology" where different mediums were used and collected throughout time, creating a three-dimensional "collage" that took form in the game. This approach, which Jamali "borrows" from the theories of Anthony Dunne, leads to a creative and possibly generative assemblage within the digital realm.

The techniques used by Ryan Jamali "reclaim", in many ways, the work of Oscar Niemeyer. Other acts of reclaiming can be found in both the digital and physical worlds, as well as in other industries. In many works of fiction, a world is imagined by a person (or a small group of people) so as to cater for a story. The story comes to life through a movie and its characters, which is then released to a broad physical audience throughout the world. The virtual and imagined world starts living through its audience, through shared memories and discussions, as well as critique. It suddenly becomes physically present and culturally relevant (figs. 6 and 7).

As is often the case, works of cinematographic fiction create a distorted reality to convene an affect that is difficult to recreate in the real world. Be it through technical prowess or through computer-generated imagery (CGI), these fictional worlds trespass the limitations of the physical

Figure 5. Aerial view of the Rachid Karami International Fair

Figures 6 and 7. A quiet and peaceful view from inside the Fair, in contrast with the chaotic outskirts in ZM_LostFair. The dome of the Experimental Theater as well as the Helipad are clearly visible.

world and send the viewer into a radically new paradigm where his or her imagination interacts with the world they are confronted with in ways that sublime reality. Here, the notion of hack is present in that the access to these spaces is created through the medium itself, but what is even more present is the idea of "borrowing" an existing architecture or style, giving it an entirely new definition in this crafted environment. This process of "reclaiming" is widely accepted as a creative ethos within the film industry, but not fully in architecture.

In ZM_LostFair, a culturally relevant physical space is taken out of its physicality to become fiction. In that fiction, it is not the space that is imagined but rather the stories surrounding the space, and the way people interact in and with the space (and with one another in the space) that becomes novel while unfathomable in its physical reality (fig. 8).

Figure 8. The Guest House as seen in ZM_LostFair

These works use the virtual and the physical space, but very differently. They create a new reality, one that is understood only through the personal lens of the person interacting with the medium. Both cinematographic fictions and digital games are purely digital and meant to stay digital. They exemplify, each in their own way, how layered, complex, and unbounded the possibilities are when using these mediums. Such mediums are in fact portals that allow the human mind to become emancipated in a totally boundless way.

The internet, with its ability to process, store, and showcase all forms of digital media, becomes the base layer of this digital ecosystem. It allows existence in a public, dematerialised space, where users react and interact anonymously or pseudonymously, freeing themselves of stigmas and boundaries. As a social and political space, it becomes an enabler of new forms of action and accountability, empowering civil society movements to challenge corruption and hegemonies of state bureaucracy (figs. 9 and 10).

Metaphysical Liberation

Ultimately, computation is not merely a tool for speculating and reinterpreting. On one side of the spectrum, it is largely used to visualise and analyse, be it for a project in conception or for a structure already built.

A case in point at the Tripoli Fair was an initiative led by UNESCO as part of a training project for the Directorate of Antiquities. Using a technique called "drone photogrammetry", they were able to create a 3D mapping of the site and, in particular, of the Grand Arch, whose structural integrity was in question. Rather than simply reproducing the shape in a digital format, this technique allowed for a very fine detailing of the faces of the arch, representing and remodelling in a picture-perfect manner the details (and imperfections) of the concrete. This model was later used to assess the damages to the structure and to test – first digitally – solutions to remedy its decay. Later, through private funding, the structure was repaired using the solution proposed by the model.

The digitisation of the physical structures mapped allows for precise archiving, at a precise point "T" in time. It is that same technology that Google uses to map Google Earth, the main difference being the scale (and subsequent detailing) of the mapped structures. However, according to Google, the average age of the imagery is one to three years, whereas the project mentioned earlier was a "one-off" instance. Since "historical imagery" is embedded in the

Figures 9 and 10. Image from the TV series *Logan's Run* (1978) (right) showing the interior of a theatre, closely resembling the Experimental Theater at the Fair (left)

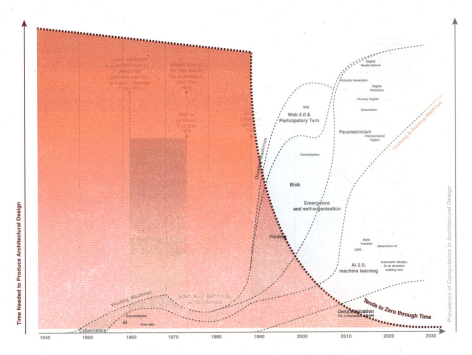

Figure 11. "Time Needed to Produce Architectural Design": a diagrammatic representation of the "exponential decay" of the time needed to produce architectural design. It starts in the 1990s, in direct correlation to the exponential prevalence of computation in architectural design.

programme (the ability to go back in time), it is thus highly likely that, since the first release of Google Earth in 2001, the world has its most updated archive of the physical built environment, capable of tracing the rise, evolution, and decay of any structures, anywhere in the world. With such data, readily available at a click of a mouse, the Earth since 2001 will never hide a mystery.

In an expected turn of events, artificial intelligence – and in particular large language models (LLM) such as Midjourney or DALL-E – is making us question reality anew. The ability to generate images through text prompts is probably only the tip of the iceberg. In the field of architecture and the built environment, text to 3D models are already being tested and image to 3D models are only months away. What this means is that the mode of architectural production will entirely change, and with it a whole economy. As explored above, the prevalence of computers in architectural design is exponential, and both worlds will inexorably blend through time. In direct correlation to the latter, one could say that the time to produce architectural design using a computer will be of exponential decay: it will become so fast that it will tend to zero through time. This means that the architectural design, from conceptualisation to production, could soon be fully taken over by computers that both "think and draw", breaking the barriers of entry to a profession that has long been seen as one of the hardest to learn and succeed into (fig. 11).

While these technologies are liberating and remove many of the physical constraints of the analogue world, one should reflect on the future role of architecture and architects within this technological realm.

As Mario Carpo argues in his 2018 essay "Republic of Makers: From the Digital Commons to a Flat Marginal Cost Society", "computers calculate and design objects the way a very smart artisan could, not the way any modern engineer or scientist would. In short, both as tools to *make* and as tools to *think,* computers are closer to the traditional, pre-industrial way of doing things, than to the modern, scientific, industrial world as we know it."[5]

In other words, and especially since the advent of artificial intelligence, which qualifies as "one of the most disruptive, revolutionary innovations of all times", the world is tending towards a place where digital creation and manufacturing will be so fast and so cheap that mass stand-ardisation, which was invented for that same purpose, will not be needed. In a world of "digital mass-customisation", where scale doesn't matter, the physical and digital exist in an almost symbiotic way.[6] It is a world where time is no longer representative of any effort, as creation and production costs are slashed. It is a world where masterpieces are created in seconds, and where architecture would no longer be seen as a service rendered.

In many ways, AI will commodify architecture and banalise it at once. With infinite amounts of data stored in invisible archives, it will be able to create iterations of everything, everywhere at any time. In that world, the role of the architect is very different, and so will be architecture.

Ryan Jamali believes that cities will be remoulded based on social interactions on digital platforms. With ZM_LostFair, Jamali's game is a glimpse of what the architect of tomorrow might look like: one that creates new portals inviting us to re-experience, modify, and reclaim our world (fig. 12).

1 Mario Carpo, "A Short but Believable History of the Digital Turn in Architecture", e-flux Architecture, March 2023, www.e-flux.com/architecture/chronograms/528659/a-short-but-believable-history-of-the-digital-turn-in-architecture/.

2 Ibid.

3 Ryan Jamali in conversation with the author via Zoom, 17 April 2024. All further quotes by Jamali originate from this conversation.

4 Anthony Dunne and Fiona Raby, *Speculative Everything: Design, Fiction, and Social Dreaming* (Cambridge, MA: The MIT Press, 2013); Jose Sanchez, *Architecture for the Commons: Participatory Systems in the Age of Platforms* (New York: Routledge, 2020).

5 Mario Carpo, "Republics of Makers: From the Digital Commons to a Flat Marginal Cost Society", e-flux Architecture, January 2018, www.e-flux.com/architecture/positions/175265/republics-of-makers/.

6 Ibid.

Figure 12. Tripoli Fair, AI generated. In the foreground, the Lebanese Pavilion reflecting on a shallow water pond, while in the background the dome of the Experimental Theater can be seen.

Play Is Progressive
Amale Andraos in Conversation with Raafat Majzoub

In this conversation, Raafat Majzoub explores with Amale Andraos the evolution of public spaces in the modern Arab city, and the architect's endeavour to redefine the brief through examples from her practice, with a particular focus on the Beirut Museum of Art (BeMA). Andraos emphasises the importance of rewriting the architectural brief to create more complex and provocative projects, and highlights the role of play in her practice as an approach that invites public engagement and rethinks architectural limits.

Raafat Majzoub In 2019, you chaired the jury of the open International Architectural Design Competition for the Knowledge and Innovation Center (KIC) in Tripoli, which is situated within the grounds of the Rachid Karami International Fair. From over 100 submissions, the jury awarded first and second place to underground projects that preserve the Fair's pavilions as ruins rather than adaptively reuse them. Could you tell us more about that decision?

Amale Andraos Yes, it was a fascinating competition: the jury included experts from around the world, such as Francesco Bandarin, Farès el-Dahdah, George Kunihiro, Suha Özkan, Jad Tabet, and Bassam Ziadeh.[1]

It was intriguing that so many people participated in the jury despite the uncertainty of the competition's outcome. Another surprising aspect was the number of international entries from all over the world. This highlighted the Fair's resonance with people regarding Lebanon's engagement with modernity and its unresolved proposition.

The two winning schemes, both underground, reflected a desire to preserve the Fair as a ruin. There was a clear reluctance to intervene in Niemeyer's work, which I found interesting. The site was never in use, so it felt like preserving the promise of something yet to be completed, rather than something to be reused. The Fair, in its ruined state, possesses a unique agency, pointing more to the future than the past, which few ruins or monuments manage to achieve today.

RM I'm going to be the devil's advocate here and ask if you see the "ruin fetish" aspect of awarding these projects? It's something we've been dealing with in the architecture scene in Lebanon, the Beit Beirut project being probably one of the most recent case studies.

AA One specific issue to Lebanon is that we've never really dealt with the desire to become a nation and what that meant. The Fair poses this question: What was this nation to be formed for, and for whom? Nor have we dealt with the war. Downtown Beirut, for example, was like, let's clean this up, keep a few monuments to create a new narrative that can attract foreign investment, and pretend nothing happened.

Unlike many other places, particularly in the West where every incident is met with years of dealing with its trauma, there is the sense as Lebanese that we can just pop a Valium and move on. There's also something interesting about the conversation between Beirut and Tripoli. Tripoli was supposed to decentre Beirut, and the Fair occupies this repressed unconscious. It's a reminder of past aspirations, while also holding optimism for the future.

For me, it undermines the notion that nation-building was meant to fail, or that modernity was simply imposed. We can't know if it would have failed, because it never had the chance to be. The Fair complicates that narrative in a good way.

RM And do you feel like the fact that neither of these projects were actually executed has anything to do with the design strategy? Or is it the usual Lebanese mystery?

AA Probably the Lebanese situation. But that's what was interesting. The whole process, from the competition to the jury, was conducted very professionally, against all odds, even with the recognition that this was probably a futile exercise.

Yet, it was important to make a point about the value of public competitions. That was Jad Tabet's emphasis: that believing in and supporting the process is important. There was an effort to go through the motions, recognising the significance of this site for architects, architecture, Lebanon, the region, and the Global South more generally. It was about rethinking modernity, regardless of whether the winning entry would be realised.

RM If you were to intervene in the Fair, what would be more exciting for you: to write the brief for the competition or to have your own design intervention?

AA Oh, that's a good question. I would first write the brief. I believe it's crucial to create an exciting and complex brief for this Fair, rather than the usual ideas like establishing a new tech hub or renovating public space.

There's a lot of room to complicate things and write a brief that raises questions about preservation generally as well as issues specific to this site. I think it would be fascinating to craft a truly provocative brief.

RM Would you imagine it could be something that encompasses the entire Fair or would you have a more piecemeal approach?

AA My gut feeling is that it would have to be a landscape project first and foremost – a landscape and preservation project. It would be about rethinking the grounds of the Fair and letting the buildings be. I remember how Jad Tabet drew a sketch situating the Fair relative to the port, highlighting the broad geographical questions that needed to be addressed before dealing with the buildings.

As architects, we often focus on the buildings, but Adrian Lahoud's "Fallen Cities"[2] is great because it emphasises the scale and topography of the Fair's grounds instead. The pavilions are quite small, so I think a landscape project would ask questions about the Fair's boundaries, scale, and siting. Adrian carefully shifts from the significance of the built structures in the Fair – downplaying the representational qualities of their architectural expression as well as their intended function as meaningful sites of cultural production – to focus instead on the design and scale of the landscape experience that never came to be.

With the Fair's buildings only occupying one third of what was conceived as a vast public park – with the canopy of trees and the mirroring bodies of water which would also have dwarfed the buildings – Adrian makes the claim that it is the constructed topography of the Fair as park which would have constructed the new Lebanese citizen, with its distributed ramps that would have moved people up and down, letting them become individuals as they emerge out of the crowd below and then, again, join back down to be a part of this new collective.

RM In your projects you often negotiate the brief and consider the architect a stakeholder in developing the program. Could you speak about where this occurred in your practice and some of the takeaways?

AA I think that's why I would want to write the brief, because we always start by rewriting the brief internally. As a practice, our position is to never take what is given for granted. We look for the hook in the program or the context that can turn things inside out and allow us to layer an additional purpose on the project. Whether it's building a new collective, making a civic gesture, or giving something private a more public dimension, these are things architects can bring. But you have to find and slightly subvert a part of what is given.

Figure 1. Rhode Island School of Design Student Success Center by WORKac, 2019

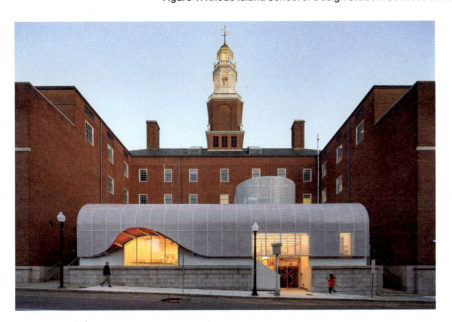

Figure 2. North Boulder Public Library model

For example, at the Rhode Island School of Design (fig. 1), the initial program was an interior renovation that created flexible spaces for Financial Aid, the Registrar, and Career Services. We found a line item for a Mail Room, which was interesting because students received packages from all over the world. We decided to make this space the focal point of the project, turning it into a contemporary post office. This expanded from a tiny mail room to a shared storage and delivery zone, an auditorium, and became a new intervention that turned the campus inside out, creating a civic presence relative to the city.

Similarly, for the North Boulder Public Library (fig. 2), the community wanted after-hour access to a Community Room. We organised the whole building to provide this access, creating an accessible ramp that serves everyone. With each project, we gravitate towards the one piece that adds value in terms of community, environment, and more, beyond just serving the initial brief.

RM WORKac's practice is characteristically playful. I would imagine that play enables a platform for serious issues to become collaborative, maybe offering a safe space for shared authorship, but could you share more about that aspect of your practice, maybe through project examples or strategies?

Figure 3. Public Farm 1 by WORKac at MoMA PS1, 2008

AA We are intent on making our work approachable and inclusive. We want people to feel a sense of ownership and generosity towards our projects. Play serves as an invitation, encouraging discovery, surprise, and engagement.

For example, with Public Farm 1 (fig. 3), we envisioned plants, people dancing, and chefs participating. We created a narrative and a network of people to build it and maintain it. We didn't initially think of kids, but they were the first to appropriate the structure, punching through its speakers and making it their own. It was amazing to see that takeover.

We believe our work should invite people to engage and transform it. It shouldn't be so precious that it resists change; it should survive and thrive through transformation. Play allows our projects to remain open for interpretation and appropriation, rather than being a top-down imposition. I think play is progressive. It's an action for the future. And we would like architecture to still have that intention despite its past failures. Despite the fact that we messed up a lot of things as architects, we can't give up – I'd rather hold on to utopia. But I think we're also playful in recognising our limits. Play invites you to say: We don't have much power, but why don't we still try to do this differently? Or why don't we come together differently? I do think that there is more room than ever for architecture to do this.

RM Play as progressive . . . spot on! You've studied the modern Arab city extensively. Could you speak to the public and share spatial elements in the design of these cities? And what do you think the role of contemporary Arab architects can be in their continuity?

AA That's a really important question. When I use the term "Arab city", it's always polemical. There isn't an essential Arab city, yet it's a useful concept to think about what has been projected as the Arab city, whether in a traditional and/or conservative way, as a modernist idea, or as a contemporary approach.

It's interesting to trace the evolution between old and new centres in the Arab world and to see how ideas about the Arab city transfer. The absorption of modernity is always transformed by the context of different Arab cities, such as in the ways climate influences the development of balconies and ideas about shade in certain Arab cities, which are not intrinsic to European modernism.

In the modernist period in particular, many projects were collaborations between local and international architects, creating a two-way exchange rather than a one-way imposition. When I interviewed the Iraqi architect Hisham Munir in the context of my Arab city seminar, it became clear that, in his work with Gropius and The Architects Collaborative (TAC) in Baghdad, there was a mix of influences at play. These collaborations are important to highlight, undermining the notion that modernism was merely applied from outside. It's about an exchange and a desire to be progressive.

On the question of public space, it's hard to make generalisations about the Arab city. Shared spaces existed, like courtyards in traditional Arab cities, with their intricate boundaries between public and private spheres. These shared collective spaces take on different forms with modernism, where the private and public are more defined compared to the blurred boundaries found in traditional settings.

In Lebanon, for example, there's sometimes an Orientalist notion that people don't know how to deal with public space. However, in New York, parks also suffer if left without competent government management, as seen in the 1980s with Tompkins Square Park. This is about policy, not cultural characteristics. It's problematic to essentialise what is Arab and what is not. Architecture, urbanism, and policy management are key to addressing these issues.

Figure 4. Beirut Museum of Art rendering by WORKac

RM But architects in Lebanon, and to some extent in the region, need to carry that burden of broken governance systems. This lends itself to your intuition to rewrite the brief, but could you speak more to how you reconcile with that?

AA As an architect in Lebanon, you need to mobilise architecture, planning, policy, mission-defining, and institution-building more than in a lot of other places. For the Beirut Museum of Art (BeMA) (fig. 4), what's been fantastic, honestly, is that before building the building, we've been building the institution. As an architect, I've been involved in reconceptualising the institution.

The original competition envisioned a contemporary museum as a black box, positioning Beirut within a global network of contemporary art cities. That vision slowly shifted. I feel I was instrumental in that shift, along with the board, the co-directors Taline N. Boladian and Juliana Khalaf Salhab, as well as BeMA's amazing team including artistic director Clemence Cottard and conservation director Kerstin Khalife. Today, the museum's mission has been recentred on the national collection – a treasure that so few have been able to engage with and learn about, and which tells the story of Lebanon's attempts to become a nation and engage with modernity and questions of identity. This collection, which starts with paintings from the late nineteenth century, has become the core of the museum.

This shift has unlocked ideas of heritage, preservation, storytelling, and the creation of an archive for people to reread and reinterpret their histories. We are conceptualising the museum as a platform and an archive for people to rewrite the brief for their place in the world.

Lebanon is often projected as "neither this nor that". For instance, Egypt has a strong narrative tying its artistic history to its relationship to France and decolonisation. Iraq has its grand nationalisation narrative. Art in Lebanon, however, has mostly been articulated as a loose collection of individuals, working without much coherence or relation to one another – as if reflecting common misconceptions about the nation itself. Indeed, Lebanon has often been depicted, if at all, as a historically provincial and derivative site of artistic production without much worth revealing. Retelling the story or discovering new stories, together with rebuilding the museum's mission, has been crucial over the past years.

The building was conceived as a fragment of the city, almost incomplete without the city around it, borrowing from Beirut's residential typology, to create an inviting, open, and porous "house" for all. Today, its expression has evolved to borrow from the earliest expressions of modernism in the city, which echoes the beginnings of the collection, mixing Arab, Ottoman, European, and traditional Lebanese elements and reflecting the museum's recentred mission and focus on the national collection. This possibility to continuously evolve is unique to this project, but also something we strive to do with every project. We aim to do more than just respond to the given brief.

RM How does your understanding of the urban scale and its transformations inform possibilities for architectural interventions on ruins? Can thinking about the city, rather than the monument, help conceptualise architectural renovation differently?

AA I think the urban and historical contexts are crucial. In the case of the Fair, focusing solely on the pavilions and their architectural expression is less interesting to me than considering scale, topography, landscape, and location in relation to Tripoli and its old quarters. These broader negotiations provide richer insights.

Zooming out is essential. Our preservation projects succeed when we are able to tell a story larger than material preservation itself. We don't believe in the autonomy of the architectural object or in strict boundaries. These boundaries are useful for practical reasons, but buildings are inherently porous – interconnected systems, people, and histories move through them.

For example, with BeMA, we wanted the museum to be as porous as possible, reflecting this idea of a living museum. For the Fair in Tripoli, shifting the lens from the building structures allows us to put reverence aside, and to give more freedom to the transformation and understanding of how the Fair could operate. It opens up new ideas about what the pavilions could become. We stop obsessing over structures and their expression, and instead focus on what is around and underneath them. This shift offers a broader perspective on architectural interventions.

RM From your experience as an educator and dean of the Columbia Graduate School of Architecture, Planning and Preservation, what would you say needs to be developed in architectural education to adapt to rapid planetary change?

AA Maybe this is the flip side of what I was saying earlier. While it's crucial to understand and make visible all these relationships, it's not enough to just make them visible or rewrite the brief. In architectural education, for example, it can be useful to set an arbitrary boundary for students, such as the scale of the building. This boundary should be seen not as finite, but almost as a plate where every food item's origin is understood, both separate and integrated.

In architectural education, especially in the United States, although perhaps less so in Europe or the Middle East with institutions like the American University of Beirut (AUB), we need to hold together the idea that we can map and understand large-scale relationships, while acting at the scale that is within our agency.

Students often feel overwhelmed by the complexity of issues, from climate to refugees. In my teaching, I invite students to understand these relationships and then frame a boundary within which they can act. This helps them navigate the entangled nature of contemporary challenges.

RM Architect as politician?

AA Modernist architects were politicians in the sense that many of them, like Niemeyer, were politically engaged. In his text, which I mentioned above, Adrian Lahoud humorously notes that Niemeyer was both a communist and a dilettante.

There was a strong relationship between architecture and nation-building, public works, and large-scale projects. However, this relationship has weakened due to planning failures and harsh criticisms of large-scale interventions, as well as to the undoing of public funding. This led architects to lose faith in their ability to hold a political position, resulting in the problematic idea of the autonomy of architecture. This idea, which began as a political form of resistance in Italy, later evolved into justifying a purely formal approach in the United States.

The role of the architect as a political figure comes and goes. Today, there's a gap between the belief in agency that architects hold in schools and the reality of their limited agency in practice. That's why I still think we shouldn't entirely give up on the scale of the building. It remains a territory where we have agreed-upon agency.

It's not about architects doing everything but about collaboration. We need planners and policymakers. While we don't need to be politicians ourselves, we should work within a strong framework of collaborations and expertise.

RM Following up on that perpetual negotiation of architectural agency, your proposal for BeMA appropriates the balcony in order to negotiate the relationship between the public and private territories in a museum. It's an interesting use of an architectural element that is familiar, valued, and highly versatile in Beirut. Could you speak about this decision in relation to making a "Lebanese" museum?

AA It wasn't so much about being specifically Lebanese, but about using the balcony as a clear transformational device – one that is both spatial and historical.

For us, the balcony represents the anti-museum. Traditional museums are elite, closed, iconic, and distinct from generic residential buildings. The balcony, on the other hand, is generic and residential. Everyone understands and relates to it. We took this familiar typology and repurposed it for the museum, turning it into something that opens up the museum and makes it feel more like a house. The balcony is also a device that cuts through architecture in Lebanon historically: from the earliest vernacular rural houses, to the elaborate verandas of Art Deco buildings in Beirut, to the modernist balcony and its appropriation during the Lebanese Civil War to expand interior spaces, as well as to today's reinventions as seen in contemporary projects.

A German newspaper once called BeMA "A Porous House", which I thought was great – it's meant to be an invitation, a house for everybody, not just a museum. The architectural expression of the balconies at BeMA isn't generic; like an urban fabric, or even a vertical archaeological dig, the balconies are more intricate, open-ended outdoor rooms which can be read, appropriated, and programmed in many different ways.

280

RM And balconies are extremely versatile here. Everyone seems to appropriate their balconies for something: social spaces, outdoor kitchens, lush gardens, closed off with glass curtains or those iconic flashy coloured striped fabric ones, et cetera. Is this flexibility reflected in the program?

AA It is. There are two main aspects. The first is that some of these outdoor rooms can be used for community meetings or, like on the second floor, for educational programs and planting – the museum site is very small, so we envisioned a vertical outdoor sculptural garden on the facade, turning it into a vertical park. The second is that they can be curated as outdoor galleries with work that is in conversation both with the present city outside and with the collection inside, to project new possibilities for the future.

In addition, we also thought initially that the competition brief's total program area requested was too large. We suggested building a smaller museum and possibly expanding into the balconies later. This idea was somewhat theoretical but it was built into the concept. This expanded notion of flexibility and potential for transformation is central to the design.

RM The location of the museum is also quite unique. It's on the demarcation line that split the city in the Lebanese Civil War, from which the country is still recovering – a few minutes away from the National Museum of Beirut, the Charles Corm Foundation, and the Institut Français – and it is part of the campus of Saint Joseph University. How does the design respond to that positioning within the city?

AA Yes, well, a few things come to mind. The site is located on the civil war's east–west divide of the city, and it was important to register Damascus Street as the conflict's Green Line. This invited us to create a sense of openness and an invitation for everyone to join in.

Beyond Damascus Street itself, the building's orientation and the way the balconies wrap around are designed to provide panoramic views of the city. We calibrated windows and the scale of the outdoor rooms to align with landmarks like the National Museum and the Hippodrome. This anchors the building on the Green Line as a symbol of the past, while also pointing to possibilities for the future as represented by the cultural and educational institutions along what's being called the Museum Mile, speaking to a hopeful future.

Being on the campus of Saint Joseph University (USJ) also emphasises its role as a university museum. It's about supporting education and fostering new scholarship. There are already collaborations with the AUB as well as conversations about new degrees at USJ and the idea of students across Lebanon coming to do archival research, aligning with BeMA's contributions as part of the country's academic ecosystem.

Including an educational component in the projects that contribute to the nation-building ecosystem of Lebanon is important for the impact of new projects in the country right now. Going back to the Fair, I particularly admire the recent Niemeyer Guest House renovation by EAST Architecture Studio, for example, in which the project has gone beyond the idea of preservation to host an educational facility for carpenters in Tripoli (fig. 5), a trade that is intrinsically connected to the identity of the city's past, but also to expand its potential for the future. In this same sense, if architectural form is the platform, I like to think that the core of our work is to enable collective possibilities and exchange.

Figure 5. The educational facility for carpenters at the Niemeyer Guest House

1 Francesco Bandarin, former Director of the World Heritage Centre and former Assistant Director-General for Culture at UNESCO, Farès el-Dahdah, then Director of the Humanities Research Center at Rice University and member of the Fundação Oscar Niemeyer board, George Kunihiro, architect and professor at Kokushikan University in Japan and a UIA representative, Suha Özkan, former Secretary General of the Aga Khan Award for Architecture, and Jad Tabet, then head of the Lebanese Federation of Engineers and Architects, Beirut, and Bassam Ziadeh then head of the Order of Engineers and Architects, Tripoli.

2 Adrian Lahoud, "Fallen Cities", in *The Arab City: Architecture and Representation*, ed. Amale Andraos and Nora Akawi (New York: Columbia Books on Architecture and the City, 2016).

Restitution against the Ruins of a Modern Temptation

Akram Zaatari

Following Egypt's defeat in the Six-Day War with Israel in June 1967, the Egyptian filmmaker Shadi Abdel-Salam started working on his feature film *Al-Mumia,* aka "The Night of Counting the Years". The choice of historical context and date of events suggests a hypothetical question: What if the rise of a local political consciousness in Egypt did not get aborted by the British campaign of 1882? An underlying conviction is embedded in the film narrative; people's awakening was bound to happen organically, and Egypt was about to modernise itself from within, as per Ahmed Urabi's uprising against Ottoman rule (1871–82), but that project got aborted by the British campaign, eventually turning into a long occupation that extended beyond Egypt's independence in 1922, until 1956.

The film is set at the eve of that campaign in 1881. It summarises events within the twenty-four hours that followed the death of the leader of the Al-Hurabat tribe in upper Egypt. The film follows one of the leader's two sons, Wanis, who is tormented by a question of enlightenment, a question that belongs to modern times: Do I obey my tribe on evil, trafficking archaeological finds off clandestine excavations? Or do I quit tribal ties, desert my tribe, stay in line with the law, work on the advancement of knowledge, and thus belong to the age of reason?

In what is to unfold through the film as an awakening of consciousness, Wanis goes through an internal struggle that leads him to cross from darkness to light, parting with tribal ties and with rural or feudal communal bonds. That isolated position represents a seed that could have reproduced and led organically into a wider or shared renaissance. Wanis learns his father's secret; his tribe has been living for years from trafficking archaeological finds, which his father and uncles extracted out of a secret subterranean hideout. This is revealed in the end as being the infamous Royal Cache in Deir El-Bahari, in southern Egypt, also known as TT320. The film is based on a true story.

During Egypt's twenty-first dynasty, and following a wave of tomb robberies, high Amun priests excavated their buried royalty out of different tombs in order to save what remained from vandalism. They re-mummified and re-buried them all together in a different cache; Mummies of eleven pharaohs from the seventeenth to the twenty-first dynasties were found there. They had been re-buried inside the tomb of the High Amun Priest, Pinedjem II in Deir Al-Bahari, with many other members of royalty and high-ranking officials.

In Abdel-Salam's movie, learning the secret of the hideout triggers in Wanis a feeling of guilt, whereas, in his own words, not knowing would have represented a greater guilt. The truth haunts and torments him over twenty-four hours until he decides to go meet the chief archaeologist on the boat that brought him from Cairo and tell him the truth. His journey and personal struggle lead to an awakening of sorts; aligning oneself with people of reason, against one's own tribe, is the first sign of turning, profoundly, modern. As much as the film is meant as an allegory of archaeology, implying that it is not possible to keep something where it has always been, buried underground in the dark – because looters will end up digging it out – Abdel-Salam's movie is meant to be the fable of awakening, of turning modern. All of a sudden, the bas-reliefs that cover ancient Egyptian temples, which Wanis perceived as decoration, as a child and then an adolescent, turn in his eyes today into records of history inscribed in stone. They turn into testimonies by his ancestors meant to address him and his people, to be read across the distance of time.

The discovery of the Royal Cache is detailed in Gaston Maspero's 1884 memoir titled *Les momies royales de Deir El-Bahari* (The Royal Mummies of Deir El-Bahari).[1] He tells how Mohamed Abdel-Rassoul led the authorities to the hideout. But, in difference to the story told in Abdel-Salam's film, Abdel-Rassoul tells the authorities the secret only after two of his younger brothers were arrested and interrogated for more than a month and after disputes had erupted at home, following their release, over compensation and shares. Both the rift within the family and the news about the authorities' determination to find the hideout sooner or later played a role in Abdel-Rassoul's decision to reveal the secret. It was his only way out. Abdel-Rassoul's collaboration with authorities did not happen as a result of any political or cultural awakening, but as a way to save himself. The turn to consciousness was Abdel-Salam's transposition of Urabi's uprising onto Wanis's character, imagining that this decision could have exemplified people's awakening, thus making him (Wanis) embody the fable of national consciousness. In other terms, it is a displacement of Urabi's uprising, which had been taking place since 1879 and was still ongoing the year TT320 was unearthed, a displacement of the anger against Ottoman rule, namely for the privileges it had extended to European powers in Egypt, including privileges to conduct excavations, a displacement into an anger against ignorance as represented in dealings with archaeological finds, thus wasting irreplaceable shared cultural heritage.

But, why did Abdel-Salam slightly change the facts while writing his film? In that twist lies a form of restitution.

Al-Mumia was produced in 1969 but had been written in the two years that preceded it, following Egypt's *naksa,* in 1967, and the loss of Sinai to Israel, which occupied the peninsula until 1982. A feeling of great defeat must have triggered Abdel-Salam's imaginary story of an aborted turn to consciousness that could have taken place before the British occupation of 1882. Can we imagine that our people would have dropped feudalism and tribalism themselves, without being forced to? Can we imagine that people would have claimed their right to self-determination and liberation, thus turning modern? Can we imagine that people would have gravitated to light, would have left ignorance and headed organically towards reason? Maspero is portrayed in the film as an illuminated modern figure, a "good guy", keen on protecting archaeology from looters. The looters are represented as being ignorant of the cultural value of finds they trade with.

Wanis cousins are happy to exchange ancient statuettes for sex with local prostitutes. They have been trading timeless and singular finds, supposedly beyond material value, against ephemera. In simple terms, they get to be represented as the "bad guys", even if they were Egyptian. Maspero is represented as a "good guy" even though he is a citizen of a colonial power.[2]

Most critics and film historians note how the film is based on a true story, without any mention of the details. Thus, Abdel-Salam's changing of facts remained quite unnoticed in film registers.[3] In 1967, Israel occupied Sinai entirely and Egypt faced another occupation of its territories, which brought back memories of the invasions of 1956[4] and that of the British occupation of 1882. The note that Abdel-Salam plays, though very subtly through his turning of facts, is that inclination to reason has no nationality, no colour, and belongs to no class. With the French hegemony and the British occupation of Egypt, Britain and France became "the enemy" in the eyes of many Egyptians, who started addressing all the values of their occupiers with rising suspicion.[5] Even the inclination to reason, which – according to Abdel-Salam – was bound to happen in Egypt, was gradually getting faced with suspicion, opposition, further religious radicalisation, and often with accusations of blasphemy.[6] Abdel-Salam knew that he could not reverse or wash away that suspicion. So, his film is in between an outcry and a lament suggesting that "we will always have faith in humanity". At a time when Egypt was at the height of its disagreements with a number of world powers, Abdel-Salam was keen on finding shared values with them, and the film proposes that it is not important where care came from, as long as archaeology is safe from vandalism.

In 1962, when Lebanon invited Oscar Niemeyer to build one of his abundant universal schemes in the northern city of Tripoli, the independent Lebanese state was only nineteen years old, although that building type with a late nineteenth-century programme was becoming outdated, and less and less fashionable. Lebanon was (and still is today) limited in natural and capital resources and has so many social issues awaiting pending resolutions, such as the recent influx of Palestinian refugees into its territories following the declaration of the State of Israel in 1948. Lebanon never had a particularly industrial economy to promote trade deals, but it had a strong service industry that could have immensely benefited from such a project. Furthermore, such a monumental scale would have been a great promotion of Lebanon as a state that embodied difference(s), that looked up to universal values, that cherished a shared future with humanity, while keeping a foot in tradition. The result of that commission is an elegant mix of traditional motifs incorporated into a universal scheme produced with concrete, which secured plasticity of shapes, volumes, and monumental metre spans with a very limited attempt at providing an elegant mix of traditional motifs incorporated into one part of the building. The site looks like an attraction park of little density, a great breathing space when compared to the fine-grain dense fabric of both Tripoli's modern downtown and its historic centre.

The declaration of Greater Lebanon in 1920 as a result of the Sykes–Picot Agreement following the collapse of the Ottoman Empire designated new borders that included Tripoli, which had formerly been an Ottoman province that extended from Byblos (in present-day Lebanon) to Latakia, including Hama and Homs in Syria. The detachment of Tripoli and its surroundings away from Syria was opposed by Tripolitan elites and was seen as a random imposition of borders, and found to be insensitive to the economic, cultural, and social links that tied Tripoli to its natural extension in Syria. Was Greater Lebanon built on a set of imaginary bonds? Or was it tailored to the promotion of a symbiosis that was expected to take place? In other terms, was it like a speculation that needed to be illustrated, reinforced, and promoted through new projects like national monumental structures before it got to be lived or inscribed into the body of the new republic? Embedded into this proposal was indeed a promise of a better life.

Youssef Howayek's infamous sculpture[7] represents two women, interpreted back then as a Christian and a Muslim, holding hands, united in mourning their children, who had paid with their lives while rebelling against Ottoman rule in 1916 (fig. 1). It is just one example of the very early public-work commissions that celebrated national unity in a country that wants to be seen as cherishing equally its regional traditions, on the one hand, and Western European trends, including the modernity trends that accompanied them, on the other. One of the two women in the sculpture wears the traditional *yashmak,* which is a garment used by some Muslim women to

Figure 1. Youssef Howayek's commission for Martyrs' Square in Beirut, 1930, is now installed at Sursock Museum. Photographed on 6 August 2020 following the Beirut port explosion.

cover their faces in public, except for the eyes, whereas the other woman represented in the sculpture does not wear it. The sculpture is at once an illustration and a celebration of ideas that were at the backbone of the Lebanon's inception. The same ideas appear to have played a role in the commission of the Tripoli Fair's grounds, which featured a few regional architectural elements incorporated into a scheme built of bare concrete. But it was way more impactful on real estate than a small public commission, way costlier to build than a sculpture, and it represented for Tripolitans an edifice suspended in time, often seen as the miracle that would one day provide them with solutions to Tripoli's misery. It was a national project that looked towards the future. But one could legitimately wonder if Lebanon really needed a fairground structure of this scale? And if so, did it need to be in Tripoli?[8] The project was stopped right before its completion in 1975, at the beginning of the Lebanese Civil War, which kept recurring until 1990. Towards the end of the war, the structures on site remained fairly sound except that the building, intended to be residential, suffered heavy damage after it had turned into Syrian army barracks until the army withdrew entirely from Lebanon, in 2005 (fig. 2).

The initial proposal that had pointed at the virtues and benefits of such a project might have gone wrong, and therefore the initial commission might have been a mistake in the first place. Or, the assessment might have been legitimate, but the project's scale, its choice of architect, could have been debated. Regardless of the case, the fact remains that Tripoli's Rachid Karami International Fair never opened, and like many bare structures in Lebanon, it has become frozen in time, inaccessible, and dilapidated. It has turned into a location for torture and possibly other forms of shady business as different militias took control of it during most of its life in addition to the Syrian Army. For a state where civil marriage isn't even possible, where governance, the electoral system, and even national bonds to a large extent are still dependent on class and religion, not to say stuck in religious feudal orders, imagining a necessity for such a project – a year following the failed military coup attempt of 1961 – is to want to belong to a modernity that Lebanon, to a large extent, had certainly missed until then.

International Style architecture's broad reach was underlined by a promise built into modern discourse. In shallow, simplified terms, it campaigns to swap one's traditional home with a modern one and to see how positively this would reflect on one's lifestyle, and how positive its implications would be for the larger urban context. It is how modern ideas worked their way mainly through photographs and films, but also through novels, literature, and other printed matter. A typical call from that period would be the movie *Al-Mo'guezah* (The Miracle) by Hassan Al-Imam (Egypt, 1962[9]), in which an activist journalist saves a pickpocket from her dark fate and helps her become a good citizen. The film ends with the demolition of an entire old neighbourhood to give way to modern white multi-storey apartment buildings. The film promotes the belief

Figure 2. This photograph captures a Syrian soldier washing himself after a gymnastics session at the unfinished Tripoli Fair in 1996

that modern architecture helps to eradicate misery and ensures a brighter future for its resident community. It is this promise that I find embedded in the implementation of superstructures like the grounds of the Tripoli Fair.

Many large-scale modern projects built in the Third World were looked up to by their communities, because they were often parachuted onto problematic zones with an expectation of change. Michel Écochard's Taamir[10] district near Ain El-Hilweh in Saida, South Lebanon, is another example of a failed modern project that had capitalised on moving people away from their miserable homes in the old city, following the earthquake of 1956 (fig. 3). Écochard planned the development of the New Saida, a residential district made with the repetition of five different building types. People moved there in the early 1960s and gradually transformed their generic modern apartments to fit their needs, but the district slowly turned into a highly problematic zone on so many levels: military, security, social, and political. Ironically, their former homes in the old city are doing so much better today than the homes where they moved in the early 1960s.

One may rightly ask: Do architectural stylistic shifts necessarily reflect societal shifts? In other terms, did the population of Lebanon turn entirely modern so that residents require/deserve such a modern facade? Introducing some building types is inevitable, given how technology has evolved, internationally, and how the notions of leisure, travel, and entertainment have become intertwined. The Beirut airport opened in 1954. Casino du Liban was built in 1957. Lebanon Television was founded in 1959. An international fairground could have been a great

Figure 3. Michel Écochard's Taamir housing project towards its completion in Ain el Helweh, early 1960s

addition to that bouquet, but the war, itself a result of unresolved conflicts, of contradicting wishes for different futures, put an end to it. And by the time the war was over, that format and that scale of a project were becoming old-fashioned. But you cannot destroy that site, and taking care of it means reconnecting it with a life and a community around it, which it actually never aimed for or opted to address or consider, neither as a programme nor as a site – except raising the real-estate value of the residential neighbourhood facing it. Nevertheless, when the site was liberated from its military occupiers, questions about possibilities for its reuse in the near future were immediately raised, acknowledging its great potential, but also acknowledging that something has gone wrong with it. To reconsider a programme that has been at the origin of the project, to restore a life that wasn't given a chance to be, is to engage in an act of restitution, in other terms a creation that responds selectively to incongruent or sometimes antonymous parameters, which are possible to imagine but not obvious to configure.

The Middle East's tryst with modernity, its heritage, as well as the idea of architectural conservation, renovation, reuse, produces a landscape rich in contradiction, gaps, misunderstandings, ambition, and layered identity, very often disputed. Are we Arabs or is "Arab" one of our many features? Does religion dictate how we perceive history? Does it at all play a role in the conservation or the classification of monuments nowadays? Or in the appointment of key government positions?

There is a rift between being modern and going through modern times. These two were often conflated or even confused with one another. The Middle East was about to "rise", maybe, or undergo a major *nahda,* but it is not the erection of a modern building that makes a modern society. It might be the opposite. But a modern building might as well be the desired future of that society or what it was dreaming of looking like. The ruins of modern building might be a sign of an accelerated modernity or a conflict with modernity. A picture where people act modern is not necessarily a sign that they were actually modern. There are layers of practices, wishes, trends to unpack – as much in an urban fabric as in photographs.

How to read modernity in photographs, in cities and monuments, is very tricky. Both photographs and monuments mirror the wishes of their makers. Photography often presents, or projects, what is fantasised about but is missing. It is a result of the performative nature of the pose and the possibilities of encoding sittings socially or politically. Sometimes people acted modern only for the sake of and in the presence of the camera. The thousands of photographs of people dressed up in clothes that didn't belong to them, holding things that the studio offered them, while being pictured. Sunglasses, a pencil, pistol, book, bicycle, flute, guitar, an unlit cigarette, and even a life-size cardboard blonde woman are all examples of wishes or desires folded into pictures. The scratched negatives of Mrs Baqari, photographed by Hashem el Madani at his Studio Shehrazade in Saida in the late 1950s, would be a perfect example of a misleading picture.

292

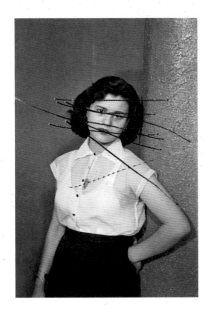

Figure 4. Direct print made from the scratched negative of Mrs Baqari's portrait
Figure 5. Digitally restored direct print made from the scratched negative of Mrs Baqari's portrait

A lady is wearing a modern dress and looking at the camera without smiling. One can see her bra through the thin textile of her white dress. She had been photographed before by the same photographer, before she got married, and continued to visit the studio for more portraits after her engagement. But the 35mm negative of that photograph has been violently scratched (fig. 4). Had this negative not been scarred by the jealous husband to prevent its future use, one would have imagined that the woman lived a perfectly modern life. But the scratch serves to remind us of a social conflict with certain aspects of modern living. Scratches, fissures, or missing parts tell us about objects or photographs that clash with their times, with social norms, and sometimes with political ideas. Such traces become indicators of things that happened. Even when seen as scars or glitches, they have a potential to communicate stories and become records of some sort, and thus could be turned into language. When exploring possible restitution, these traces become useful in reconstructing any object biography. But traces could also become a useful language within creative practices.

It is through conflict that one measures a trend's relevance to its times in a specific society like the portrait of Mrs. Baqari, and like the Tripoli Fair. Any attempt to read the portrait of Mrs Baqari without the scratch is to confuse a young woman's wish with her very different and oppressing sad reality. One could easily consider the scratch to be a hostile element alien to the original photograph or to the wish itself. In this vein, one could indeed digitally restore the photograph on the negative to its initial state, retouching the scan of the negative to eliminate the scratch, therefore restituting the portrait to the negative's undamaged state (fig. 5). Or one could decide to print the negative with the scratch to show how violent the whole might look. Both would be equally legitimate restitutions, although to eliminate the scratch is to consider the photograph at face value, locked at birth, like a valuable icon to care for and keep forever safe from glitches, unchanged, or regularly restored to appear brand-new, as if a machine were to be reset periodically to "factory settings".

Implicit in the term restitution[11] is the idea that something has gone wrong, somewhere, sometime in the past. Something has either been broken or perished, got lost or transported against the wishes of its people, when it shouldn't have been so. In simple terms, an object has been displaced away from its location and is missed there. Restitution could mean bringing it, or a copy of it, back to where it used to be, like a reversal of an action found undesirable, or an apology of some sort. But restitution is also an act of potential repair or closure even when repair isn't perfectly possible. It proposes alternative restitutions to every loss, even an immaterial loss like the loss of pride or order or rights, for example. Yoko Ogawa's novel *The Ringfinger,*[12] originally published in Japanese in 1994, is full of creative restitutions which sound like a set of performance art gestures that take the form of prescriptions, like those in the medical field. These are the result of a creative process that involves imagination, and not any kind of scientific or legal resolution. Answers to questions of restitution could be elastic and might turn impossible to manage or proceed with at a national scale, such as the Rachid Karami International Fair. If the desire to restitute comes from a feeling of loss, then sometimes it is very difficult to identify, or agree on, "loss" collectively, in order to identify possible avenue(s) for its restitution. Like restitution, loss is difficult to measure with scientific tools.

Rethinking certain architectural monuments against changes in times is necessary, otherwise the market would do it from a lucrative perspective. Architecture reuse today needs to reconnect to, or at least not disregard, the complex intentional and accidental layers that represent a building's biography. The wider avenue of restitution is a creative practice and not an expression of nostalgia for origins or authenticity. Internationally, institutions have transitioned the relationship with heritage and its artefacts into an issue of navigation, isolating cultural objects through access bureaucracy, for example. But culture cannot be experienced or perceived only through its navigation. The essence of a creative engagement with the past lies in recognising that buildings and cultural artefacts are not merely inanimate objects but, moreover, repositories of memories, including those we dislike, experiences, including those we want to forget, and changing identities, including the constantly disputed ones and those evolving and changing over time.

The creative practice involving objects of cultural significance and the pursuit of restitution of a life an edifice has missed, thus, become acts of reimagining – of spaces, of identities, of histories. Whether it is through archaeology, material conservation, or the dissemination of reproduced images, the essence of restitution lies in seizing the complexities of our accumulating heritage with a sense of creativity, responsibility, and an understanding of the socio-political undercurrents that shape our world. For national monuments, and in the absence of consensus over who we are and where we are heading as a nation, there would not be room for creative imagination to take place. Instead, a set of performative and ephemeral interventions could play notes found missing in the original scheme, or imagine a relationship that never happened against the ruins of a modern temptation, delayed by the fears of some, aborted by the wars we have led in the name of justice, liberation, and sovereignty.

1   Gaston Maspero, "Les momies royales de Deir El-Bahari", published in *Mémoires publiés par les membres de la mission archéologique Française du Caire*, vol. 1 (Paris: Leroux, 1884), fasc. 4.

2   Gaston Maspero arrived in Egypt in November 1880 to lead the French archaeological mission in Cairo. A year later, he was appointed director-general of excavations and antiquities of Egypt.

3   This remained unnoticed until Magdi Abdel Rahman included the details mentioned in Maspero's report in his contribution to *Al-qāhirah Journal*, where he mentions that Abdel-Salam changed some details of the story, but not its essence, to suit his creative vision. See Magdy 'abdel-Rahmān, "Yā man taḏhab sata'ūd", p. 232, in *Al-qāhirah Journal for Contemporary Art and Thought*, special issue "Šādy 'abdul-Salām.. Šu'ā' min Misr.", issue no. 154, Cairo (December 1994), pp. 228–40.

4   Following the nationalisation of the Suez Canal in 1956, the United Kingdom, Israel, and France led the Tripartite Aggression against Egypt, which was a military attack on Sinai and Suez in order to force Egypt to reopen the Suez Canal and the Straits of Tiran.

5   The antithesis to *Al-Mumia* is another Egyptian movie entitled *Al-Gabal* (The Mountain) by Khalil Shawky (1965). The plot revolves around efforts to bring a specific tribe at the Luxor's West Bank to move down from the mountain, where its men sell the finds they excavate, into new mud-brick homes built specifically for them at the foothills in New Gourna. The architect – whose figure was inspired by the Egyptian architect Hassan Fathy – tries to convince them to quit the risky clandestine digs, yet without being able to promise them any sustainable life in return. He is represented as an idealist who is stuck between stubborn rough conservative mountain dwellers, who do not want to leave the mountain, and, on the other hand, Europeanised, spoiled, corrupt, and greedy urbanites, who sponsor him hoping that they would get the mountain treasures for themselves. They kill him in the end.

6   Even the most renowned Egyptian writer Taha Hussein was accused of blasphemy following the publication of his book

On Pre-Islamic Poetry, a Descartian approach to studying the language of pre-Islamic poetry. The book was published in Egypt in 1926, before being withdrawn immediately from the market until Hussein revised it and republished it in 1927 under the title *On Pre-Islamic Literature*.

7   Commissioned under the French Mandate to represent the new nation's unity while struggling against Ottoman rule, the sculpture was installed in 1930 at the Martyrs' Square in Beirut, the site of the infamous hanging of intellectuals and activists on 6 May 1916. The sculpture was removed after it had been vandalised in 1958, but reinstalled at Sursock Museum in Achrafieh in 1993.

8   Tripoli has always been a city central to trade in its wider geography, which included Homs and its surroundings across the borders with Syria reaching to the Akkar District in North Lebanon. When Greater Lebanon was announced in 1920, Tripolitan leaders and its mercantile power opposed themselves to the newly drawn borders because this meant depriving Tripoli of its natural and vital area of economic influence. The same thing happened in South Lebanon central cities like Bint Jbeil, which was pivotal to the region of Galilee but became marginal following the declaration of Greater Lebanon in 1920, and almost economically strangled following the closure of the Lebanon–Israel border in 1948.

9   Ironically, the commission of the Tripoli Fair and the making of the films *Al-Mo'guezah* and *Al-Mumia* happened within the same decade when Jacques Tati produced his two films that are highly critical of modern architecture and International Style: *Mon Oncle* (1958) and *Playtime* (1967) represent a satire of modern times and a critique of modern architecture's failed promise.

10 Taamir means, literally, building or constructing.

11 From *restituere* in Latin, which means to "set up again, restore, rebuild, replace, revive, reinstate, re-establish"; see Etymonline.com.

12 Yoko Ogawa, *L'Annulaire*, translated from Japanese into French by Rose-Marie Makino-Fayolle (Arles: Actes Sud, 1999).

Contributor Biographies

Nora Akawi is a Palestinian architect, and an assistant professor at The Cooper Union, New York. She focuses on erasure and bordering in settler colonialism and works at the intersection of architecture with border studies, cartography, and archive theory. Prior to joining The Cooper Union, Nora taught at Columbia University's GSAPP, where she was the director of Studio-X Amman since 2012, and the founding director of the Janet Abu-Lughod Library and Seminar since 2015. She curated *Al Majhoola Min Al-Ard* (This Earth's Unknown) at the Biennale d'Architecture d'Orléans (2019) and co-curated *Sarāb: Wadi Rum,* a festival of experimental electronic music and performance from the Arab worlds (2019), and *Friday Sermon* at the Venice Architecture Biennale (2018). She co-edited the books *Friday Sermon* (2018) and *Architecture and Representation: The Arab City* (2016). Together with Eduardo Rega Calvo, in 2019 Akawi co-founded the interdisciplinary research and design studio Interim Projects.

Noura Al-Sayeh Holtrop is an architect and curator based in Bahrain. She co-curated *Reclaim,* Bahrain's first participation at the 12th Venice Architecture Biennale in 2010, which won a Golden Lion, and was Deputy Commissioner General for *Archaeologies of Green,* Bahrain's National Pavilion at Expo Milan 2015, which earned a Silver Medal. Since 2015, she has led the "Pearling, Testimony of an Island Economy" UNESCO World Heritage project, awarded the Aga Khan Award for Architecture in 2019. She has created various installations and worked as an architect in Jerusalem, Amsterdam, and New York. Currently, she is Advisor for Heritage Projects at the Bahrain Authority for Culture and Antiquities (BACA), overseeing cultural institutions, museums, urban rehabilitation, and public space creation. She holds a master's degree in architecture from the École Polytechnique Fédérale de Lausanne and is a board member of the Palestinian Museum in Birzeit, Palestine. Noura Al-Sayeh Holtrop served as an On-Site Reviewer for the Aga Khan Award for Architecture in 2022.

Elias and Yousef Anastas lead AAU Anastas, a multidisciplinary architecture studio based in Bethlehem, dedicated to bridging crafts and architecture across various scales, from furniture design to territorial explorations. The studio champions contemporary structural stone use, particularly in Palestine, promoting low carbon footprint structures, resilient cities, and ethical quarry exploitation. Elias and Yousef are co-founders of Radio alHara, an online community radio fostering global solidarity through sonic experiences, where they aim to link diverse contexts and strengthen critical global discourse. Their latest initiative, The Wonder Cabinet in Bethlehem, gathers artisans, artists, and technical experts to cultivate a culture of global provincialism through innovative cultural productions.

Amale Andraos is a Principal of WORKac which she co-founded with Dan Wood. The practice's work around the world emphasises a deep engagement with local cultures, climates, and histories, with a focus on public, cultural, and institutional projects. Andraos is also Professor and Dean Emeritus of Columbia University's Graduate School of Architecture, Planning and Preservation (GSAPP), the first woman to have become dean of the school. Her publications include: *The Arab City: Architecture and Representation* (2016, co-edited with Nora Akawi) and *We'll Get There When We Cross That Bridge, 49 Cities, and Above the Pavement, the Farm!* (2017, in collaboration with Dan Wood). Andraos served on the Master Jury of the Aga Khan Award for Architecture in 2022.

George Arbid is an architect with successive teaching positions at the Academie Libanaise des Beaux-Arts, the American University of Beirut, and the Lebanese University. He received a Diplome d'Etudes Superieures in Architecture from ALBA and was a Fulbright Visiting Scholar at the History, Theory and Criticism Program at MIT. As well, he holds a Doctor of Design degree from Harvard University. Arbid is the co-founder and director of the Arab Center for Architecture and has served on several competition and award juries, including the 2019 European Union Prize for Contemporary Architecture – Mies van der Rohe Award. He co-curated the Pavilion of Bahrain at the Venice Architecture Biennale in 2014 and authored *Architecture from the Arab World (1914–2014): A Selection* (2014). Arbid recently co-edited *Designing Modernity: Architecture in the Arab World 1945–1973* (2022) with Philipp Oswalt, published in English and Arabic.

Aaron Betsky is a critic of architecture, art, and design living in Philadelphia. He was previously director of the Netherlands Architecture Institute, the Cincinnati Art Museum, the 11th International Venice Architecture Biennale, and the School of Architecture and Design at Virginia Tech, as well as president of the School of Architecture at Taliesin in Arizona. His most recent book, *Don't Build, Rebuild: The Case for Imaginative Architecture* (Beacon Press), is forthcoming in the fall of 2024.

Sibel Bozdoğan, retired professor of modern architecture, taught at MIT, Harvard University Graduate School of Design, and Boston University (1991 and 2023) and part-time at Istanbul Bilgi and Kadir Has universities (2006–17). Her publications include *Modernism and Nation Building: Turkish Architectural Culture in the Early Republic* (2001), the recipient of the 2002 Alice Davis Hitchcock Award of the Society of Architectural Historians, and *Turkey: Modern Architectures in History* (2012, co-authored with Esra Akcan). She received the Turkish Chamber of Architects' National Award for "lifetime contribution" in 2018 and served on the Master Jury of the Aga Khan Award for Architecture in 2022.

Costica Bradatan is the Paul Whitfield Horn Distinguished Professor of Humanities in the Honors College at Texas Tech University, and an Honorary Research Professor of Philosophy at the University of Queensland, Australia. He has also held faculty appointments at Cornell University, Miami University, University of Wisconsin–Madison, and University of Notre Dame, as well as at universities in Europe, Latin America, and Asia. Bradatan is the author and editor of more than a dozen books, including *Dying for Ideas: The Dangerous Lives of the Philosophers* (2015, 2018) and *In Praise of Failure: Four Lessons in Humility* (2023). He also writes book reviews, essays, and op-ed pieces for such publications as *The New York Times, The Washington Post, The Times Literary Supplement, Literary Review, Aeon,* and *Commonweal.*

Aziza Chaouni is the founding principal of Aziza Chaouni Projects (ACP) with offices in Fez, Morocco, and Toronto, Canada, and an associate professor of architecture at the University of Toronto. She directs the Designing Ecological Tourism (DET) research platform, focusing on sustainable design in developing regions. Her research integrates architecture and landscape with sustainable technologies in arid climates and modern heritage preservation. Chaouni co-authored *Desert Tourism and Out of Water,* and led preservation projects like the Sidi Harazem Thermal Bath Station, supported by the World Monuments Fund and Getty Foundation. In 2017, she co-founded the NGO Joudour Sahara. Chaouni holds a Master of Architecture from Harvard and a Bachelor of Science in Civil Engineering from Columbia University. Chaouni served as an On-Site Reviewer for the Aga Khan Award for Architecture in 2019.

Civil Architecture is a cultural practice preoccupied with the making of buildings and books about them. The work of Civil asks what it means to produce architecture in a decidedly un-civil time, presenting a new civic character for a global condition. Since its founding by Hamed Bukhamseen and Ali Ismail Karimi, the practice has attracted a strong following for their provocative works and offer of an alternate future for a nascent Middle East.

Marco Costantini is an art historian and the director of mudac, Museum of Contemporary Design and Applied Arts in Lausanne, where he organised the exhibition *Beirut: The Eras of Design* in 2023. Previously, at the Museum of Fine Arts in Lausanne, he was in charge of research for its transition from a museum to PLATEFORME 10. Costantini initiated several other independent exhibitions for contemporary art spaces in Switzerland and abroad. He was a lecturer at the School of Design and High School of Art of Valais, after having been a lecturer in the Department of Art History at the University of Lausanne, as well as at the Polytechnic School of Lausanne. He is the author of numerous articles published in scientific books and exhibition catalogues specialised in design and contemporary art.

Farrokh Derakhshani is the director of the Aga Khan Award for Architecture and has been associated with the Award since 1982. Derakhshani trained as an architect and planner at the National University of Iran and later continued his studies at the School of Architecture in Paris (UP1). His main field of specialisation is the contemporary architecture of Muslim societies. He lectures widely and has organised and participated in numerous international seminars, exhibitions, colloquia, workshops, and international competitions. He has served as a jury member at various international competitions and schools of architecture and collaborated on a large variety of architecture-related publications.

Fadi El Abdallah is a published author, poet, music critic, and lawyer. He earned a PhD in Law from Paris II University, and lives and works in The Hague, Netherlands. He has taken part in several contemporary art activities across the world. His recent publications include *l'Orient sonore* (ed., Actes Sud and MUCEM, 2020), *Fragility as Foundation: Encounters with Lebanese Writings* (Al Jadid, 2023), and *In Pursuit of a Fascination: On Music and Critique* (Kotob Khan, 2024), in addition to several poetry collections.

Farès el-Dahdah is a professor of art history and the Mamdouha El-Sayed Bobst Dean of the Faculty of Arts and Sciences at the American University of Beirut. He has written extensively on Brazil's modern architecture and has been involved in several projects with Casa de Lucio Costa and Fundação Oscar Niemeyer, two Brazilian cultural foundations on the boards of which he serves. In recent years, data science, digital art history, and cloud adoption have increasingly become central to his research and so has the creation of online geospatial platforms in the areas of cultural heritage, public health, social justice, disaster response, and climate change.

Nicolas Fayad is an architect and founding partner of EAST Architecture Studio. He studied architecture at the American University of Beirut before earning a master's degree in architecture with distinction from the Harvard University Graduate School of Design. He is a recipient of the Aga Khan Award for Architecture, 15th Cycle, for EAST's Renovation of the Niemeyer Guest House at the Rachid Karami International Fair in Tripoli, Lebanon, and was recently awarded the American University of Beirut's Distinguished Alumni Award, honoring his achievements. In 2021, he was a visiting assistant professor of architecture at MIT and is currently an assistant professor of practice in architecture at the American University of Beirut.

Sarah Mineko Ichioka is a strategist, urbanist, curator, and author. She is the founding director of Desire Lines, a consultancy for environmental, cultural, and social-impact organisations and initiatives. In previous and parallel roles, she has explored the intersections of cities, society, and ecology within leading international institutions of culture, policy, and research. She is co-author of *Flourish: Design Paradigms for Our Planetary Emergency* (with Michael Pawlyn). Ichioka has been recognised as a World Cities Summit Young Leader, one of the Global Public Interest Design 100, a British Council / Clore Duffield Cultural Leadership International Fellow, and an Honorary Fellow of the Royal Institute of British Architects. She served as an On-Site Reviewer for the Aga Khan Award for Architecture in 2019.

Charles Kettaneh is an architect and founding partner of EAST Architecture Studio. He studied architecture at the American University of Beirut and Pratt Institute, graduating with honors, and later pursued management studies at INSEAD. Before founding EAST Architecture Studio, he worked with RSVP Studio, Perkins Eastman and Nelson in the United States, as well as Raed Abillama Architects in Lebanon. He is a recipient of the Aga Khan Award for Architecture, 15th Cycle, for EAST's Renovation of Niemeyer Guest House at the Rachid Karami International Fair in Tripoli, Lebanon.

Bernard Khoury studied architecture at the Rhode Island School of Design and Harvard University. He was awarded the Borromini Prize (honorable mention) by the municipality of Rome, which is given to architects under forty years of age (2001), the Architecture + Award (2004), and the CNBC Award (2008). He co-founded the Arab Center for Architecture (2008)and was a visiting professor at several universities, including the Ecole Polytechnique Fédérale de Lausanne and L'Ecole Spéciale d'Architecture in Paris. Over the years, he has developed an international reputation and a diverse portfolio of projects in over fifteen countries and has lectured and exhibited his work in over 150 institutions. He was the architect and co-curator of the Kingdom of Bahrain's national pavilion at the Venice Architecture Biennale (2014). Khoury was nominated by the French Ministry of Culture for the Chevalier des Arts et des Lettres (2020).

Raafat Majzoub is an architect, artist, writer, and educator based between Boston and Beirut. He is the editor-in-chief of the *Dongola Architecture Series* and co-editor of *Design to Live* (MIT Press, 2021). He is the co-founder of the award-winning magazine *The Outpost* and the creative director of The Khan: The Arab Association for Prototyping Cultural Practices. In 2024, he received the Aga Khan Program for Islamic Architecture research fellowship at MIT, and will be lecturing at the institute's Program in Art, Culture and Technology, where he is also an alumnus. Majzoub has previously lectured at the American University of Beirut, MISK Art Institute, and Ashkal Alwan, among others, and has published and exhibited his art internationally.

Nader Tehrani is the recipient, for his contributions to architecture as an art, of the Arnold W. Brunner Memorial Prize awarded by the American Academy of Arts and Letters, the highest form of recognition of artistic merit in the United States. He is also the recipient of awards from the American Academy of Arts and Sciences, the National Academy of Design, and the Design Visionary National Design Award by Cooper Hewitt and the Smithsonian Design Museum. Tehrani is the founding principal of NADAAA, an interdisciplinary practice with a body of work in infrastructure, urbanism, architecture, and installations. Tehrani is also the former dean of The Irwin S. Chanin School of Architecture at The Cooper Union. The works of Nader Tehrani have been widely exhibited at MoMA, LA MOCA, and ICA Boston. Tehrani served on the Master Jury of the Aga Khan Award for Architecture in 2022.

Ana Tostões is an architect, architecture critic, and historian, currently serving as president of Docomomo International and editor of the *Docomomo Journal*. Since 2010, she has transformed Docomomo into a global network, and the journal into a key international periodical for modern movement architecture and its reuse. A full professor at Técnico, University of Lisbon, she teaches theory of architecture and critical history, and directs the Architecture Scientific Board. Since 2012, she has led the architectural PhD programme. Tostões has taught at numerous universities worldwide, including Tokyo, Lausanne, and Barcelona. Her research focuses on contemporary architecture's critical history and theory, and she has published extensively, curated exhibitions, and coordinated research projects, such as *Modern Architecture in Africa: Angola and Mozambique,* and was awarded the Gulbenkian Prize 2014.

Sumayya Vally is the principal of the architecture and research practice Counterspace. She is the youngest architect ever commissioned for the Serpentine Pavilion, completed in 2021, and the artistic director of the inaugural Islamic Arts Biennale in Jeddah. A TIME100 Next list honoree, World Economic Forum Young Global Leader, and Dezeen's Emerging Architect of the Year 2023, Vally has been identified as someone who will shape the future of architectural practice and pedagogy. She is Honorary Professor of Practice at The Bartlett School of Architecture, and an honorary fellow of the Royal Architectural Institute of Canada.

Jozef Wouters is a Brussels-based scenographer and theatre-maker. His work often relates to a specific location and initiates a dialogue between strategic spaces, social processes, and the power of imagination. Since 2017 he has been an autonomous artist in residence with Meg Stuart / Damaged Goods. In 2016, Wouters and his technical director Menno Vandevelde founded Decoratelier, a constantly evolving project in a former factory in Brussels, which functions as an accessible workspace and platform for artistic collaborations, residencies, nightlife, and social experimentation. In 2020, he published his notes on scenography in the book *Moments Before the Wind.*

Akram Zaatari has produced films, videos, books, and countless installations of photographic material, all sharing an interest in writing histories, in the production and circulation of images in times of war, and in the play of tenses inherent to various letters that have been lost, found, buried, discovered, or otherwise delayed in reaching their destinations. The act of digging, or the excavation itself, has become emblematic of his search for objects, narratives, and missing links, while trying to restitute connections lost across time and geography.

EAST Architecture Studio

Founded in 2015 by Nicolas Fayad and Charles Kettaneh, EAST Architecture Studio is an award-winning collective practice committed to architectural design and experimental research. The studio is an open laboratory continuously in search of architectural typologies that reconsider the intersection between spatial experience, form, and technology while adjusting to changing social, economic, and political environments. Projects emerge from the studio with optimism, translating visionary ideas into an architecture of the present – a reality that the team embraces, with a particular interest in intellectual pursuits and design research. Emphasis on history, culture, and the territory are an integral part of the adopted design methods, defining an architectural response that engages with the challenges of our time. Based in Beirut and the United Arab Emirates, EAST Architecture Studio works internationally with networks spread across four continents.

Image Credits

All copyrights belong to the respective owners listed below, to whom we are grateful for the honour of presenting their work in this book.

Courtesy of AAU Anastas: p. 181 (left); Abaca Press / Alamy Stock Photo: p. 28; Aga Khan Trust for Culture / Maxime Delvaux: p. 189 (bottom); Aga Khan Trust for Culture / Cemal Emden: pp. 7–9, 77 (right), 87 (right), 186–88, 192, 205, 208, 282–83; Aga Khan Trust for Culture / Danko Stjepanovic: p. 190; AGB Photo Library / Alamy Stock Photo: p. 108; George Arbid: pp. 34–35; Arcaid Images / Alamy Stock Photo: p. 185; Iwan Baan: pp. 232, 240 (left), 242; Courtesy of Bahrain Authority for Culture and Antiquities (BACA): pp. 152, 154, 189 (top); Courtesy of Bahrain House of Photography: p. 153; Uwe Bergwitz / Alamy Stock Photo: p. 107; Frans Blok / Alamy Stock Photo: p. 98; Adrian Boot / urbanimage.tv: p. 238 (right); Built by Nature: p. 97; Mikaela Burstow: p. 180; Aziza Chaouni Projects: pp. 120, 121 (right), 123, 126, 132; Ceddyfresse / Wikimedia Commons, Creative Commons Attribution-Share Alike 4.0 International license, https://commons. wikimedia.org/wiki/File:Fazl-Moschee_2010.jpg: p. 234; Civil Architecture: pp. 163–70; David Corio: p. 233; Courtesy of Charles Corm Foundation: pp. 245, 247–49; Counterspace: p. 231; Bruce Damonte: p. 273; George Darrell: pp. 238 (left), 240 (right), 241; Roman Deckert / Wikimedia Commons, Creative Commons Attribution-Share Alike 4.0 International license, https://commons.wikimedia.org/wiki/File:TripoliLebanon Fair_OscarNiemeyer_OpenAirTheatre6-Roman Deckert14102018.jpg: p. 191 and https://commons.wikimedia.org/wiki/File:TripoliLebanonFair_OscarNiemeyer_ LebanonPavilion2-RomanDeckert14102018.jpg: p. 197 and https://commons.wikimedia.org/wiki/File:TripoliLebanon Fair_OscarNiemeyer_LebanonPavilion-Helipad-RomanDeckert14102018.jpg: p. 218; Maxime Delveaux: p. 157; Dhun, Jaipur: p. 101; Michel Écochard Archive, courtesy of Aga Khan Documentation Center, MIT Libraries (AKDC@MIT): p. 65; EAA – Emre Arolat Architecture Archives: pp. 198–99; EAST Architecture Studio: cover, pp. 74–75, 77 (left), 78–80, 82–86, 87 (top), 87 (left), 214–16, 302; Michel Faublée Archives: pp. 124–25; Elizabeth Felicella: p. 275; Murat Germen: p. 201; Francesco Giardina: pp. 148–49; Pol Guillard: pp. 139, 146 (top); Miguel de Guzman: p. 274; Denis Guzzo: p. 99; Natheer Halawani: p. 13; Jonathan Hillyer: p. 211 (top); Courtesy of Studio Anne Holtrop: p. 156; John Horner Photography: p. 212 (top); Raoul Jahan / Arab Center for Architecture: p. 45; Ryan Jamali / taken from the game ZM_LostFair: pp. 260–61, 264–65; Joseph Philippe Karam Archives / Arab Center for Architecture: p. 43; Charles Kettaneh / derivation based on Mark Garcia and Steven Hutt, "Prevalence of Computation in Architectural Design," 2023 (cited in Mario Carpo, "A short but believable history of the digital turn in architecture," Chronograms of Architecture, e-flux, March 2023); text additions are in color, the black text being true to the original graph: pp. 259, 267; AI image prompted by Charles Kettaneh and generated by MidJourney AI, 27 June 2024: p. 269; Bernard Khoury: pp. 46–59, 61, 62–63, 67–69; Karol Kozlowski Premium RM / Alamy Stock Photo: p.111; Kubik: p. 100; Eric Lafforgue / Alamy Stock Photo: p. 39 (right); Tommy Larey / Alamy Stock Photo: p. 91; Raafat Majzoub: pp. 24, 27, 29–30; Vladimir Miller: p. 146 (bottom); Samer Mohdad / arab-images.com: p. 290; Alfred Moussa: pp. 246, 251; Andreea Muscurel / Aziza Chaouni Projects: pp. 121 (left), 122, 129–31; NADAAA: pp. 211 (bottom), 212 (bottom); Valerio Olgiati: p. 158; Dick Ossemann / Wikimedia Commons, Creative Commons license 4.0 International, https://commons.wikimedia.org/wiki/File:Istanbul_Museum_of_Modern_ Art_Exterior_in_2024_5632.jpg?uselang=de, p. 202; Photo 12 / Alamy Stock Photo: p. 266 (right); Pgre / Alamy Stock Photo: p. 114; Bas Princen: p. 159; Reply.rajrewal / Wikimedia Commons, Creative Commons Attribution-Share Alike 4.0 International license, https://commons.wikimedia.org/wiki/File:HALL_OF_NATIONS.jpg: p. 196; Tim Ring / Alamy Stock Photo: p. 239; Rami Rizk: pp. 10–11, 15, 38, 263; Rio Cinema Archive: p. 237 (right); robertharding / Alamy Stock Photo: p. 39 (left); Roman Robroek / Alamy Stock Photo: p. 266 (left); Image Courtesy Roti Kitchen: p. 237 (left); Lorena Samponi / Alamy Stock Photo: p. 112; Michael Sparrow / Alamy Stock Photo: p. 236; Spuntik 360 / Alamy Stock Photo: p. 113; Amman Sanctuary, Amman, Jordan Courtesy of SUGi: pp. 102–03; Edmund Sumner: pp. 178–79, 181 (top), 181 (right), 182; Trinity Mirror / Mirrorpix / Alamy Stock Photo: p. 235; WORKac: p. 277; Jozef Wouters: pp. 140–41, 145; Muammer Yanmaz: p. 200; Akram Zaatari: pp. 288, 291, 293; Ariadne Van Zandbergen / Alamy Stock Photo: p. 117; David Židlický, courtesy of Villa Tugendhat: p. 90

Beyond Ruins
Reimagining Modernism

With contributions by Nora Akawi, Noura Al-Sayeh Holtrop, Elias and Yousef Anastas, Amale Andraos, George Arbid, Aaron Betsky, Sibel Bozdoğan, Costica Bradatan, Aziza Chaouni, Civil Architecture, Marco Costantini, Farrokh Derakhshani, EAST Architecture Studio, Fadi El Abdallah, Farès el-Dahdah, Nicolas Fayad, Sarah Mineko Ichioka, Charles Kettaneh, Bernard Khoury, Raafat Majzoub, Nader Tehrani, Ana Tostões, Sumayya Vally, Jozef Wouters, and Akram Zaatari.

Editors: Raafat Majzoub and Nicolas Fayad

Project management: Nadia Siméon, Marlene Schneider, Cristina Steingräber

Image editing: Isabelle Griffiths, Marlene Schneider

Copyediting: Dawn Michelle d'Atri

Art direction: Julia Wagner, grafikanstalt

Production: Sonja Bröderdörp

Reproductions: Optische Werke, Hamburg, Germany

Printing and binding: Gutenberg Beuys Feindruckerei GmbH, Langenhagen, Germany

© 2024 Aga Khan Award for Architecture, ArchiTangle GmbH, and the contributors

Aga Khan Award for Architecture
P.O. Box 2049
1211 Geneva 2
Switzerland
www.akdn.org/architecture

Published by
ArchiTangle GmbH
Meierottostrasse 1
10719 Berlin
Germany
www.architangle.com

ISBN 978-3-96680-031-0

Use the QR code to access additional digital content such as videos.